THE

Byline

BIBLE

Get Published in 5 Weeks

SUSAN SHAPIRO

WRITER'S DIGEST BOOKS

WritersDigest.com
Cincinnati, Ohio

FOREWORD BY *NEW YORK TIMES* EDITOR PETER CATAPANO

908.02
SHA

For more resources for writers, visit www.writersdigest.com.

22 21 20 19 18   5 4 3 2 1

Distributed in the U.K. and Europe by F+W Media International
Pynes Hill Court, Pynes Hill, Rydon Lane
Exeter, EX2 5AZ, United Kingdom
Tel: (+44) 1392-797680, Fax: (+44) 1626-323319
E-mail: postmaster@davidandcharles.co.uk

Library of Congress Cataloging-in-Publication Data

ISBN-13: 978-1-4403-5368-0

Edited by Amy Jones
Cover designed by Alexis Estoye
Designed by Liz Harasymczuk and Katelyn Summers
Production coordinated by Debbie Thomas

Dedication

To my Fantastic Five: Jack, Mickey, Brian, Eric, and Mike,
with eternal love and gratitude

Table of Contents

Foreword

PETER CATAPANO

One of the fun things I get to do in my job as a *New York Times* editor is visit Sue Shapiro's writing classes at The New School and disagree with her. This is bad manners on my part, since Sue has always been very nice to me (and my books) and frequently invites me to speak to her students, which is flattering, probably good for my résumé, and is something I actually, really, truly like to do. It can also turn out to be embarrassing because Sue is usually right.

For example, Sue will tell one of her students trying to sell a short personal essay or op-ed piece, "Make it timely!" (There are often exclamation points at the end of things Sue says, I just know it.) I will add something dangerously misleading like, "We've got timely up to *here*. Why not make it weird, obscure, and also timeless?" I do this at least once per visit, partly because I truly am fond of odd and offbeat writing, but also because it reinforces my long-cherished notion of myself as a rebel who has no use for practical advice, either giving it or taking it. A week or so later, I will find myself rejecting an odd and offbeat piece and accepting another one because it is more timely. And so it goes.

I do this a few times a year in my capacity as a member of the Opinion section of *The New York Times*, where I develop and edit online series, usually weekly installments of first-person essays or commentary on a range of topics such as mental health, psychology, philosophy, music, religion, war, and peace. These venues are not restricted to "experts" in their chosen field; they are platforms for people from all walks of life and levels of experience. We welcome new writers, not just "experts," as long as they can write well and make compelling arguments or tell great stories that will appeal to our readers.

Many of Sue's students, coached by her on the ins and outs of narrative technique, to-the-point pitching, and common sense publishing etiquette, have found their way into *The New York Times* as well as other newspapers, websites, and magazines. These clips have led to more than one hundred books. So she and her recruits are doing something right.

Sue has told me that one of the reasons she invites me back every term is that I'm "optimistic"—something no one who has had to live with me would agree with. What I think she means by this is that I firmly believe these are good times for writers, and that, with new publications and websites sprouting up every day, and new readers with new interests and appetites wanting to read them, the landscape for writers looking to publish their work is far more promising than it has ever been. The days when one had to print out his work with a cover letter, put it in an envelope, lick the stamp and affix it, then send it off in a mailbox like a message in a bottle only to wait weeks, sometimes months, for a reply—usually a polite "no"—are over. These are boom times (for words, if not pay). Today, I can honestly encourage a classroom full of aspiring writers.

Sue's classes—and by extension this book—are like a journalistic and literary boot camp. They provide a set of rigorous practical steps that few new writers would ever dream up themselves. You must write and write fast—don't be fussy about it, because Sue doesn't tolerate dawdling. Develop strategic plans to identify and pitch editors just as quickly. Do your homework. Figure out who edits what. Take names. Didn't get the nod on your first piece? Brush yourself off and do it again. Ding! Then again. Write some more while you are at it. And move that middle part to the top—that's the hook right there, and you buried it. Brush it up, check your spelling, your flow. Be sure the pitch is short and to the point. And never send it on a Friday. Need to follow up? Be polite but persistent. All the things I never learned but should have when I was starting out as a writer. (It is the rare editor who didn't start out wanting to be a writer.)

In class, I field questions from new recruits, rapid-fire, about thirty in an hour, on the practical aspects of writing and publishing. These

Q&As are a little like speed dating, without the prospect of a date. Part of what I try to offer new writers is a sense that editors—particularly editors at higher profile places like *The New York Times*—are humans, rather than rigidly judgmental authority figures stamped out of a culture machine. Each one of us has our own tastes and inclinations, with passions, pet peeves, and sometimes odd obsessions. Most have hectic schedules, exploding e-mail inboxes, and lots of actual editing to do. But for the most part, we are happy to discover new writers, and we'd much rather say yes than no.

Another thing I never fail to mention: A writer who can produce good, skillful copy on time and conduct all the business of pitching, writing, and revising in a calm, professional manner is an editor's dream. That is the sort of writer this book is meant to produce.

I am also sometimes asked about how I got to do the job I now have. (I sometimes forget that it is a rare and wonderful one, and that question reminds me.) In the interest of the whole "editors are really just people" theme, I cough up a few details: Growing up in a Catholic working-class Staten Island family, I cared more for baseball than books and set my sights on the typical career choices of clueless boys—race car driver, big league pitcher, or if none of those worked out, a firefighter, like my dad. But a transformative head-on collision with Kurt Vonnegut in Mrs. Jocelyn's sophomore English class, and a realization that I couldn't break the town speed limit with my fastball, set me on another path. I had fallen in love with literature (as well as the cute, book-loving girl who sat in the next row). I was going to write.

I could have used a book like this in 1986 when I moved back to New York after graduating college. I arrived with a degree in history from Cornell University (thanks to financial aid, student loans, and my dad, who took on a second job) and a plan. It involved writing, yes, but it was devoid of the practical steps regarding what I might do when the writing was done. I figured my brilliance and undeniable talent would simply manifest itself, at which point an agent, an editor, and a publisher would materialize unbidden to nurture my genius. I would be discovered.

Much to the dismay of my parents, who were still paying off my student loans, I avoided steady work so I could write short stories, poems, and eventually, The Novel. I enrolled in an M.F.A. program and scraped by as a waiter, a bartender, a tutor, a drummer in a few rock bands, a middle school science teacher, and a part-time copy boy at *The New York Times*, where I delivered piles of breaking news updates, on actual paper, that came chattering off the wires, and where I began the slow process of learning about the business.

I wrote a handful of music reviews and profiles—of a jazz club owner, a bus driver, and a musician working in an Indian restaurant on Sixth Street—but I didn't have much guidance on how to be a working writer. Eventually, I lost my focus, and more important, my discipline, and gave up on the idea that I could figure out how to make a living from my first love.

What Sue's class and this book offer is not so much advice as a game plan, a practical to-do list that you'd never figure out, let alone follow, on your own. Think of Sue as your personal writing coach.

Working as an editor on the lookout for new writers has kept me busy. I have not yet written that novel. But so far, the publishing gods have been good to me. I have co-edited two essay collections, *The Stone Reader* and *Modern Ethics in 77 Arguments*, published by Liveright Publishing Corporation. And I still hammer out the occasional essay. The most recent, which ran in *The New York Times*, recalled how my mother wouldn't let me play football when I was a sports-mad kid. As Sue joked, except for the high-profile report on the dangers of playing football released just days before, which I linked to the piece, it wasn't timely at all.

—Peter Catapano, Editor, *The New York Times*

Introduction

"You're gonna sell your poems on the sidewalk?" my father asked. "Stop wasting time writing. Go to law, medical, or business school and get a real job."

As a Jewish kid growing up on Manhattan's Lower East Side, he'd carried blinds and fabric up broken tenement steps for my grandpa's window shade store. My parents met in the neighborhood as teenagers. My mother was an orphan who'd lost her parents young, already moonlighting as a secretary by tenth grade. "Just got into medical school in Chicago. Ya coming or not?" was his marriage proposal, according to family lore. They worked hard to give their four kids what they never had.

Yet I was an overly sensitive outcast in my big Midwest clan. I had a brilliant but conservative doctor dad I couldn't please, a redheaded domestic goddess mom I paled next to, and three sharp science-brain brothers who called me "Morticia" for my dark hair and clothes. They trashed my Dylan music, lefty politics, and poetry. When arguing, I couldn't finish a sentence without interruption. I felt silenced, inferior, outnumbered. Scrawling my hurt into secret notebooks was soothing. My fantasies of being an acclaimed author were fueled by the desire to be heard.

At the University of Michigan (which my dad called "The People's Republic of Ann Arbor") I was pleased to have my prose printed in a literary journal, though they only paid in extra copies. As an NYU grad student, I studied with Nobel and Pulitzer prized luminaries whose published work I revered. Sitting around a table in class after my poems were praised, I asked my professor, "Which editors do you submit to?"

"If you're worried about selling your work so soon, you're not serious," he sniffed.

I *was* serious. And desperate to learn if the obsessions I explored in verse might be expanded to prose I could earn money for. Nobody knew or would tell me. So after six years of higher education with two degrees, I didn't even know how to craft a cover letter to submit the pages I'd spent years perfecting. My folks urged: Move back to Michigan, marry, have kids, get a "normal" career. But I didn't want to be normal. I wanted to be a writer.

Miraculously, a former professor I hounded recommended me for an editorial assistant job at *The New Yorker*. I was overjoyed, though it was mostly typing and paid only thirteen thousand dollars a year, before taxes. Coincidentally, my first week at work, Monica, a fellow peon, introduced me to a *Cosmopolitan* editor in charge of the "Outrageous Opinions" column. The glossy magazine offered me five hundred dollars for a humorous essay about my confusion when using labels like "date," "guest," and "plus one" when referring to the guy I was seeing, who wasn't really my boyfriend. (Among others, I suggested: "I just met the man I want to father the children I don't want to have.") How jazzed I was to find stars in the margins and edits on my draft from their famous editor-in-chief, Helen Gurley Brown!

At twenty-three, seeing my name in a national magazine was exhilarating. When it came out, I ran ten blocks in heels to a newsstand, buying all the copies they had. Getting the check for my first byline was redemptive. Writing allowed me to talk without being interrupted. Publishing was like winning a prize for my words.

"I owe you my life!" I told Monica. She sort of took me up on it when she married my surgeon brother, moved near my parents, and had four kids, becoming the daughter my parents always wanted. I chronicled my jealousy over this triangle ("My Best Friend Stole My Brother") for my next piece, earning one thousand dollars. As Nora Ephron once said, "Everything is copy." At twenty-four, I met a *New York Times* editor who assigned me book reviews. Soon I had my own paperback column at *Newsday* that was syndicated across the country.

These early feats convinced my skeptical parents that I should keep trying. Not wanting to stay on the editorial route, I left my full-time nine-to-five to focus on writing. Since I was single and soon broke, my mother complained, "You're freelance everything!" After earning anywhere from one hundred to five thousand dollars each for many clips over several years, I still couldn't afford my rent. To cover my bills, I taught feature writing at NYU's journalism school by night. I loved teaching, which pleased my father who said, "Finally, a real job!" Yet I was disappointed by the administration's dismissive attitude toward helping students get bylines. My department heads pushed me to assign 8,000-word third-person term papers to my classes, instead of the intimate three-page stories using *I* that editors coveted. "Nobody will buy long researched coursework from newcomers," I argued. "But editors pay for good essays based on firsthand experience every day."

"We don't care about publication or payment. We're not a trade school," I was told.

My higher-ups shared the opinion of many in the ivory tower. They charged as much as business, medical, and law schools, seventy thousand dollars a year, to study great works. But unlike those other fields, they never shared practical guidance to help students land well after graduation. I was confused and frustrated by the discrepancy between what top educational institutions taught and what was needed to launch a profitable career. It was a glaring gap, as if wanting to support yourself with the craft you studied was greedy and shameful.

Most writing courses I took focused on reading famous texts and studying syntax, structure, and subtexts, relevant mainly in academia. So in 1993, when The New School offered me a job teaching classes for people of all ages, they let me try something different: I assigned short pieces editors wanted. Remembering how early bylines fueled my self-esteem, the goal of my course was: "Write and publish a great piece by the end of class." Parodying my impatience, with a nod to the late, great Carrie Fisher, I titled my method "Instant Gratification Takes Too Long."

I sped up the results by critiquing assignments not only on whether they were *good* for the classroom, but if they were *publishable* in the marketplace. Instead of analyzing metaphor or meter, I questioned if the story was engaging, original, wise, topical, or relevant to readers. We studied the best short nonfiction pieces. I showed my classes how to make their pages fit a specific newspaper or magazine column, which editor to try, and ways to craft a cover letter to get it read ASAP.

Best of all, The New School allowed me to invite wonderful editors to speak to my class, like the charmingly contrarian Peter Catapano! We'd go around the room to ask specific questions: "Which kind of pieces are you open to?" "How long?" "What should new writers never do?" Editors answered! These amazingly generous pros—twenty per semester—not only gave clear, smart, technical inside advice, they encouraged my students to submit work. "The worst that will happen is I might say 'No, thank you,'" Peter reassured, in a compassionate way that eliminated their fear.

In my initial New School class of twelve, many heard "Yes." Eight students got published and four made one thousand dollars or more. I instituted a rule: If anyone earned four figures from my assignments, they owed me dinner. I've rarely paid for a meal since. By giving the same homework and hosting varied editors, half of my classes published each term. Others sent clips and links later. With each student who sold a piece, I felt a vicarious thrill, remembering the euphoria of seeing my first byline.

Over two and a half decades of teaching, I learned that everybody has a story. But few know how to tell it well, where to send it, or how to convince an editor to pay for their words. The process seems insurmountable for someone new. Yet ironically, many editors would rather promote a debut over reprinting familiar voices. That's why it has been rewarding to show my students the steps to success.

Of course, even with a dramatic, burning story to tell, it's difficult to dive into feature journalism with no experience. But you don't have to be an English major, college grad, or take a class to get published. You just need a strong idea, three great pages, and a seasoned editor or guide to help navigate the process. I taught a workshop at Holy Apostles Soup Kitchen for thirteen years with *New Yorker* humorist Ian Frazier, helping homeless members—some without high school diplomas—sell beautiful, dark, honest work about their experiences on the streets. It inspired an anthology, *Food for the Soul*,[1] which was featured on NPR and *The Today Show*. Several contributors said seeing their name in print was life changing.

For twenty-five years, despite several recessions, aspiring authors and non-writers alike have filled my courses and seminars. With the rise of social media, it's easier to make your opinion and narrative known. Anyone with access to a computer can submit work to an editor who'll pay. Everyone from teenagers looking for a sideline, to students applying to colleges, to professionals, to retirees on fixed incomes, can benefit from creating a platform and reaching a big audience fast.

I've become practically psychic in figuring out where a piece might land, and I love moonlighting as a literary matchmaker. I joked to my students that getting "clips," copies of published pieces, is addictive: Like crack, you keep wanting more. Three people who studied with me joined *The New York Times* staff; one was hired at *The New Yorker*. So far, 105 books by my students have been sold to mainstream publishers (with $5,000 to $500,000 advances), many launching projects from their very first essay. When I offered endorsements to anyone who began their book in my class, I had no idea more than one hundred plugs would cause my book editor to call me "a blurb whore." Several students had the nerve to get bigger offers on books that sold more copies than mine.

After acing my fifteen-week class, the CEO of Mediabistro asked if I'd teach a five-week version for their adult education wing. On my college syllabus, we had five-month semesters to go from rough idea to completion. Yet even in my shorter five-week version, students sold pieces by the fifth class—or sooner. It was not only doable, it was fun to be more focused. As they say, "Obsession rids the mind of clutter." Undergrads and graduate students appreciated having the whole term to develop their work. But adults who were broke, impatient, and time- or

---

1. Seabury Books, 2000

childcare-challenged voted for the thirty-five-day version. When Mediabistro was sold, I kept teaching the short classes on my own. Tons of successful five-weekers took the class repeatedly to up their game and land bigger clips and book deals.

Lots of old-schoolers scorn the speed of e-publishing, lamenting the loss of lead times and big bucks for print pages. Yes, you're now more likely to get one hundred than one thousand dollars for a debut piece. Still, I rejoice in the vast opportunities provided by such websites as *Salon, Slate, Quartz, BuzzFeed, VICE, Vox, Bustle,* and *Tablet,* who are eager to pay newcomers for original work. Newer online versions of top newspapers and magazines like WashingtonPost.com, TeenVogue .com, and Esquire.com pay less to start, but unknowns can break in every day with first-person stories.

While I've personally mined my dating, mating, and addiction disasters, my students tackle more global issues, harnessing the power of the press to speak out on topics they're troubled by, in profound pieces this book will share. Alex Miller detailed his trauma as an African-American Navy vet fighting the U.S. Department of Veterans Affairs system in a *New York Times* op-ed. In *Tin House, Psychology Today,* and *The New York Times,* Aspen Matis revealed she was raped on her second day of college. Haig Chahinian depicted the difficulties of a gay Armenian man raising a biracial daughter for *The Washington Post, Los Angeles Times,* and *O, The Oprah Magazine.* Daisy Hernandez confessed she'd avoided explicitly telling her conservative Spanish-speaking New Jersey mom about her girlfriend by using the code words "I'm staying in Nueva York" in *Ms.* magazine. English wasn't his first language, yet my Muslim student Kenan Trebincevic chronicled surviving the ethnic cleansing campaign in his Bosnian hometown for *Esquire, Slate,* and *The Wall Street Journal.* A twelve-year-old victim became a thirty-year-old champion for his people.

Getting published is not only empowering and transformative—it can be lucrative and lead to more career triumphs. After his *New York Times* piece, Alex, the Navy man, was offered a full-time hospital job. Aspen's essay on her sexual assault led to a book and paid lectures for

RAINN (the Rape, Abuse & Incest National Network). Kenan became a Bosnian spokesperson against genocide, earning as much as seven thousand dollars per speech, lecturing around the country, as did Kassi Underwood, who published two pieces and a book on her abortion. Che Kurrien, an Indian-born undergrad, penned a *Newsday* op-ed on the culture shock of being a Mumbai immigrant in Manhattan. He contacted me ten years later to say everything I'd taught also applied to his job in his homeland, where he's now the editor-in-chief of *GQ India*.

Meanwhile as I aged, I tried longer, more literary ventures. When I showed a mentor my novel about two sisters-in-law who switched lives, she said: "You have no imagination whatsoever. Quit fiction." Fearing she was right, I took my own advice to "write about your obsessions." I chronicled quitting self-destructive relationships, cigarettes, drugs, and alcohol. At forty-one, I sold my debut memoir to Random House. That led to a stream of nonfiction books, two that were bestsellers. But I never gave up revising my novel, which finally sold to St. Martin's Press thirteen years after I started. Instead of a book launch, I threw myself a book mitzvah. My publishing motto: No never means no. It means keep revising until it rocks. In a student's parody of my class, a perky teacher character critiqued a piece, saying, "This is really fantastic. Now just rewrite the whole thing and make it much better."

When students asked a seasoned editor visiting my class if the successful writers he knew had the most talent, he answered, "No. They're the most obsessed." To quote Goethe, "At the moment of commitment the entire universe conspires to assist you." Indeed, my method is no longer shunned. I recently traded up to the Ivy League for a term, teaching a Columbia University M.F.A. course and Skyping into a journalism seminar at Harvard taught by a star ex-student. While many of my protégés are flourishing at a young age, it took me until my forties to live well doing what I love. Still, how many people nail their dream?

Last summer, I received a missive from Olaf, the doctor taking care of my eighty-five-year-old father in the hospital. "Your dad says you're a very important author and a generous professor who assists aspiring writers," Olaf wrote. "I could use your advice." I helped Olaf publish his first piece in *Quartz*, where my former student was his editor, which tickled my dad.

"So what did you tell Olaf about me?" I asked him.

"That I'm proud of my successful daughter," he said, melting me. "He says you're the real deal."

"Why don't you ever tell me that?"

"I am now," he said.

I flashed to *Cosmopolitan* editor Helen Gurley Brown, who grew up poor in Arkansas feeling like an ugly outcast "mouseburger." She discovered that success and power produce their own kind of beauty. I'm grateful she gave me the chance to see my words go national and to pass along the honor of giving voice to others.

After spending a quarter of a century teaching the class I wish I could have taken, I've now written the guide I'd needed to read, sharing the inside secrets for landing an impressive byline in lightning speed. Focusing on longer projects, I thought I'd tire of short nonfiction. Yet it turns out the best way to generate interest in a book at any stage is to publish three pages on the topic. This past fall, when I sold a short piece mentioning *The Byline Bible* in my bio, it wound up going viral. I was trending for ten minutes, my smartphone burning up and buzzing during class. I walked home on air. Even after doing this for three and a half decades, it's still magic to see how quickly three pages can change your life.

CHAPTER 1

Where to Start

ASSIGNMENT #1

The best way to break into publishing is with a great three-page double-spaced personal essay.

There's nothing more engaging than an intimate tale told with insight, humor, or candor. That explains the acclaim of such anthologies as *The Best American Essays*, moving first-person forums like *The New York Times'* "Modern Love" column and podcast, NPR's popular *This American Life*, and all the memoirs on nonfiction best-selling book lists—often sprung from one essay. Unfortunately, not all first-person narratives are as compelling for the editor and audience as they are for the author. Still, there's no reason you can't turn your private experiences into wise, eloquent, and publishable prose.

Early in my career, I sold short, provocative pieces to women's magazines about relationships, family, and work problems. Coming from a confessional poetry background, I knew that a surface-level appreciation of one's mate, parents, or children would not lead to brilliance. Love letters and light slices of life rarely engendered profundity. Showing off how great you are is superficial and will make readers hate and resent you. Writing usually becomes much richer when you focus on your vulnerability and explore your regrets and struggles. Think in extremes: the night that changed your life, the lover who shattered your heart, the embarrassing addiction you couldn't get over. Trying to tackle unfinished, messy, and uncomfortable conflicts led me to authentic, meaty subjects and often a cathartic release, not to mention money, success, and acclaim.

STEP ONE: WHAT SHOULD I WRITE?

The most frequent mistake newcomers to nonfiction make is to pick a subject that's lackluster, self-congratulatory, or just a diary-like rendering of something mundane they went through. Sorry, but no editors I know want to publish a piece about how cute your cats, gardenias, or grandchildren are. I know it's counterintuitive, but what makes you successful and lovable in real life might make you unlovable and unknowable on the pages of a short essay. So if you portray yourself as strong, wealthy, good-looking, and happily married, audiences might stop reading after the third line. I learned this the hard way when I first brought a piece into my writing workshop about an ex-boyfriend whose surprise visit rattled me.

"She comes off like a well-off, white, forty-year-old married woman with a good husband [but] who still has feelings for her old flame. I hate her guts," one critic told me.

I was hurt and confused by the negative response, since I was the "she" being critiqued. Clearly there was something wrong with the way I was telling my story. I wound up reorganizing the details and reframing the events, offering a deeper, more vulnerable context. In my revision, I confessed that I was going through difficult infertility treatments and rejections from a series of book editors my literary agent had contacted on my behalf. It was at this moment that the college beau who'd unceremoniously dumped me twenty years earlier showed up at my doorstep. To make the timing worse, he handed me a book he'd just published—though he'd been a biology major who used to tell me that my English degree was "worthless." I weaved in the humiliating events that had happened the day before my ex came over when I'd received two phone messages. In the first, my fertility doctor shared disappointing results of tests my husband and I had taken, proving it was unlikely I'd be able to get pregnant. In the next call, my agent informed me that five editors had rejected the novel I'd spent five years on.

"I felt like she was saying, 'The only baby you have is ugly and we don't want it,'" I wrote, holding back tears.

"Wow, you should have gotten old and bitter a long time ago, because this rocks," remarked the critic after she heard the new passages a week later. Indeed, that much more dark and vulnerable revised version of my essay wound up being published in *Marie Claire* magazine and launching a first memoir about all my horrific breakups: *Five Men Who Broke My Heart*.[1]

After learning how important it was to express vulnerability on the page, I began my first feature journalism class by asking everyone to write a "humiliation essay," revealing *their* most embarrassing secret. I shared the basic, technical writing rules for the type of short nonfiction personal essays I'd had so much luck with.

1. **AIM FOR 500–900 WORDS**, around three double-spaced typed pages, the most likely length an editor will publish fast by a new scribe. Not 3,500 words. Stick to the word count.

2. **PUT EVERYTHING IN *NEW YORK TIMES* FORMAT**, which most publications use. You can buy their style manual,[2] or just pick up their Sunday newspaper and emulate the way they title every piece, put bylines under those titles, and indent for each new paragraph and line of dialogue.

3. **PICK A STORY THAT YOU CAN PUT YOUR REAL NAME ON.** *The New York Times, The Washington Post, The Wall Street Journal, TIME* magazine, and others will not allow you to use a pseudonym (though a few women's and men's magazines might allow you to use a maiden name or "anonymous").

4. **DON'T USE FAKE NAMES FOR THE OTHERS**, which many editors will also not allow in nonfiction. To avoid specific monikers, try using labels like "my old best friend," "my former flame," "my ex-girlfriend," "my relatives," and/or using pronouns throughout. Sometimes you can get away with saying, "My ex, let's just call him Pete," as long as you indicate to the reader and editor you're making a change. Or you can use real nicknames or labels you make up, as

---

1. Delacorte Press, 2004
2. *The New York Times Manual of Style and Usage*, Three Rivers Press, 2015

I did in my memoir (about Mr. Studrocket, Beach Boy, Root Canal, Hamlet, and The Biographer).

5. **SHARE YOUR BACKGROUND AND ETHNICITY** so people can picture, relate, and like you. You're familiar with your family lineage, background, and physical looks. But your photograph or bio won't necessarily accompany your pages. So describe yourself with unique, idiosyncratic details. My student Saba Ali began her first *New York Times* piece: "Born in Kenya of Indian heritage, I came to the United States at age six, settling with my family in upstate New York, growing up Muslim in suburban America." Include specific religious, ethnic, cultural, and class conflicts, especially since multiculturalism is hot.

6. **FOCUS ON ONE CURRENT SCENE OR ONE PROBLEM IN ADULTHOOD.** Since most editors are over eighteen, it is much harder to publish a piece about childhood, though strategic flashbacks later in the piece can work.

7. **SHOW, DON'T TELL.** Use very specific, fleshed-out details, including dialogue, external settings, and physical descriptions. Some novice writers think staying general is more universal, but it's just the opposite.

8. **DON'T OVERLOAD THE READER WITH BACKSTORY** or expository facts that ruin the momentum. Nobody wants to read "then-this-happened-then-that-happened." Playwright David Mamet says only three things are relevant to drama: Who wants what from whom? What happens if they don't get it? Why now? Make sure you answer those questions on your first page. If you need to, you can subtly weave in important background details later.

9. **DON'T LIE.** In nonfiction, you can't make things up. While you can exaggerate a little or re-create dialogue from the best of your ability, you can't make up stories, actions, or characters. Everything you write has to have really happened. Some editors work with fact-checkers or will Google you to test your veracity. *The New York Times'* "Modern Love" editor often shows a piece to the ex-spouse, mother, or brother in the story to double-check the essay's accuracy.

10. **GATHER PROOF.** Just in case an editor, fact-checker, or book publishing lawyer asks in the future, keep your old diaries, letters, and photo albums. Ask if you can tape conversations with loved ones (several ex-boyfriends surprisingly agreed when I interviewed them for my first memoir). File printed-out e-mails and texts, as many journalists do. In order for someone to win a lawsuit against you in nonfiction, he'd have to prove you lied, with malice intended, and show damages. So keep any evidence that shows you're telling the truth.

11. **CLARIFY YOUR EMOTIONAL ARC.** There's a saying you should "start in delight, end in wisdom." Though I can also understand the Seinfeldian rule "no hugging, no learning," you certainly don't want to start angry and end angry. Something has to be resolved or changed from your first line to your last. What did you learn or have to unlearn? What did this occurrence teach you? How can this experience help others? In my *New York Times Magazine* essay "The Bride Wore White—and Black," I was proud to wear all black to my cool, bohemian wedding, shunning convention. I concluded with the second ceremony, where I wore a white dress, with a rabbi and cantor, and we married all over again, for my mother, realizing it was worth it to make her happy.

12. **DON'T START BY GIVING AWAY YOUR END.** While provocation can get attention, if you confess "We broke up and then my first love died" right away, why would we keep reading? Add suspense, intrigue, mystery, or counterintuitive irony. Let your last line contain a big surprise.

During the second week of that initial class, my students turned in chronicles of their bad breakups, addictions, illnesses, and domestic fissures, as well as assaults, racial discrimination, sexual harassment, and trouble with their families, bosses, and the law. I was so blown away by all of the brave, beautiful, and distinctive and dramatic essays they handed in—and later, by how many of those wound up published—that it soon became my signature assignment. It's tough to argue with stellar results. Over the last twenty-five years, this exact prompt has led to thousands of wise, well-crafted first bylines for my students. (Many I'll quote and offer links to throughout this book to make them easier to look up and read.)

While some critics find confessional writing to be self-indulgent, editors of almost every newspaper, magazine, webzine, and book publisher buy them constantly. That's because audiences love to read personal writing, the most popular of all types of pieces. Best-seller book lists show millions of memoirs sold every year. The chance to get paid for a big byline has been dwindling—along with newspaper and magazine pages. Writing the "humiliation essay" is one of the best ways to beat the odds and break in.

Your first idea may not be your best one. So write a list of several topics you might consider. My student Sarah Herrington, a yoga teacher, at first complained, "But I don't have anything humiliating to write about." After hearing the other students' ideas she came up with: "Teaching a kids' yoga class, a little girl had a panic attack. I helped her through it since I'd had panic attacks myself." That wound up in *The New York Times*, the first of a long series of revealing essays Sarah went on to publish. Here's the advice I give my classes when it comes to figuring out good essay topics for my infamous humiliation essay assignment.

1. **LEAD THE LEAST SECRETIVE LIFE YOU CAN** (without getting sued, divorced, disowned, killed, or arrested).

2. **EXPLORE YOUR WORST ADDICTIONS OR OBSESSIONS THAT YOU CAN PUT YOUR NAME ON.** Pick a subject you find enthralling or that you have expertise on, especially if it's in the news or permeating current culture. My only students who've published pieces about the Iraq, Afghanistan, or Vietnam wars have been veterans, military spouses, or children of vets. Conversely, pupils have aced essays on being addicted to buying makeup at an all-night Duane Reade drugstore, getting tested for HIV, and firing a nanny after reading her X-rated blog. Don't worry if the subject is small compared to world events. You'll bring a theatrical freshness to what fascinates you.

3. **FOCUS ON DRAMA, CONFLICT, AND TENSION.** Don't write an idealistic appreciation of your spouse, parents, or children. Confront unresolved emotional issues about something that's bothering you. As writer Joan Didion said, "I write entirely to find out what I'm thinking."

4. **FAILURE IS FASCINATING.** Do you remember losing an internship, job, lover, friendship, money, contest, or your pride? Go back there! An author friend suggests starting when you're about to fall off a cliff (literally or figuratively).

5. **CUT TO THE CHASE.** In a 900-word essay, there's no time to meander, explain your entire history, or include the highlights of your résumé. Be as blunt as you can about what your humiliation is. "In December, my husband stopped screwing me" was the first line of a piece I published in *The New York Observer* that led to a book deal. (Of course, I would not have sent that piece to *The New York Times* or *The Christian Science Monitor*. I chose *The New York Observer*—known for Candace Bushnell's "Sex and the City" column—because I knew they preferred very revealing first person.)

6. **AVOID THE OBVIOUS.** While being opinionated or sardonic is great, we already know that terrorism is bad, public schools need money, breakups hurt, and online dating can suck. Be counterintuitive, find idiosyncratic angles, play devil's advocate, twist clichés. When my student Rainbow Kirby explored her thirty-year-old boyfriend's living at home, she smartly began with the film *Failure to Launch*, which had just opened, and sold the flip side—the perks of dating a man residing with his folks—to *Newsday*. My protégée Amy Klein's *New York Times'* "Modern Love" column about being addicted to JDate ended with her missing her Internet stalker.

7. **EDIT YOURSELF.** Just because something really happened is never enough reason to write it. Much of life is boring. Try to get rid of the in-between actions, all tedious back-and-forth talk, and stage directions ("and then we went to the parking lot, got in the car, put on our seat belts, and turned on the engine"). Only include the most significant, fascinating beats to your story.

8. **END AS A VICTOR, NOT A VICTIM.** Personal essays must get personal. But even if you bravely revisit your worst struggles, acting victimized and reciting a litany of injustices inflicted on you is boring and cliché. Question, challenge, reveal, and trash yourself more than others. One colleague wrote about her ex-husband of twenty years who was an abusive alcoholic, listing all of his evils. When she admitted she knew he was a problem drinker after the first year, I suggested refocusing on why she stayed for nineteen more. Turned out her father was a drinker and her mother helped him give up the sauce—at age sixty. So that was her model for marriage. Her revision was a standout.

9. **DON'T FORGET THE WISDOM.** If you heard good advice, repeat it with attribution and share your own solutions to your problems. My favorite essays about quitting addictions include the nitty-gritty on how the writer nixed cigarettes, alcohol, heroin, pills, pot, rampant sex, shopping, or sugar. For example, I chronicled how, when I was going through nicotine withdrawal, my addiction specialist instructed my husband to hold me for one hour every night, without speaking, as we watched a TV show or film. That calmed me down and replaced my toxic habits with love.

10. **REMEMBER, THE FIRST PIECE YOU WRITE THAT YOUR FAMILY HATES MEANS YOU'VE FOUND YOUR VOICE.** (If you don't want to offend anyone, try writing a cookbook.)

LIST HUMILIATING MOMENTS TO MINE

Like Sarah Herrington, many of my students at first complained that they couldn't come up with any enthralling ideas. I could relate. I always feared my life was too boring to compete with such internationally acclaimed authors as Mary Karr, Salman Rushdie, Zadie Smith, Etgar Keret, Alison Bechdel, or A.M. Homes. After all, I was a straight white girl from Michigan who'd had stupid affairs and addictions. Moving to Manhattan, therapy helped me quit my toxic habits and I married someone nice. That was it. I'd become a workaholic who sat at the computer most of the day. My parents were not raging alcoholics. I wasn't adopted. I had no children. Nobody important in my childhood died on me. I wasn't a world traveler. I'd never been in a war, race riot, on food stamps, in the hospital more than overnight, divorced, or the subject of a fatwa. There were many other typical freelancers and teachers like me in the world. What could I possibly add to the cultural conversation?

Luckily I learned you don't need a wildly dramatic existence to be a successful nonfiction writer. It turned out that by being brutally honest and extremely revealing about many of the dull day-to-day issues I'd been through made me stand out. Even my silly-seeming exploits and minor adventures resonated with top editors and readers. In fact, Gustave Flaubert advised writers to "Be regular and orderly in your life, so that you may be violent and original in your work."

Here's a list of embarrassing topics I explored for national magazines and webzines over the years. Since they had big audiences across the country, I tried to make my stories both idiosyncratic and universal at the same time.

1. Although I lie and pretend otherwise, I really get sick of seeing all the pictures of my friends' kids. (Goodhousekeeping.com)
2. I started a secret Facebook friendship with my ex's wife. (Elle.com and picked up on Redbook.com and Esquire.com)
3. I fixed my brother up with my best friend and lost them both. (*New Woman*)
4. After a bad breakup, I felt suicidal and needed therapy to save me. (*Cosmopolitan*)
5. Though I was happily married, I developed a crush on a physical therapist half my age. (*New York* magazine)
6. My best friend stopped returning my phone calls and e-mails, breaking my heart. (Oprah.com)
7. I was a feminist who intentionally avoided female doctors. (*DAME* magazine)
8. I was sure I was the type who never held grudges. But then I realized I was incapable of forgiving anyone unless they give me a full-out apology. (*Salon*)

9. Because I was broke and desperate, I had to ask my conservative father—a doctor—to write me a prescription for birth control pills. (*Jane* magazine)
10. I couldn't see that criticizing my husband was ruining my marriage. (*Marie Claire*)
11. In graduate school, I dated a professor I felt harassed by, but later realized I was the aggressor and he was the victim. (*New York* magazine)
12. When my husband stopped initiating sex, I started overeating. (*Psychology Today*)
13. I thought quitting diet soda would be easy. Then I stopped and went into withdrawal. (*Newsweek*)
14. I gave away two old Barbie dolls to a friend's young daughters, then missed them. (*Daily Beast*)
15. I won't let anybody take selfies of me because I hate how I look in candid photographs. (*Yahoo*)
16. I was secretly ashamed of my family's politics. (*Salon*)

Here are my personal essay topics that I made more timely or specialized to publish in particular newspaper or web sections.

1. Though I swore I would grow old naturally like Gloria Steinem, at the first sight of a gray strand, I ran to the beauty salon to get my hair dyed. (*The New York Times Magazine*)
2. After I quit smoking and drinking, I'd swim a mile every day in my Greenwich Village roof pool—until I got the only back injury in the world that made swimming impossible. (*The New York Observer*)
3. After I lost my favorite job, reviewing five books a week, my boss hired someone to take my place and let her do only three books weekly for the same salary. (*Quartz*)
4. The friend who fixed me up with my husband danced the hora at my wedding, then stopped speaking to me. (*The Forward*)
5. I needed a shrink to help me write a book with my Manhattan shrink. (*The New York Times* Opinion)

THE BYLINE BIBLE

6. I de-friended people on Facebook who had political opinions I disagreed with. (*The Washington Post* Opinion section)
7. Although it was supposed to be nonaddictive, I got hooked on smoking pot and don't celebrate all the marijuana reforms. (*Los Angeles Times* Op-Ed section)
8. When my best friend from high school visited me, I found myself completely jealous of her domestic life in Israel. (*Tablet*)
9. The first day I tried to quit cigarettes, I wound up searching the garbage for half-smoked butts at three in the morning. (*The New York Times*)
10. After I quit cigarettes, alcohol, pot, gum, and bread, I became addicted to quitting things every New Year. (New York *Daily News*)

WHAT IF MY TOPIC IS TOO ORDINARY?

My students sometimes get hung up on finding the perfect, original idea that will go viral, propelling them into print, book publishing, or notoriety. I tend to agree with the late British novelist and critic Sir Arthur Thomas Quiller-Couch, who said there are only seven stories in the world: Man against Man. Man against Nature. Man against himself. Man against God. Man against Society. Man caught in the middle. Man and Woman. (Feel free to update with your own gender and pronouns.)

So it's not necessarily the saga itself that will get you noticed, paid, and published, but the way you tell it. To quote the German-born architect Ludwig Mies van der Rohe: "God is in the details."

That said, some tales really have been told too often for editors to keep printing. The frequency of a universal issue getting covered doesn't imply you can't attempt another go. But be conscious what you're up against, be innovative, and add a signature spin when visiting places many others writers have already trod.

"Losing a loved one is the most common essay theme we see," a top editor once told my class. "My bosses declared: 'We have a moratorium on dead parent stories.' There are too many, they're too depressing, and they're mostly the same, so they're rejected."

Many other editors I know have echoed that sentiment. It doesn't mean you can't write about the intense pain of losing your mother, father, or grandparents. To publish it, you just have to be more creative in the way you spin that saga. Here are some examples of unusual twists that worked.

1. In "Agreeing to Accept and Move On," my student Elizabeth Koster's *New York Times'* "Modern Love" piece centered on how—while her mother was sick with cancer—Koster desperately tried to find a husband so she could introduce them before it was too late.

2. My student Bryan Patrick Miller's *New York Times Magazine* piece "Return of Glavin" chronicled how he tried to fulfill his mother's deathbed request that he visit their ancestral home in Ireland, where their lineage was highly regarded. Turned out, their bloodline was filled with scoundrels who'd been run out of town.

3. "Rhode Island Author Searches for Father's Forgotten Grave," the *Providence Journal* essay by my student Judith Glynn, centered on her quest to find out exactly where her divorced, estranged late dad was buried and visit him there.

4. My friend Alice Feiring's *New York Times* piece "Writer's Block at the Tombstone" is about how, after her brother Andrew passed away, she and her mother were appalled that her sister-in-law only etched "Beloved husband and father" on his tombstone, without also putting "brother and son."

5. The *Salon* essay by Rebecca Lanning called "Death Doesn't Come Like It Does in the Movies" delineated what her mother's last days with cancer taught her about our right to die and the importance of assisted dying.

6. In his *New York Times* essay, "A Son's Initiation in the Fraternity of the Lawn," my colleague Rich Prior remembers all the gardening and landscaping advice his late father gave him over the years while Rich mows the grass at his own summer house.

7. "The Way They Were," my colleague Gabrielle Selz's *New York Times* piece, dissected the contrasting ways her parents dealt with death. Her shy, late mother never mentioned any last wishes and died in

the hospital. Her take-charge, still-living ninety-six-year-old father, on the other hand, has been obsessively preparing every detail of his demise for the last twenty-six years, including drafting his obituary and buying his burial plot, along with the gravestone to mark it.

WRITE A HOLLYWOOD MOVIE PITCH

It helps—for many reasons—to condense the idea of your essay in one or two succinct fun or fascinating lines. Try to slip in specific idiosyncratic details about yourself, whether it's your age, religion, color, ethnicity, or background. Be witty, provocative, or vulnerable. Here are descriptions of humiliation essays that my students pitched me, and editors over the years, which sold to national magazines. While a small percentage of the publications or sections might no longer exist, many do. I've included some pieces in full, and most of the others you can look up online. Because these ideas are so crazy, weird, or heartfelt, I bet they'd sell just as quickly today.

1. I wasn't afraid of going to bed with him. I was afraid to sleep with him—because he didn't know I was a sleepwalker. (Kathleen Frazier, *Psychology Today*'s "Two-Minute-Memoir")
2. I couldn't wait to flee my suburban family and escape to Los Angeles—until a back injury left me no choice but to move home so they could take care of me. (Lawrence Everett Forbes, *Newsday*)
3. During my difficult divorce at forty-three, I decided it was okay to let my two daughters see me cry. (Beverly Willett, *Good Housekeeping*)
4. I had a big schnoz everyone told me to get fixed. (Sarah Liston, *Marie Claire*)
5. I tried to cure my obsessive-compulsive disorder with prayer. (Abby Sher, *SELF* magazine)
6. Meeting my missing father for the first time, I was afraid he'd think I was a failure. (Kelley Brower, *Cosmopolitan*)

7. None of my friends or co-workers knew I was a Muslim refugee who'd survived ethnic cleansing at age twelve before I became an American citizen. (Kenan Trebincevic, Esquire.com)
8. My gynecologist incorrectly decided my husband had abused me when he hadn't. (Aspen Matis, *Psychology Today*)
9. As a kid, I was sexually abused by a neighbor. As an adult, I was afraid to tell anyone. (Jake Cooney, *Newsweek*)
10. I cheated on my husband—with food. (Kara Richardson Whitely, *SELF* magazine)
11. Nobody knew I spent my first eighteen years in America as an undocumented immigrant. (Maria E. Andreu, *Newsweek*)
12. My voice was so high-pitched that people thought I was female. (Mark Jason Williams, *Out* magazine)
13. Studying in Africa made this white girl appreciate her big behind. (Amy Karafin, *Jane* magazine)
14. I was afraid to go out or show my arms and legs because I had a skin disorder called vitiligo. (India Garcia, TeenVogue.com)
15. As a first-generation Chinese-American woman who wears a size 36D bra, I can testify to the power of the American fast food diet. (Jennifer Tang, *Newsweek*)

Here are some newspaper and web ideas my students sold:

1. When my elderly mother was sick, I slept in the same bed with her. (Peter Napolitano, *The New York Times*' "Modern Love" column)
2. I was fired from my job for sexually harassing a young co-worker while I was drunk and I didn't even remember doing it. (Mark Hoadley, *The Washington Post*'s "Solo-ish" column)
3. After a long estrangement with my mother, I tried to connect with her on Facebook. (Adane Byron, *Salon*)
4. I'm a liberal New Yorker who has a gun I named Roxy. (Amaya Swanson, *The Frisky*)
5. At forty-four years old, I'm a nomad who has lived in eighteen temporary residences in six years. (Susan Marque, *The Washington Post*'s "Solo-ish" column)

6. As a nice Jewish guy named David living in Queens, for two weeks in 1977, the police thought I was the serial killer Son of Sam. I liked being seen as dangerous. (David Kempler, *The New York Times*)

7. I've been petrified I'll die any second for fifty-seven years, ever since I was diagnosed with diabetes. (Dan Fleshler, *The New York Times'* Opinion section)

8. Facebook suggested I befriend my rapist. (Dorri Olds, *The New York Times'* Opinion section)

9. At thirty-seven, I moved back in with my parents, becoming the rebellious teenager I never was. (Joel Schwartzberg, *The New York Times Magazine*)

10. As a life coach, I hated helping my clients too much. Because when they became successful, they quit me. (Stacy Kim, *Quartz*)

11. My name is Arpard Herschel Fazakas—or at least it was until last year, when, at age fifty-one, I changed it. (Art Segal, *The New York Times Magazine*)

12. As an undergraduate, I fell in love with a guy who had to wear an ankle bracelet because he'd been accused of raping another student. And I hated how passive he was sexually. (Ashley Cross, *The New York Times'* "Modern Love" column)

13. I never should have followed my dreams and left my boring job, because now I'm broke, out of work, and even more depressed. (David Sobel, *Salon*)

14. As an Asian man, I was afraid to tell my family I was most attracted to blonde American girls. (Tuan Nguyen, *New York Press*)

15. I thought I could handle getting an abortion, but when my ex-boyfriend had a baby with another woman three years later, I flipped out. (Kassi Underwood, *The New York Times'* "Modern Love" column)

16. I tried to become a spy to get away from my conservative parents. (Carolina Baker-Norko, *Slate*)

17. Ever since a car accident landed me in a wheelchair, I've done more immoral, illegal things. (David Birnbaum, *The New York Times Magazine*)

18. My whole family was out of work at the same time. So how could I help my daughter find employment when I couldn't get a job myself? (Lisa Reswick, *The Wall Street Journal*)
19. I was roofied at fifty—and nobody at the school function where it happened did anything about it. (Linda Kleinbub, *The New York Observer*)
20. My Asian parents didn't care if I got Cs in school. They weren't tigers; they were pussycats. (Kate Chia, *The New York Times'* "On Campus" column)
21. I had "man boobs," a condition called gynecomastia, and I never told anyone I had an operation to fix it at age fifteen. (Zachary Valenti, *Salon*)

FIGURE OUT YOUR MAIN GOAL

So you've picked your subject. Before trying to decide where you might publish a piece, I ask my students to first figure out exactly what their goal is. Here are some typical responses.

1. "I've never published before, so I just want to see my work anywhere, even if I don't get paid." In this case, I would research *The Rumpus, Tin House, Honeysuckle Magazine, The Brooklyn Rail,* and *McSweeney's,* which usually don't pay for pieces, but publish many short essays by new writers all the time.
2. "I'd like to get paid something, as long as my piece will be published quickly." If this is how you feel, check out *AMNY, Metro, The Villager, The Establishment, Ravishly,* and *Bustle,* which sometimes pay only fifty dollars but come out quickly.
3. "I want a prestigious byline, no matter if it just pays one hundred dollars." The more respected a publication, the more competition you'll have. So make sure to first peruse many pieces from *The New York Times'* Opinion and Well Family sections and its "Modern Love" column, as well as *The Wall Street Journal, The Washington Post, Salon, Slate, The Nation, The New Republic, The Atlantic,* and *The New Yorker.*

THE BYLINE BIBLE

4. "I'm hoping to make the most amount of money possible." When finances are your main motivation, I recommend buying and studying the hard copies of such women's and men's magazines as *Esquire*, *GQ*, *Men's Journal*, *Men's Health*, *Marie Claire*, *Elle*, *Cosmopolitan*, and *Redbook*, which often pay between one and four dollars a word. (I have a karmic theory that if you want to get paid from a publication, you have to buy the paper version, you can't just read it online for free.) But be warned: The higher the fee, the slower and more difficult it will be. In some cases it can take a year or two to get a yes, a clip, and a check. Some publications pay on acceptance—not necessarily a good thing. *The New Yorker* once famously bought a piece it didn't run for fourteen years!

5. "I'm aiming for the best publication in the world." If you want only the top, study *The New Yorker*, *The New York Times*, *Harper's Magazine*, *The Atlantic*, *The Paris Review*, and *O, The Oprah Magazine*. But again, you might need to take the long view.

6. "I want to get published but there is no way I can ever put my name on this." I've never known *The New York Times* or *The Washington Post* to allow the author of a first-person essay to use a pseudonym. However, *Cosmopolitan* and *Marie Claire* have published my students' work under an alias or "anonymous." Focus on women's and men's magazines. Make sure to let the editor know in your cover letter you won't be able to use your legal name, knowing that might be a deal-breaker.

7. "My dream is to launch my book project with an essay." From my experience, the best places to make a splash that will interest literary agents and book editors are *The New Yorker*, *Tin House*, and *The New York Times'* "Modern Love" column—the latter has inspired about fifty books so far, according to editor Daniel Jones. But he also takes three to four months to get back to you on submissions. So don't submit your Valentine's Day story on February 1. And the minute you submit your piece, start something new.

READ WHAT YOU WANT TO WRITE

"When writers asked me, 'What kind of pieces do you like?' I used to answer, 'We like the kind of pieces that we run,'" said former *New York Times* editor Frank Flaherty.

It seems obvious, but an amazing number of aspiring freelancers ask editors this kind of general (and usually inappropriate) question all the time. It can easily be answered by reading their publication and their section carefully.

If you commit to writing a great personal essay, don't craft it in a vacuum. Even accomplished copywriters, or authors who have published poetry, mysteries, or novels, make mistakes leaping into this genre. So you need to first study the specific format and style of the publication you want to emulate. If you don't do your homework, you could blunder by sending an essay about getting sexually harassed by your boss to an editor who just did a special issue on that very topic the previous week. Or you might submit a screed on how you quit drinking, thinking it's brilliant and original. Until the editor asks, "Why didn't you reference the three current best-selling books on that exact topic?"

For an overview of the genre, check out Phillip Lopate's *The Art of the Personal Essay*.[3] Linger over fifty lovelorn stories in *Modern Love*,[4] curated by *New York Times* editor Daniel Jones. Memorize Daphne Merkin's work. To get a sense of the current field and what's already been done and done well (and who your competition is), study pieces by David Sedaris, Roxane Gay, Joan Didion, and Ian Frazier, to mention a few of my favorite living essayists.

Read at least twenty recent pieces from the publication you have decided to aim for. Pay careful attention to the length, tone, and topics they cover. When I wanted to break into the "Lives" column of *The New York Times Magazine*, I spent a day in the library reading hundreds of past issues. I saw most of their essays were on such heavy topics as death, illness, and abortion. My idea (about being a feminist who wore a black dress to my nontraditional wedding but became a Bridezilla nonethe-

---

3. Anchor Books, 1995
4. Broadway Books, 2007

less) was too light and amusing. So I completely revised it to focus on the darker, more embarrassing angle of the story: After I married in a hip downtown New York ceremony wearing a black dress, my Jewish mother—who'd been an orphan—freaked out that I wouldn't allow her to plan her only daughter's wedding. She insisted I put on a white gown and get married again before a rabbi and cantor, and under a chuppah in Michigan. After an emergency therapy session with my shrink, I acquiesced. That was the topic that made it into the column.

Had I not read so many essays that editor had already published, my original lighter piece would have been rejected. Do your homework! As the saying goes, "The harder I work, the luckier I get."

IDENTIFY YOUR TARGET AUDIENCE

Once you decide what you want to write about, you need to get a broader idea of who might be interested in your particular subject, age group, or regional or political bent. After you pick the demographic you're aiming for, you can better readjust your story around their focus, emulate their style, and emphasize their concerns. If you're targeting "Modern Love," for example, the details of how you met your spouse will be extremely relevant. If you're aiming for *Forbes* or *The Nation*, not so much.

Here are some choices to consider:

1. **PARENTHOOD** is a huge growing subgenre. Check out *Redbook*, *The Washington Post*'s "On Parenting" column, the Well Family section in *The New York Times*, *Aeon*, *Babble*, *Parents*, *FamilyFun*, and *Brain, Child*. Aside from pieces on being a mother or father, these editors also run work by people who were adopted, have complicated issues and reconciliations with their own parents, and those who are child-free.

2. For those **IN HIGH SCHOOL OR COLLEGE**, many magazines cater to this group: *Seventeen*, *Teen Vogue*, *Cosmopolitan*, *Boys' Life*, *Girls' Life*, *CICADA*, and *Teen Graffiti*. *Newsday* and other newspapers have sections specifically for teenage reporters, and *The New York*

Times' "Modern Love" column and *Glamour* have a special college contest every year you should look up.

3. If you are retiring or chronicling **PEOPLE OVER 50**, aim for places that care about that demographic. While mainstream publications might be interested in universal issues, it won't hurt to take a good look at *Next Avenue* and *Purple Clover*. *AARP The Magazine* is known to pay fifteen hundred dollars for a short piece.

4. **TRUE STORIES ABOUT DATING AND MATING** are wildly popular. Aside from *The New York Times'* "Modern Love" column there's the *Los Angeles Times'* "L.A. Affairs" and *The Washington Post*'s "Soloish" columns, which want the issues of singles addressed, as well as *DAME* magazine. Also read *Cosmopolitan, SheKnows,* and *The Frisky,* which care about the social lives of young women. For men, check out the online versions of *Esquire, GQ, Men's Journal,* and *The Good Men Project,* which accept lots of essays from freelancers.

5. Are you writing about **HOMOSEXUALITY**? While some mainstream editors welcome pieces about lesbian, gay, bisexual, transgender, pansexual, and gender fluidity issues, they are covered much more frequently and extensively in *The Advocate,* the *Washington Blade, POZ, Instinct, Out, Metrosource, Curve, Them, Pink* magazine, and *BuzzFeed's* LGBT section.

6. While it is not easy to write about **WRITING** (since most national editors fear it doesn't "play in Peoria"), a few places that do are *Publishers Weekly*'s "Soapbox" column, *Writer's Digest, The Writer, Poets & Writers,* and *Literary Hub.*

7. Many publications run stories about **ILLNESS, RECOVERY, MENTAL AND PHYSICAL HEALTH**. Check out *Psychology Today, Dr. Oz The Good Life, Health, Men's Health, Men's Fitness, Muscle & Fitness, Women's Health, Prevention, SELF,* and *Yoga Journal.* I've sold pieces on my breast cancer scare, my journey through genetic testing, and how—though I'm a feminist—I didn't see my first female doctor until I was 48.

8. Not all publications care about **POLITICS**, especially from non-experts. But if you have a platform and can make the personal political with a timely peg, consider *Slate, Salon, The Nation, The New Republic, Foreign Affairs, The American Conservative, The American Spectator,* and *The Atlantic.* But remember to first read many recent pieces they've already run to see what their bent is. I sold a piece to the left-leaning *Salon* about coming to terms with relatives who voted for Donald Trump that would have been scorned by editors at the right-wing *The American Conservative* or the *New York Post.*

9. **WILD AND CRAZY CHRONICLES**: While shamelessly confessing your past sins is almost a requirement for relationship and addiction memoirs, most publications avoid profanity, graphic language, and titillating tales involving sex-and-drugs-and-rock-and-roll. Thus I often ask students to consider toning down their racy rhetoric and pay attention to guidelines. (If you're aiming for *The New York Times* but put "motherfucker" in your first line, you clearly didn't do your homework.) I usually aim for a PG-rating myself. Still, there are editors who relish the daring and indecent. Blatant sexuality and swearing do not scare off *BuzzFeed, Salon, The Village Voice, VICE, Out, Rolling Stone, The New Republic,* or *The New Yorker*—though your time frame and topic have to be relevant to their readers, and the writing up to par.

START STRONG

The prolific *New Yorker* writer John McPhee says that the beginning of a piece (referred to as the "lede") "like the title—should be a flashlight that shines down in the story. A lede is a promise." In the kind of short essays I write and assign to my classes, there's no time to build up to brilliance. You have to grab readers by the throat immediately, mesmerize, humorize, or offer intrigue.

About ten years ago, a generous *New York Times* editor who came to my class said he preferred essays "to be focused on a turning point or a single scene, and be surprising." He shared these great opening paragraphs of pieces he'd bought.

When I was sixteen, my father left my mother and me for his pregnant mistress, who happened to be a jockey at the racetrack and didn't ride sidesaddle, if you know what I mean. Well, we're from Houston; off-color divorce is our municipal hobby. Mother's first words after reading Daddy's Dear Jane letter—'All that goes back tomorrow!'—referred to a cluster of shopping bags we collected earlier that day at Neiman's and addressed the real problem for both of us: with my father gone, the gravy train was over.

("Son of the South" by Robert Leleux, November 4, 2007)

Let's make this fast. I was molested when I was a child and then I wasn't anymore and then I skated competitively as a kid and then I quit skating and then I started drinking when I was a teenager and then I quit drinking and then I started therapy when I was an adult and then I married and then I still had therapy and then I had children and then I still had therapy and finally I decided I was tired of all this therapy, all this talking like a talk machine.

("Feet to Brain" by Amy Fusselman, April 15, 2007)

The last place my increasingly forgetful eighty-five-year-old father wanted to be was sitting beside me in the office of a geriatric specialist. The doctor leaned forward at her desk and locked eyes with my father. 'Has it been difficult for you to remember things recently, Mr. Cooper?'

("Spell 'World' Backward" by Bernard Cooper, January 8, 2006)

The first time I was pregnant when I didn't want to be, I was a college senior. That year I wasn't on the pill, because of migraines, and other birth control was less reliable, especially when you didn't use it. My roommate had just had the flu, and at first I thought I had caught it.

("Confession of Choice" by Kathryn Rhett, June 25, 2006)

In late August, on the eve of our thirtieth anniversary, my husband and I took two carloads of friends and relations to our favorite swimming place on Cape Cod. When we arrived, we seemed to be intruding on what we took for a cult ceremony. A circle of seven men stood chest-deep in water, their hands cupped over their brows—to cut the glare, we learned, as one of the men had discovered the absence of his wedding band. Friends and random swimmers had gathered to help him find it.

("Ring Cycle" by Rebecca Okrent, September 23, 2007)

My own *New York Times* piece that I mentioned, "The Bride Wore White—and Black" began: "I was married twice last summer. I wore two different dresses in two different colors in two different cities."

Here are ledes to other provocative *New York Times* essays my students and colleagues published.

I'm an Irish George Constanza. Single, bald and paunchy around the middle, past my prime for anything but a midlife crisis. In May I sat in my doctor's office; the tests were in. I flunked cholesterol. How could that be? I crammed wholesome food for an entire week. Dr. Lopachin prescribed medication, but I insisted I could get my blood in shape with diet and exercise. So with only six weeks of training, just days after my forty-eighth birthday, I'm ending my health problems by jumping into the Hudson River next Sunday for the New York City Triathlon.

("Cholesterol Countdown On Sea, Land and Wheels" by Rich Prior, *The New York Times* Sports section, June 20, 2004)

I was standing on a ladder in the closet, cleaning out the shelves, when I noticed Gracie, our standard poodle puppy, throwing up in the corner. "Ethan, could you please help?" I asked my husband. He wiped up the mess with a few paper towels, but she threw up again, and then again.

"I'm taking her to the vet," he said, grabbing her, practically carrying her limp, dehydrated body out the door. He came back empty-handed.

("A Dog's Grace" by Kimberlee Auerbach Berlin, *The New York Times* Opinion section, October 18, 2012)

Last winter, after more than three decades of silence, I desperately wanted to reconnect with my mother before it was too late. Not to make amends, really. I wanted to see her once and not be afraid. I had been courting her in recent years, sending flowers, fruit, and candy for her birthday and holidays, asking to visit. She acknowledged my gifts with terse handwritten notes. She sent back the designer jelly beans with the scrawl: "I prefer dark chocolate." In the past, she ignored me completely or ended with "you stupid idiot." We were making progress. Yet she still refused to see me.

("The Most-Hated Son" by Frederick Woolverton, *The New York Times Magazine*, November 12, 2010)

After reading an article on Bosnia's tourism boom, my brother Eldin and I decided it was time to face down our past. We reasoned that we were really doing this for our seventy-two-year-old father, Senahid. If he didn't see the country of his birth or his childhood friends soon, he never would. Yet within days I became obsessed with creating a to-do list for our trip: 1. Take a picture of the concentration camp my brother and father survived. 2. Visit the cemetery where the karate coach who betrayed us was buried. 3. Confront Petra, the neighbor who stole from my mother.

("The Reckoning" by Kenan Trebincevic, *The New York Times Magazine*, December 2, 2011)

For a long time, I didn't like telling people what I did for a living. How many mothers do you know who would be proud that their college educated 45 year old son is a professional dog walker? Born of mixed race in Taipei during the Chinese zodiac Year of the Dog, me and my eight siblings were raised in a pack environment. My designated chore was walking Casey, our orange/faun field spaniel. I spent hours with Casey, teaching him tricks. I imaged we were connected: I was also adopted, having been given up by my birth mother at three days old. My family history made me feel an unspoken kinship with pets.

("I got out of debt, fell in love and found my true calling—as a dog walker" by Ryan Stewart, Quartz, November 20, 2015)

TRY TOPICALITY

As mentioned in my stubborn ongoing argument with Peter Catapano, my feeling is: If you can't be sexy, scintillating, or brilliant to start, at least be timely. The Rolling Stones' song "Yesterday's Papers" asks, "Who wants yesterday's girl?/Who wants yesterday's papers?/Nobody in the world."

That's true of most publications. They usually don't want outdated stories. So go out of your way to make the beginning of your piece new, fresh, or set in the future to grab the impatient reader's attention right away. To quote a successful fellow journalist: "It's called *news*papers, not *old*papers." Many editors I know admit they won't read more than the title and first few lines from a writer they don't know who submits an unsolicited piece. So never sound dated, stale, or cliché by starting in an overdone way, in the past, or with someone else's quote we've heard before. If you can flip your beginning to comment on the current world, you'll have more work.

While telling a good story is important, framing it well is also essential. So be on the lookout for prominent upcoming books, award-winning movies, recent studies, and news stories on your subject to peg your personal essays to. I constantly buy hard copies of newspapers and magazines to peruse and clip anything on my topic. (My theory: How can I expect to be paid from publications if I'm reading everything for free?) If I see something that might be helpful, I print out a copy and underline. Here's how some students of mine transitioned from topical references to their own stories, giving their ideas a current connection, contemporary context, and more universal appeal.

> When I first learned of the fires decimating Northern California, my stomach clenched and my pulse quickened, even though I was three thousand miles away in New England. ... I couldn't stop thinking about the people I knew in Northern California and those I don't, the

exhausted firefighters who saw no containment in sight, the people were able to outrun the flames and those who were consumed by them. When I was seven years old, my parents had refused to evacuate for a massive brush fire ...

("The Brush Fire We Stayed For" by Kelli Auerbach, *Lenny*, October 20, 2017)

"What's so funny?" asked my mother, my laughter so loud she could hear it from three rooms over. I was watching *Will & Grace*, my favorite television show. Of course, as a closeted nineteen-year-old in a very Catholic household, I was afraid to tell her ... Excited by *Will & Grace*'s return to television, I dug out my DVDs. ...

("Years ago, *Will & Grace* helped me come out. Now I'm hoping it'll grow up" by Mark Jason Williams, *The Washington Post*'s "Soloish" column, September 26, 2017)

It might be funny to watch a forty-ish single mom try to pass as a twenty-something to get her old publishing job back on the new TV series *Younger*. Or the middle-aged protagonist of another show, *Happyish*, try to hang onto his advertising job after a pair of callow Swedish boy geniuses take over his company. But it's probably more amusing if you aren't sixty and watching while downing your fourth glass of wine to help you recover from your very own aging-in-the-workplace daily reality show.

("I'm 60. My boss is a 20-something. It's awkward." by Lisa Reswick, *The Washington Post*, October 6, 2015)

As I looked down at the small bag of crystals that resembled rock salt in my hand, I had no idea what I was actually holding. When my friend Ian pointed out that it was crystal meth, I broke into a sweat. I was no Jesse Pinkman, the meth addict *Breaking Bad* had introduced just before I arrived in Australia. I was more like Dorothy of Oz: naïve, well-mannered, and lost in a foreign land.

("How a Breakup Inspired My Attempt at Breaking Bad" by Melanie Gardiner, Nerve.com, October 10, 2013)

Tonight, my Chinese family and I will be at a restaurant in Brooklyn's Chinatown eating fried tofu and Peking duck while Donald J. Trump attends Inaugural Balls. If you'd told me a year ago that we would be commiserating banquet-style while an Internet troll was sworn in as president, I would have snorted derisively into my illegal shark fin soup. Growing up in Manhattan, the American-born child of immigrants from Hong Kong, I was embarrassed by my family's strange holidays. I never learned to speak the language, or even use chopsticks. Disney's *Mulan* felt like a caricature of every stereotype I was teased about in school. When *Fresh Off the Boat* aired on television, it seemed that people like me were the butt of a nationally understood joke—especially when Chinese people were portrayed by Korean actors.

("What Trump Taught Me About Being Asian-American" by Stephanie Siu, *The New York Times*, January 20, 2017)

Here are two timely ledes of my own:

My childhood rabbi once explained that on Yom Kippur, the saddest day of the Jewish calendar, sins we make before God are mercifully erased, but not offenses committed against fellow humans. To come clean, we have to approach those we've wronged, specify our misdeeds, and beg forgiveness. But what if I was the person who was wronged and the one who hurt me refused to express any regret?

("The Forgiveness Tour" by Susan Shapiro, *Salon*, October 11, 2016)

Hillary Clinton and I have been having communication problems. As a New York Democrat of her generation, I related to her recent troubles involving 62,320 e-mails. Okay, I can barely be my own secretary while she was Secretary of State. Still, not growing up with computers, electronic mail storage can be confounding.

("Storage Wars: My Hillary-Like E-mail Crisis" by Susan Shapiro, *The New York Observer*, April 2, 2015)

CRUSTY WAYS NOT TO COMMENCE

"But there's nothing timely about my topic," students often complain. All it takes is Google to research your theme and come up with a fresher intro. Here are outdated first sentences and how they can be quickly revamped so your words seem more zingy and in the zeitgeist.

1. Old: "Twenty-two years ago, when I was a nerd in high school …"
   New: "On this season's hot TV hit *Riverdale*, Betty is a high school good girl like I used to be …"
2. Old: "In 2010, when I saw the Rockettes at Christmas …"
   New: "After the Rockettes' political tussle with the presidential inauguration, I wonder if their upcoming Christmas show will feature …"
3. Old: "In the immortal words of Mark Twain …"
   New: "In the immortal words of Roxane Gay …"
4. Old: "As a toddler, I was supposed to have been sweet, quiet, and shy …"
   New: "The best-selling book on introverts could have been written about my childhood …"
5. Old: "The first time I voted in 1987, I wasn't sure how to press the lever."
   New: "As both sides alleged voter fraud in the recent controversial election, I kept flashing back to my first ballot box …"
6. Old: "At Thanksgiving a month ago, I decided I needed to diet."
   New: "This Easter I'm skipping the candy eggs and doing Weight Watchers, like Oprah …"
7. Old: "Watching the Grammy Awards last Sunday night, I was struck by all the ugly outfits …"
   New: "On the upcoming Academy Awards, I can't wait to see which stars flunk fashion …"
8. Old: "My grandmother used to tell her six grandkids …"
   New: "This week's *People* reported that Goldie Hawn just became a grandma for the fifth time …"
9. Old: "Before I ever used a computer …"
   New: "When Apple launches their latest mobile device next month, I'll be the first in line …"
10. Old: "As the sixteenth-century saying goes, 'All it takes for evil to flourish is for good men to do nothing …'"

New: "'This is what democracy looks like!' political protestors in DC cried out this week ..."

AVOID FIRST-PERSON MISTAKES

1. **DON'T PEN A PIECE IN SECOND OR THIRD PERSON, OR WRITE ABOUT WHAT HAPPENED TO SOMEONE ELSE.** It's easiest to use first person and focus on yourself. There's a different type of essay called "As Told To" where you chronicle someone else's story, which along with ghostwritten pieces, most editors I know won't publish. For the humiliation assignment, I've found it's best for beginners to use the word *I* and center on you.

2. **DON'T PLAGIARIZE ANYBODY ELSE'S WORK AND PASS IT OFF AS YOUR OWN**, even if it's just lines from a famous poem or sentences from Wikipedia. If you are reusing more than a phrase you've heard elsewhere, put it in quotes, with an attribution. While titles of a book, song, or movie can't be copyrighted, I often credit the late comedy writer/actress Carrie Fisher for her "instant gratification takes too long" quip—though I just use five words from a line of hers in the novel *Postcards From the Edge* for my class and this book's working subtitle.

3. **DON'T MAKE UP CHARACTERS OR WRITE ABOUT EVENTS THAT DIDN'T HAPPEN.** Nobody will expect you to remember past dialogue verbatim; just approximate to the best of your knowledge. But if your story is not true, don't label it a "personal essay" or "nonfiction." Call it "fictionalized," a "short story," "novel," or "novella." While the well-known writers Ruth Reichl and Peter Carey made up characters in their memoirs, they came clean with their creative strategies in their author's notes. If you say, "This is based on a true story," it's considered fiction. No newspaper or magazine editors I know will accept a "fictionalized essay" or a "fictionalized memoir" from an unknown writer. These are contradictions to the normally understood terms. If you're playing with form or combining genres, aim for literary journals that take experimental work, and clearly explain your concept in a cover letter.

4. **DON'T USE GENERALITIES INSTEAD OF SPECIFIC, FLESHED-OUT DETAILS AND DIALOGUE.** In a piece about marrying late, instead of a line mentioning that I'd grown up with a conservative suburban mother, I remembered a scene where my beautiful redheaded mom walked into my pink carpeted bedroom when I was four, saw Barbie dolls strewn all over the floor, and screamed, "No man is going to marry such a slob!"

5. **DON'T OVER-FOCUS ON YOUR CHILDHOOD.** While you can aim for *Highlights for Children* or *Teen Vogue*, almost all newspapers, magazines, and webzines have adult audiences, and the top editors I work with are over thirty and won't care about your toddler years unless you're famous or they're as dark and interesting as Frank McCourt's first page for *Angela's Ashes*: "Worse than the ordinary miserable childhood is the miserable Irish childhood, and worse yet is the miserable Irish Catholic childhood ..."

6. **REVAMP COMMON STORIES.** If you're writing about a parent's death or a difficult breakup, try a timely lede, new spin, humor, or unusual emotional insight to make it stand out.

7. **PUT A DAMPER ON DELUSIONS.** Don't write one draft, decide it's brilliant at three in the morning, and without receiving any feedback, send it to *The New Yorker*.

HOW TO SHOW AND TELL

New writers are often advised: "Show, don't tell." Many have no idea what this means.

"Showing" can be defined as painting a vivid picture of what's going on, using the kind of physical description, humor, pathos, and dialogue that immediately bring readers into a scene in novels, short stories, poetry, and on the screen.

"Telling" is when you report facts from an unemotional distance, the way you'd share résumé highlights on a job interview. It gets a bad rap. Mark Twain instructed: "Don't say the old lady screamed. Bring her on and let her scream." And best-selling writer Janet Evanovich wrote: "If your character walks out of his apartment house, pulls up the collar of his coat, and goes searching through pockets for his gloves, you don't have to tell us it's freezing."

Yet Twain and Evanovich are known mainly for their fiction. While you don't want to list everything that happened to you from birth on in nonfiction, there are often important reasons you should "tell" factual elements in an essay. Still, sharing data didactically can be typical and boring. If you pick up President Barack Obama's eloquent memoir *Dreams From My Father,*[5] you'll see he doesn't present his story chronologically. He begins the first chapter when he's twenty-one years old in New York, getting a phone call from an aunt in Africa telling him of his father's death. Then he flashes back to his childhood to fill in the facts.

In a short personal essay, there's room to both efficiently "tell" information quickly *and* "show" the important parts, according to essayist Phillip Lopate in his wonderful, aptly titled essay collection, *To Show and Tell.*[6] Showing is often more effective at the onset of an essay, when you have only one job: to lure the reader in. Or, as Hollywood director Billy Wilder suggested in "Rules for Screenwriters[7]": "Grab 'em by the throat and never let 'em go."

At the start of his heartfelt *Quartz* piece, my former student Emillio Mesa *showed* a dramatic scenario with the first lines: "I eventually erased my mother's frantic voicemail, but it still beats inside me, like a second heart. 'Your brother is dead! Please come home,' she screamed."

In the next line Emillio *told* the reader what had happened: "A sudden heart attack claimed my brother's life at thirty. He died in his sleep, found by his eldest son." Emillio later wove in more facts. "A year after I was born in the Dominican Republic, my mother divorced my father. She left me in the car of my grandparents to leave for New York City. Five years later she returned to me, with a new husband and child. That's when I first met my brother, Wesley."

In another culturally evocative piece in *The New York Times'* "Modern Love" column, "Close Enough to Touch Was Too Far Apart," my

5. Three Rivers Press, 1999
6. Free Press, 2013
7. From Cameron Crowe's book *Conversations With Wilder (Knopf, 2001)*

single, conservative Muslim student Saba Ali led by *showing* a common image within a provocative question: "Who knew that holding hands, the very act that signals the start of so many relationships, would be the end of mine?"

Then she *told* us about her background:

"Born in Kenya of Indian heritage, I came to the United States at age six, settling with my family in upstate New York. Growing up Muslim in suburban America."

In the lede of my *New York Times'* "Modern Love" piece, I *showed*: "His e-mail read:

"'Here for one night. Giants game tomorrow. Buy you a drink?'

"I was so stunned, I lost my breath. I hadn't seen him in twenty-five years. I thought I had gotten over the need to get over my first love. But eleven words on a screen and I was a nervous fourteen-year-old again."

Then, after that, I *told* specific details: "A decade ago, needing closure, I begged him for a long overdue showdown ... Now that he was here, I panicked. I had recently turned fifty, torn two ligaments in my back, was out of shape. I felt too weak to face my ex. Did he really want to buy me a drink? He didn't even know I hadn't smoked or drank in ten years."

So I started *showing* a scene to capture your attention. Then I filled in the backstory to help you understand the relevance of the episode I returned to.

BALANCE *SHOWING* WITH *TELLING*

1. **USE PAST TENSE THROUGHOUT.** It's the most honest, since the story you're writing has already happened. While in poetry, fiction, and for the screen it's more common to use present tense, fewer newspapers or magazines will publish a present-tense nonfiction essay. Since it's an artsy conceit, often to make a piece feel more immediate, I sometimes see creative nonfiction that plays with tenses in literary journals. But you usually have to know the rules before you break them. For beginners, I'd use the verb form that indicates that the action has already occurred. I find it's easier to put everything

     THE BYLINE BIBLE

in one tense. So instead of starting with past tense, then switching around to say, "I *have* always been the type to talk in my sleep," I'd write, "I *had* always talked in my sleep." Just use past tense, which is easier to write, read, and remember.

2. **RECALL AS CLEARLY AS POSSIBLE.** Nobody has a recorder that taped every word spoken in the past. Write it down in the most accurate way you recollect it happening. But you don't have to say, "I remember that …" We know you remember it, that's why you're writing it. You can also cut the line "I don't remember much, but …" Instead add how you figured it out, for example: "When I asked my mother, she was sure that …," "Family records indicated …," or "Looking through my sister's old photograph album, I saw …"

3. **DON'T OVERDO DIALOGUE.** Five or six lines of a conversation in a scene are sufficient for a 900-word personal essay. If you write an entire page of dialogue, that's a script.

4. **DON'T START AT THE VERY BEGINNING.** If I read the first line of an essay, "I was born in Columbus, Ohio, the oldest of three children of an Italian homemaker mother and a lawyer father …," I would stop reading. After all, I didn't sign up for the modern version of *Great Expectations*, just a short essay.

5. **BEGIN WITH BRAVADO.** Some of my provocative ledes: "We met the day I replaced her." (*Marie Claire*) "I was married twice last summer." (*The New York Times Magazine*) "Sliding into a booth at the gelato parlor, a shooting pain flared in my spine and I sat up straighter, the way he taught me." (*New York* magazine) "Of all possible illicit online liaisons, how did I wind up with my first lover's wife?" (*Elle*) The indelicate first line "That summer my husband stopped screwing me" (*The New York Observer*) actually led to a memoir deal. Don't be afraid to be out there, crazy, brave, revealing, and innovative. If you are using typical words that have been said many times, twist them differently. As the poet Emily Dickinson wrote, "Tell all the truth but tell it slant."

6. **DON'T BOMBARD THE READER WITH FACTS.** If there are important details to be told, weave them in later when it feels more

organic. Don't overstuff the lede. In David Mamet's rules for drama,[8] he says the audience cares only about three questions: Who wants what from whom? What happens if they don't get it? Why now? All the other stuff you shove in is irrelevant and can clunk up your first paragraph, rendering it boring or confusing.

7. **DON'T REVEAL THE ENDING TOO SOON.** If you begin your essay, "After living through the worst divorce in the history of the world, I swore I'd never get married again so walking down the aisle was a surprise," you've given away too much information too fast. There's no reason to keep reading. Instead try something more enigmatic like "When I first saw the cute, tall, bearded man with glasses, I turned away, sure he wouldn't be interested in a forty-five-year-old angry divorcée, like me." In my favorite relationship pieces, I don't know if the couple is going to break up or get married. Pretend you're writing a rom-com with a mini-mystery to solve. (Who winds up with whom?) Put a tiny clue in each paragraph, but wait until the very end to reveal the cliffhanger.

This is also true of memoirs. A wise colleague, Knopf editor Deborah Garrison, once told me, "A novel that's merely autobiographical is a great disappointment, but a memoir that reads like a novel is a great surprise."

8. **ANIMATE WITH HUMOR OR SELF-DEPRECATION.** Sybil Sage's essay "How I Fended Off My Own Personal Harvey Weinsteins" in *The Forward* started, "'Oy, this is bad for the Jews' is how my parents would have reacted to a scandal involving a Weinstein." Conversely, Kenan Trebincevic's *Wall Street Journal* essay, starts: "'I hope they're not Muslim,' I told my brother, Eldin, when we first saw the pictures of the Boston Marathon bombers. We soon found out they shared our religion, as we'd dreaded, when my Jewish college roommate kiddingly texted, 'Hey would you please tell your people to stop

---

8. "Every scene should be able to answer three questions: 'Who wants what from whom? What happens if they don't get it? Why now?'" From David Mamet's book *Bambi vs. Godzilla: On the Nature, Purpose, and Practice of the Movie Business* (Pantheon, 2007)

blowing things up?'" These kinds of dark jokes made the narrators knowable, likable, adding levity to a usually serious topic.

9. **COMMIT WHOLEHEARTEDLY TO ONE STORY.** In the middle of reading a personal essay, I can't stand when a writer tosses in the cliché, "But that's a whole other story ..." or cuts to a tangent about another character or family. I've argued with students who don't want to flash forward and give a satisfying conclusion because "I'm saving the follow-up for my next piece." Don't play games, be coy, store up anecdotes, or save the best stuff for later. Push yourself into completing this essay by telling one story as if it's the last piece you'll ever write and publish, and it won't be.

DO YOU WANT YOUR NAME ON THIS?

While I tell my students, "Your life is your own and you have a right to tell your story," there are circumstances that require discretion and certain intimacies I would not want circulating with my byline. Remember, once something is online, it can be almost impossible to get it offline.

Here's What Not to Share (If You Want to Be Taken Seriously as a Writer and Not Get Sued)

1. Naked pictures, sex tapes, X-rated tweets, or porn links.
2. Salacious stories about your infidelity or secret second family while you're still married and have minor children who don't know.
3. Inside secrets of your office if you're a doctor, commodities trader, reporter, attorney, teacher, politician, or might be one some day. Think of Donald Trump's "grab 'em by the pussy" comment made to *Access Hollywood* reporter Billy Bush, who was fired from his TV job. And Trump may have won the election, but would you want that line included in your obituary, legacy, or future biography?
4. Stories that focus on other people's secrets using real names and identifying details. In a first-person essay, the only one you should "out" is yourself, unless the offending party is dead, gives you permission, or you can disguise the identity.

5. Allegations of a crime that can't be proven, using the perpetrator's first and last name. You can, however, refer a bit more vaguely to "my dishonest old boss," "my abusive parent," "my psychotic ex," or "my rapist."

6. Crimes you've committed but haven't served time for. *New York Times* editors who published pieces by my students took out parts about shoplifting, shooting up heroin, and bringing marijuana home from Jamaica. The newspaper didn't want to sanction illegal activities. Plus, law enforcement can also come after you. Some crimes have no statute of limitation for prosecution. In fact, a longtime undocumented foreigner in America recently gave an interview that led to her deportation. That's probably why a former student who wanted to write about being an illegal alien did so in a novel. Don't naïvely publicize anything in nonfiction that could get you deported or land you in prison.

7. Made-up stories—which should be called "fiction," "humor," "poetry," "science fiction," or "fantasy."

8. Anything you've signed a confidentiality agreement not to disclose—at work or home.

9. Anything you are currently in litigation over. It would not be worth losing your spouse, children, job, or home for a hundred-dollar essay (though for a six-figure book deal, I might recommend first discussing it with a good lawyer and therapist).

AVOID THE POISON PEN

"What if I don't want to offend anybody?"

As a teacher of first-person nonfiction who has published countless essays and three provocative memoirs my family hates, I'm often asked this question. It's a conundrum for all writers, bloggers, and everyone who posts anything the least bit controversial on social media. The late great novelist E.L. Doctorow once told me there were stories he didn't publish until after certain relatives of his died—and he wrote fiction!

I love Joan Didion's cynical line, "A writer's always selling somebody out." I jokingly began a recent book with the author's note: "Some names and identifying characteristics of people portrayed in this book have been obscured so they won't divorce, disown, hate, kill, or sue me." But there are ways to keep the sparks flying while avoiding lawsuits, loathing, or the loss of jobs, freelance work, spouses, and friendships.

1. **GET IT DOWN FIRST.** Many aspiring scribes stress out and make themselves insane with fear before they've written one word. Preliminary agony is unnecessary because early drafts of most personal narratives suck. If yours sucks, nobody will buy it. So do the work before you worry. You'll only have a problem if your story is spectacular and you're willing to revise and compromise to kick it into shape. The narrative you envision might turn out to have different twists than you expect. So give yourself room to sketch out a very rough version before you decide whether or not to kill it.

2. **DON'T RUSH TO PUBLISH OR POST.** If you're blogging for free, don't post venomous pages about getting dumped, fired, or evicted without first getting feedback from someone with a more rational outlook and perhaps a law degree. One good reason to wait until you can sell your work to an editor is that they will evaluate if it's ready and worthy of publication, providing a filter to tone down mean-spirited (or litigious) lines you don't need.

3. **LOSE THE POPULARITY CONTEST.** If your main goal is to be nice, write cookbooks. Or switch professions. A good journalist has to be cynical. Being accused of "cranking out PR fluff" is a major insult. You have a right to tell your story in your voice. To clarify your goals, envision your *New York Times* obituary. Do you want to be called an acclaimed, sardonic author known for revealing brutal, candid truths—or a really nice insurance salesman? Oh yeah, if you're a really nice insurance salesman you probably won't get a *New York Times* obit. (Unless you do it by day while moonlighting as a writer like Wallace Stevens, Franz Kafka, and Tom Clancy.)

4. **FACE THE FACTS—PART 1.** Sometimes it's appropriate—or necessary—to show your soon-to-be published work to the real-life ver-

sions of those you depicted. Before *The New York Times* ran my student Helaine Olen's "Modern Love" essay about firing her nanny after reading the nanny's sex-filled blog, the editor showed it to the nanny. The blogosphere eventually went batty, but Helaine's veracity was proven and it ran as written. I usually don't show my work to my subjects before it sees print. But I did share an early draft of essays and my memoir *Lighting Up* with the addiction specialist I quoted throughout. He asked that I change his name and two minor details (which I did) and corrected an addiction theory I'd misquoted. When I showed an editor an early galley of my book about my mentors, she asked me to remove two insignificant details about her that I wasn't aware could have led to lawsuits.

5. **MIX VINEGAR WITH HONEY.** A while ago, while he was still a nicotine fiend, I described my father as "a chain-smoking oncologist." But I also noted that he was "brilliant," describing a high school photo of him in a black leather jacket that showed him looking "handsome like a gangster." Perhaps calling my mother "a domestic goddess" and "a cross between Lucille Ball and Ava Gardner" helped her forgive me for revealing she was "an overfeeder." Here's the deal: If the major players in your prose are just jerks, you come off like a jerk for caring about them. If your portraits are interesting, intelligent, and complex, there's a better chance you will be, too. The bestsellers *Them* by Jon Ronson[9] and *The Glass Castle* by Jeannette Walls[10] were particularly savvy in depicting oddball yet three-dimensional parents.

6. **TONE DOWN THE TOUGH PARTS.** Personal pieces are about you—not others. When Jeff, a thirty-year-old student, confessed in his gut-wrenching essay that an acquaintance had sexually abused him as a teenager, his father insisted he turn down *Newsweek*'s publication offer. I suggested Jeff delete the three lines that mentioned his parents, making it Jeff's story alone. The essay ran and his father subsequently apologized, admitting he felt guilty that he'd done

9. Simon & Schuster, 2002
10. Scribner, 2006

nothing to stop the abuse. Ultimately, he told Jeff that printing that story was courageous. Dad just didn't want to be mentioned.

7. **CONSULT A THERAPIST/ADVISER/MENTOR FIRST.** An NYU student was chronicling a secret love affair she was having that her husband did not know about. She asked me for the name of my *Marie Claire* editor. I gave her the number of a shrink instead. I worried she was subconsciously using her essay to get out of her marriage. While I salute literary ambition and often repeat my therapist's mantra "Lead the least secretive life you can" as a rationalization for my career, you have to be clear on your motives. Rage, revenge, domestic destruction, and/or humiliating someone else are not good reasons for publication—especially in an age of Internet notoriety, when you may never be able to retract it. Tech-savvy kids as young as three know how to Google their own names and those of their unsuspecting parents.

8. **NOT EVERY STORY NEEDS TO BE SOLD.** I questioned a married mother of two taking my class who wanted to publish a piece on why she approves of her first-grade son's penchant for wearing dresses to school, accompanied by a photo of him in a princess outfit. Though I applauded her political statement, this was not really a piece about her. It was about her young child who could be adversely affected by her byline later on. I worried she could harm her son's reputation with his peers in the future. (And if he turned out to be gay, transsexual, or a cross-dresser, wasn't it his decision if and when he wanted to go public?) If your mate, children, parents, or employer might wind up mortified, decide whether a clip is worth the pain you could cause to your family and yourself before pressing "Send."

9. **FACE THE FACTS—PART 2.** The Random House lawyer who vetted my memoirs explained that to win a lawsuit, the plaintiff must offer evidence that the nonfiction writer lied with *malice intended*, and show damages. If you have proof of your accuracy, there's no case. Luckily I saved pictures, articles, diary entries, letters, and printed

e-mails that substantiated my memories. If you plan to publish stories about your history, you should, too. It can pay to be a packrat.

10. **NOT EVERY RANT MAKES A GOOD ESSAY.** Although writers often get the last word, those words have to be worthy of publication. That wasn't the case when a woman I didn't know e-mailed me an essay about a man she met on Tinder in a foreign country who left her pregnant. When she told him, he pressed her to have an abortion. After she decided to keep the baby, he harassed her. Broke, she and her infant wound up moving in with his mother, whom the author described as an evil witch manipulating her to get sole custody of her grandchild. The writer sounded hysterical. She thought selling her story would earn her money and help her cause. Yet her screed was unintelligible, calling the father and his mother abusive, racist monsters and her own mother neglectful while she cast herself as an innocent, endless victim. She offered no self-insight, clarity, or emotional arc while trashing everyone else. Feeling bad for her, I referred to her a therapist, and also to a ghost editor who, like me, felt that no reputable publication would take such a slanderous rant. At some point I hope she'll be able to craft a better narrative on surviving and thriving against the odds as a single mom. As Oprah asked a guest who kept telling a horrible airless tale of her life, "I'm sorry this happened to you. But can you tell a different story now?"

11. **LOOK INWARD.** Even if it's true, nobody really wants to read a kvetch about all the bad things bad people did to you. If you are an innocent lamb tricked by unscrupulous evildoers, can you reframe your personal story? Taking responsibility for some of your problems makes your first-person piece more compelling and less likely to incite loathing and legal action. The single mother mentioned above could start with her anger, but then analyze why she wasn't using birth control for a hookup with a stranger. Contemplating her regrets might keep her from repeating mistakes while helping others stuck in similar situations. I'll repeat one of my favorite rules for first-person nonfiction: Always question, challenge, and trash yourself most. Self-deprecation could make your message

and your writing fuller, darker, and funnier. If you don't believe me, check out the work of Dorothy Parker, David Sedaris, Tina Fey, Roxane Gay, and Gary Shteyngart. My favorite book of his is called *Little Failure*.[11]

12. **PRACTICE PATIENCE.** There are some stories you can write and publish quickly. Others take longer. I was forty-three, happily married, and self-supporting by the time my first hardcover—about the worst breakups of my life—came out. That was probably good timing. Once you've finished your first draft, sometimes you should hold the ink until you're ready—psychologically, emotionally, financially—for the fallout. Or decide not to publish at all. Or wait until the inspiration for a specific character croaks.

13. **TURN TO FICTION.** Most short stories and novels are somewhat autobiographical. To fictionalize, don't just change names. It's a creative opportunity to fully dramatize your story. Add a triple murder, a suicide, or a plane crash that didn't happen. Put all of your characters on drugs, like the reverse of James Frey (who switched to novel writing after being accused of making up facts in his bestselling memoir, *A Million Little Pieces*.[12] Fiction means it's not true, so falsifying more can't get you in trouble with Oprah.

Last-Minute Checklist: What Not to Do

1. Don't lie, make up stories that didn't happen, or ridiculously exaggerate.
2. Don't switch names or details without checking your editor's policy for disguising real people. (*The New York Times* and most other newspapers will not allow pseudonyms.)
3. Don't trash somebody in anger and then rush those pages into publication.
4. Don't assume everybody wants to be written about or will appreciate your portrayal. (Some private people hate even positive mentions of themselves in the press.)

---

11. Random House, 2014
12. Nan A. Talese, 2003

5. Don't tell only one side of the story. Everything isn't black and white. Murderers and monsters often had horrible childhoods that might illuminate their pathology. Sometimes the more complex and magnanimous a writer can be, the more likable, relatable, and publishable.

Exercises

1. List your motivations for publishing the piece. If it's revenge, redemption, or making tons of money, rethink your decision.
2. Read over your work a day or two later. Ask yourself how you'd feel if this were published about you.
3. If you're worried, before you submit your work to an editor, show it to the mate, parents, child, boss, or co-worker in the piece and ask, "Will you still speak to me if this sees print?" If they say no, ask, "What can I do to change it?" In some cases, it will only require taking out a few lines to preserve a lifelong relationship.
4. Read your favorite essayists and memoirists and underline diplomatic passages chronicling their complicated relationships with their mothers, fathers, spouses, or other relatives or exes. Examine how they pulled it off.
5. List a few good traits about the person you're trashing. When I was working on my breakup memoir *Five Men Who Broke My Heart*, my writing workshop encouraged me to show a few early happy scenes of each affair, when I first fell in love and was free of the retrospective rage.

SELF-EDITING

You have three pages written. Great! But there's more work to be done before taking your piece public. Once you finish the first draft of your essay, put it away for twenty-four hours. Then reread it and revise again the next day. And the next. Read the piece aloud if you can, to hear the rhythm of the words. Here's what you want to ask yourself.

1. **IS IT BLOATED?** The trick is to convey everything simply and succinctly, without what we call "throat clearing." A student once handed in a piece that included the sentence: "And it was then I had the sudden, intense realization that I couldn't bear to be around my older sister." I shortened it to "I couldn't bear to be around my older sister," losing eleven pointless words we didn't need. It was clear the author was having a deep sudden realization, which was why she was writing it. If there are words you can delete without altering the meaning, cut away. Say everything in the fewest words possible.

2. **DID YOU AVOID REPETITION?** A smart editor I worked with insisted I could use each word only once in every essay (except for *and* and *the*). I often find pieces reiterate the same boring phrase ten or twenty times, especially when they are central to the story (like "social media," "recovery group," "memorial service," or "relationship status"). Using the same words over and over is lazy. A colleague who mentioned the "American flag" six times in three pages was able to change some of the "American flags" to U.S. banner, United States' pennant, red-white-and-blue marker, USA streamer, and symbol of the Land of Liberty. Consult a thesaurus to find synonyms.

3. **AM I USING TOO MANY ADJECTIVES AND ADVERBS?** Describing your teacher as "a tall, dark, thin, lanky, bearded, bespectacled middle-aged man" is overkill. "Bearded and bespectacled" suffices. Saying "She was very, very anxious" makes me think the writer was anxious, not the subject. If you just say, "She was anxious," we'll get it. Or better, show her tapping her fingers on the desk and bouncing her leg.

4. **WHAT'S THE WORD COUNT?** Is your essay the right length for the editor you are targeting? This is what computer programs with word counts are perfect for. If the *Los Angeles Times* "L.A. Affairs" column wants 800–900 words, 912 words are okay; 1,300 are not. "Sorry I'm writing you a long letter. I don't have time to write you a short one," the author Samuel Johnson allegedly wrote. (Though

the line has also been attributed to everyone from Mark Twain to Abraham Lincoln.)

5. **WHY NOW?** Is there any timely lede or fresh angle that makes your piece about something more than your own personal experience so it's relevant to a wider audience? If not, do research and find one. When Kenan Trebincevic started his piece about being a Muslim immigrant that wound up in *The Wall Street Journal*, he Googled and ended up referencing the story currently in the news at that time: the Muslim Boston Marathon bombers. By playing off that story and his fear of Islamophobia, his personal experience had deeper significance and sold faster.

6. **WHAT'S NEW HERE?** Has the publication you're aiming for done anything on this topic recently? Google ASAP to find out. If so, pick a different angle or editor. The first draft of my student Emillio Mesa's *Quartz* piece was only about his younger brother's death. When he added the missing iPhone's lack of iCloud backup, it seemed younger and more in the zeitgeist, and sold to a young editor right away.

7. **DID YOU DELETE WHAT'S STALE?** Get rid of all clichés like "tall, dark, and handsome" and "chip off the old block." If someone else already wrote it, invent a fresher, more idiosyncratic way to tell this story. Write the piece that only you can write.

8. **HAS IT BEEN FACT-CHECKED TWICE?** Is everything you wrote completely accurate? Can you prove it if an editor asks? She might.

9. **ARE YOU PLAYING THE VICTIM?** Listing a litany of woes that happened to you with no earned wisdom or surprising twist at the end is tedious and often unpublishable. If that's the case, revise with more self-reflection.

10. **ARE YOU TOO NASTY?** Even if your parent, ex-spouse, former bestie, sibling, or childhood clergy was unfair and abusive, as the writer you have all the power. Depicting someone as a mean monster can make you come off like a bully. In several essays and memoirs, I've mentioned that my ex-boyfriend slept with my roommate in college. But I also depict him as handsome, hilarious, and confess that

(like Rachel and Ross on *Friends*) we were "on a break." A fairer, nuanced portrayal makes your narrator wiser and more complex. And remember, you won't lose a lawsuit if they can't prove you lied with malice.

11. **IS IT FOCUSED?** Make sure your piece revolves around one specific scene or experience. If there are too many tangents or ideas, streamline or refocus on a narrower part of the story.

12. **DID YOU BOTH SHOW AND TELL?** Make sure you haven't thrown in too much expository history, overexplaining your past. But also limit the lines of dialogue so you aren't using the label "personal essay" for a poem, monologue, or teleplay.

13. **DO YOU REALLY WANT THIS ESSAY PUBLISHED?** Are you ready to see this in print or on the web with your name on it? What if it goes viral and your boss, child, mother, and spouse read about your secret addiction to airplane glue or former shoplifting phase? When in doubt, wait. And write about something else.

Great Short Pieces That Led to Books
(By my students, colleagues, and me)

1. "The Reckoning" by Kenan Trebincevic in *The New York Times Magazine* led to the memoir *The Bosnia List* (Penguin Books, 2014). www.nytimes.com/2011/12/04/magazine/lives-the-reckoning.html
2. "The Most-Hated Son" by Frederick Woolverton in *The New York Times Magazine* led to the self-help book *Unhooked* (Skyhorse Publishing, 2012). www.nytimes.com/2010/11/14/magazine/14lives-t.html
3. "A Hiker's Guide to Healing" by Aspen Matis in *The New York Times'* "Modern Love" column led to the memoir *Girl in the Woods* (HarperCollins, 2015). www.nytimes.com/2012/05/06/fashion/a-hikers-guide-to-healing.html

4. "Elvis and My Husband Have Left the Building" by Liza Monroy in *The New York Times'* "Modern Love" column led to the memoir *The Marriage Act* (Soft Skull Press, 2015). www.nytimes.com/2005/04/24/fashion/sundaystyles/elvis-and-my-husband-have-left-the-building.html

5. "Creature of the Night" by Kathleen Frazier in *Psychology Today* led to the memoir *Sleepwalker* (Skyhorse Publishing, 2015). www.psychologytoday.com/articles/201203/two-minute-memoir-creature-the-night

6. "No Release, Please! Frisky Masseur Hans Is All Hands" by Peter Hyman in *The New York Observer* led to the essay collection *The Reluctant Metrosexual: Dispatches From an Almost Hip Life* (Villard, 2004). observer.com/2003/01/no-release-please-frisky-masseur-hans-is-all-hands

7. "Ciao, Papa" by Liza Monroy in *The New York Times Magazine* led to the novel *Mexican High* (Spiegel & Grau, 2008). www.nytimes.com/2006/11/26/magazine/26lives.html

8. "Learning to Conquer My Daughter's OCD—and My Own" by Abby Sher in *SELF* magazine and *The Forward* led to the memoir *Amen, Amen, Amen* (Scribner, 2009). forward.com/sisterhood/210627/learning-to-conquer-my-daughters-ocd-and-my-own/

9. "The Crossing" by Maria E. Andreu in *The Washington Post Magazine* led to the young adult novel *The Secret Side of Empty* (Running Press Kids, 2015). www.washingtonpost.com/wp-dyn/content/article/2009/02/06/AR2009020602087.html

10. "A Hoarder's Daughter Yields to a (Little) Mess" by Judy Batalion in *The New York Times'* Motherlode blog led to the memoir *White Walls* (New American Library, 2016). parenting.blogs.nytimes.com/2013/01/04/a-hoarders-daughter-yields-to-a-little-mess

11. "I Found My Late Husband's Lovers on His Computer" by Julie Metz in *Glamour* magazine led to the *New York Times* best-selling memoir *Perfection* (Hachette Books, 2009).

12. "A Lost Child, But Not Mine" by Kassi Underwood in the *The New York Times'* "Modern Love" column led to the memoir *May Cause Love* (HarperCollins, 2017). www.nytimes.com/2011/07/31/fashion/a-lost-child-but-not-mine-modern-love.html

13. "Mentally Unfit" by Zachary McDermott in *Gawker* led to the memoir *Gorilla and the Bird* (Little, Brown, 2017) and TV option from Channing Tatum. gawker.com/mentally-unfit-1558940900

14. "Love Is the Drug, and I'm Jonesing for a Hit" by Susan Shapiro in *The New York Observer* led to the memoir *Lighting Up* (Random House, 2004). observer.com/2003/03/love-is-the-drug-and-im-jonesing-for-a-hit

15. "My Best Friend Stole My Brother" by Susan Shapiro, originally in *New Woman* magazine, then in *Marie Claire,* led to the novel *Overexposed* (Thomas Dunne Books, 2010). www.marieclaire.com/sex-love/advice/a5916/female-competition

16. "I Have Severe Scoliosis, Just Like My Mom" by Alyson Gerber in *The Frisky* and *Chicken Soup for the Soul* led to the middle-grade novel *Braced* (Scholastic, 2017). www.thefrisky.com/2010-06-24/i-have-severe-scoliosis-just-like-my-mom

17. "Staying Out" by Daisy Hernandez in *Ms.* magazine is the subject of the memoir *A Cup of Water Under My Bed* (Beacon Press, 2015).

18. "We're Checking the Wrong 'Privilege'" by Phoebe Maltz Bovy in *The New Republic* led to *The Perils of "Privilege"* (St. Martin's Press, 2017). newrepublic.com/article/121540/privilege-checking-debate-often-overlooks-income-inequality

19. "My Husband, the Criminal" by Janet Lombardi in *Salon* led to the memoir *Bankruptcy: A Love Story* (Heliotrope Books, 2017). www.salon.com/2012/07/20/my_husband_the_criminal

20. "From Hunger" by Sarah Gerard in *The New York Times* led to the novel *Binary Star* (Two Dollar Radio, 2015) and the essay collection *Sunshine State* (HarperCollins, 2017). opinionator.blogs.nytimes.com/2012/10/01/from-hunger/

21. "Choke Point of a Nation" by Tyler J. Kelley in *The New York Times* led to the nonfiction book *Holding Back the River* (Simon & Schuster, 2019). www.nytimes.com/2016/11/23/business/economy/desperately-plugging-holes-in-an-87-year-old-dam.html?_r=1

22. "Teaching Kids What It Means to Be Transgender" by Chris Edwards (Boston Globe, 2014) led to memoir *Balls: It Takes Some to Get Some* by Chris Edwards (Greenleaf Book Group, 2016) and a TV deal executive produced by Chelsea Handler. www.

bostonglobe.com/magazine/2014/12/04/teaching-kids-what
-means-transgender/sd6wYW2PJWuA8AUPrax6eN/story.html

23. "The Enemy Within: One Woman's War With a Rare Autoimmune Disease" by Wendy Shanker in *Self* magazine March 2007 led to her memoir *Are You My Guru? How Medicine, Meditation and Madonna Saved My Life* (Berkeley Publishing, 2010).

24. "Baby Envy" by Amy Klein in *The New York Times'* "Motherlode" August 7, 2013 led to agent and book deal for *What To Expect When You're Not Expecting* (Ballantine, 2019). parenting.blogs .nytimes.com/2013/08/07/fertility-diary-baby-envy/

25. "The Accident No One Talked About" by Jessica Ciencin Henriquez in *The New York Times'* "Modern Love" column led to her getting a literary agent. www.nytimes.com/2017/03/31/fashion/ modern-love-the-accident-no-one-talked-about.html

26. "Healing Sought (Bring Your Own Magic)" by Laura Zam in *The New York Times'* "Modern Love" column led to her getting a literary agent.

27. "Of Breakdowns and Breakthroughs" by Jenny Aurthur in Longreads May 2018 led to agents calling for her memoir *The Warrior Pose.* longreads.com/2018/05/04/of-breakdowns-and -breakthroughs/

PUBLISHED ESSAYS BY MY STUDENTS

THE TRUTH IS THAT RACISM IS EVERYWHERE

By Haig Chahinian; O, The Oprah Magazine; May 2017

When my husband and I adopted our newborn biracial daughter, I proudly snapped photos of her and pasted them to handwritten announcements I sent everyone we knew. I instantly loved this child. I vowed to carve out a world for her that was free of bigotry, including bigotry against gay men like her two dads. Her picture books showed people of every shade. We moved to Harlem so she could see tykes like herself on the playground. As she's grown—she's 11 now—I always thought I was succeeding.

But there was that bright, bracing

autumn day two years ago, when she and I went on a hike in the Hudson Valley. Wet leaves plastered the ground, a breeze chilled our ears, and my daughter pushed her mocha-skinned Bitty Twin doll in a stroller, straggling several yards behind me as I ascended the trail. And then I rounded a bend and saw a tall black man walking toward me.

I froze. The back of my neck tensed. Adrenaline shot through my limbs. I registered that he was moving quickly. Separated from my daughter, my instinct was to protect her, to call out to her. But what would I call? "Careful, here comes someone else enjoying the scent of pine needles!"?

By the time my girl and the oncoming hiker reached me—simultaneously—my panic had subsided. He smiled at us as he passed, using both hands to wave hello, as if he were in a parade. Embarrassed, I greeted him with a nod.

During my childhood, my Armenian parents cursed the Ottomans of the Turkish empire that murdered all eight of my great-grandparents because of their ethnicity. Yet I was forbidden to play inside the home of our African-American neighbors. My folks saw no link between their intolerance and the Turks' ethnic cleansing.

Now, ambling with my daughter, I was overcome with shame. I hated that seeing a dark-skinned man had frightened me so easily, especially since my own child had a similar complexion. I'd felt the same split-second impulse as the men who shot Alton Sterling and Tamir Rice—one similar to "gay panic," the urge to harm a queer person like me after perceiving a threat. And then I remembered: When the backpacker said hello, he'd raised his palms on either side of his head, as if to show he was unarmed. It looked like surrender—to me, his progressive, gay, urbanite aggressor.

When we adopted our daughter, I worried I wasn't prepared for the challenges of raising a child of color. Still, we took comfort in the fact that we were enlightened, that we knew better—that we were better. Hell, I'd even studied racial identity in college. But none of that had inoculated me against racist hair-trigger fear.

My daughter and I paused to catch our breath under a canopy of maple leaves. I reached into my knapsack and handed her a bag of dried fruit and nuts. She put a cranberry to the lips of her doll, then munched on it herself. Breathing in the mountain air, I recalled a saying that likened racism to smog: Although sometimes hard to see, it's everywhere. It's my job to both recognize its presence and fight against it—day by day, step by step.

PRENATAL DEPRESSION: WHAT I DIDN'T EXPECT WHEN I WAS EXPECTING

By Jessica Ciencin Henriquez,
New York Times, December 8, 2013

I arrived late, hands covering a flat stomach where a bump should have been. I watched as the other women waddled to their seats. Each mother-to-be held a pen in one hand, scratching around a protruding belly button with the other. They scrawled in their open journals, "can't wait to meet you," "felt you kick today!" With no burgeoning stomach blocking the view of my blank page, I wrote, "This is terrible."

Eight women attended the Wednesday night childbirth classes. At 26, I was the youngest. The crier. The non-sharer. Their little bundles were already bringing them joy, while mine brought paranoia instead. Our doula led us through stretches, breathing exercises and shared tips for beating postpartum depression. No one uttered the words prenatal depression, a condition that affects one in eight women. I sat there, stoic, the statistic.

"Write to your baby," our doula instructed. Theirs had known genders and names. Mine had neither. One woman next to me enthusiastically read aloud, while I resisted the urge to slap the glow right off her face. We had all shared the initial squeal seeing two pink lines on our pregnancy tests, but our experiences forked on the road to reproduction.

Months earlier, I had stared at a black-and-white photo, arrows distinguishing head from heart; immediately I fell in love. My fiancé and I weren't trying to conceive but were ecstatic that we could. He anticipated midnight ice cream runs. I envisioned stylish maternity wear and foot rubs. Reality wasn't so enchanting.

Instead, morning sickness pressed on each month, the intensity increasing. Seemingly innocent smells kept me retching. Dish soap and freshly baked bread were my unexpected enemies. Five months in, I had hardly gained a pound. An exhausted immune system failed to shield me from stomach viruses and head colds that hung in the air. Breeding was a blessing and so I accepted those plagues, along with insomnia and hot flashes, as part of my package.

My moods became beastly, unpredictable, impossible to tame. My extroversion had always turned strangers into friends. Now I kept my head down, ashamed when others found my condition more thrilling than I could. I wandered aimlessly through grocery stores, shuffling my feet, forgetting why I was there. The question "when are you due?" caused panic, the answer always "too soon." Even with a devoted partner and financial stability, I didn't feel prepared, I felt miserable. A heart beat six inches from mine, and still I felt isolated.

While crib shopping, I watched other mothers. They looked giddy, buoyant ... ready. My breath quickened. The room spun. I frantically dialed my obstetrician. She assured me, "Feeling under the weather or unlike yourself is normal." Not like this, I knew, otherwise only saints and the senseless would choose to carry a child.

I hung up and drove home cribless. Curling into bed, I was desperate for this pregnancy to end. My fiancé arrived home to a still-sobbing woman. I confessed everything. I couldn't do this anymore. "Maybe," I whispered, "I'm struggling like this because I shouldn't be a mother." I held onto him, finally defeated.

He insisted I see a different doctor immediately. I reviewed my symptoms for her, choking back sobs. When I finished, she said: "I didn't know you before your pregnancy, but looking at you now, you have no light in your eyes, like you're soulless. It shouldn't be this hard." Two souls in one body and I looked as though I had none? She handed me medication for morning sickness and the number of a therapist specializing in prenatal depression.

In our first session she described what it looked like. "Feeling empty, exhausted, angry, no appetite. …" It looked like me. "During pregnancy, estrogen and progesterone rise by about 40 times. However, in some cases the placenta doesn't produce enough progesterone; this offset causes symptoms of depression," she explained.

This was about my body's defects, not my own maternal shortcomings. I could control some things, but a lazy placenta was not one of them. The medication soon eradicated nausea. With each pound I gained, my confidence lifted. "If you want to be a great mother, you need to take care of you," my therapist insisted.

I grudgingly laced up sneakers and jogged to yoga each morning. "Exercise naturally releases endorphins that will keep your spirits up until we can discuss your postpartum medication options," my therapist said. My fiancé and I began to openly discuss our parenting fears. Were we too selfish? Could we lean on each other? By my third trimester, daydreams became more frequent than doubts. I pulled out that empty journal and tried again.

That June I gave birth to our son, 9 pounds, 4 ounces. We named him Noah, meaning comfort and rest. He was exactly what I needed and at last, I was ready to be the mother he would need.

WAITING IN LINE FOR PASTA: WHAT IT WAS LIKE, POOR AND MIDDLE-AGED, TO PLAY A MILLIONAIRE ON A HIT TV SHOW

By David Sobel, Quartz, February 25, 2018

"Make believe you're the wealthiest people in the world," the production assistant said.

I raised my wine glass and tried to imagine I was a finance mogul toasting a 10-million-dollar deal, but I couldn't do it. I was an unemployed, 46-year-old Jewish guy earning 120 bucks for ten hours as a non-union extra on *Mr. Robot*, the TV show about hackers plotting to upend capitalism. I'd only taken three acting classes in my life. I didn't even know how to pretend I was rich.

I stood with dozens of other background players on the balcony of a building near Chinatown in Manhattan. We were supposed to be upper one percenters at a party, unaware we were losing everything in a cyber-attack. The men wore suits and ties. The women were stunning in dresses and heels. A female violinist playing the theme from *Titanic*, foreshadowing our impending financial collapse.

"Did you bring homeless clothes?" a lady near me asked. Her sleeveless black dress clung to her dark, athletic body. She looked like a celebrity at a Whitehouse dinner.

"Homeless clothes?" I asked, confused. I had on a navy-blue suit and tie with black polished shoes. Nobody told me about a change of wardrobe.

"Some people had to bring them to play the same characters in a later scene."

"Are they getting a better rate?" I asked, hopeful. I'd been desperate when the casting agency called, saying yes before considering tolls, gas, and taxes. I could use the additional pay.

"I think so," she said.

Enthused, I thought about delivering a heart-wrenching performance as a broke, middle aged white guy. I'd remove my sport jacket, untuck my soaked dress shirt, and summon feelings about losing my marketing job and leaving my Upper East Side studio to live with my parents in New Jersey.

Maybe I'd be lucky enough to get noticed for a speaking part.

"I should talk to someone," I said.

"They would've told you when they called," she said.

I sighed. After I got laid off, I quickly realized recruiters weren't rushing to interview a 40-plus year old male with a music industry degree whose last job was in jewelry distribution. Desperate, I applied to everything from food service to retail, praying my luck would turn around. It didn't.

Then, an actor friend suggested I do some background work. She said lots of shows were filming in the city, and people were frequently being pulled out of the crowd to say lines. This entitled them to vouchers and the possibility of joining the Screen Actors Guild.

"You have a look," she said. "You never know what could happen."

Now, standing in the blistering heat for more takes, my hopes of being picked seemed ridiculous. When the shooting finally ended, I walked into the church that functioned as the holding center, telling myself this was a waste of time.

Then I saw the food in steaming trays on long tables.

It was a feast large enough to feed every character on *Game of Thrones*, including the ones that had been killed off. I threw my jacket over a chair and rushed to the line.

"Are you SAG?" a crew member in jeans and a t-shirt asked. An ID hung from a chain around his neck.

"No," I said.

"Sorry, union people first."

I sat down and sulked. This was the

kind of capitalist power play the writers of *Mr. Robot* were critiquing. I had been hired to act like a Master of the Universe, only to be dressed down by some kid who thought he was entitled to eat sooner because he was in some exclusive club.

I waited a few minutes before returning to the buffet. I took two plates and helped myself to paella, chicken cutlets, ravioli in pesto sauce, and heaping assortments of as much gourmet food as my eyes permitted. Dessert was cheesecake and key lime pie.

I carried my tray to a table, where an Asian woman who looked to be in her fifties was holding court with other performers.

"They just pulled me out of the crowd," she said.

"That's great," another woman responded.

"Are you acting on the show?" I said.

"Yeah," she said. "I'm a regular."

"Really?" I said, surprised.

Her name was Micheleen. Portly, with a boyish haircut and a high-pitched voice, she'd started doing this for extra money, never intending to have a career. She got noticed, and now she was a recurring character on the show. An agent was sending her out for other roles.

I wanted the same thing for myself. As more people sat with us, it became clear everyone was hoping to get a break. The Russian acupuncturist covering a rent increase, the Chelsea art gallery manager looking for some new, an office assistant who felt stuck.

The food was the most filling and delicious I'd ever had. After I finished all of it, a production assistant made an announcement to form a line and sign papers to get paid. I arrived at the table and picked up a pen, telling her the number I'd been assigned earlier.

"You can go," she said.

"You don't need any more homeless characters?"

"Sorry," she said.

I was a poor, middle aged guy, being rejected for the role of a homeless person on TV—and I hope the same thing will happen in my real life.

PHONE SEX CHANGE

By Mark Jason Williams,
Out Magazine, March 26, 2014

I recently fell in love over the telephone. He was an operator at a Poison Control Center, which I'd called after accidentally brushing my teeth with hydrocortisone cream. I was embarrassed to discuss what I'd done, but his calm, friendly demeanor immediately put me at ease.

"Don't worry; I get this call often," he said in a deep, raspy voice that I found very soothing and incredibly sexy. He assured me I'd be fine, speaking to me as if we were best friends, then listed some precautionary measures, while I imagined that he looked like Bradley Cooper and dreamed of our wedding day in Belize.

"I feel much better, thank you," I told him, then waited for a charming response like, "My pleasure. Call anytime. In fact, here's my personal number." Instead, I got, "No problem, ma'am."

Ma'am? I wanted to go back in the bathroom and swallow real poison.

This wasn't the first time someone mistook me for a woman over the phone. It happened quite frequently. A few days earlier, I called to my credit card company and the representative quipped, "Mark? Well, that's an interesting name for a woman."

A 5-foot-4, 150-pound gay playwright with soft features, including what my late grandmother called "birthing hips," I'm not the epitome of masculinity. Yet I've got a beard and hair on my chest. I look like a man; I just wish I sounded like one. Believe me, I've tried. I've seen speech therapists and vocal coaches. I consulted an endocrinologist, who asked me my least favorite question, "Any pre-existing conditions?"

"Leukemia," I said. But I hate telling people of my childhood illness. It's always compelled them to look at me with a doe-eyed sadness and ask me a bunch of dumb questions: Did it hurt? Were you afraid of dying? I bet you can't donate blood, huh? Thankfully, the doctor just nodded and scribbled as I recounted five years of chemotherapy, radiation, blood-transfusions and near death-experiences.

"But the worst part was the hospital food," I added. "The pizza tasted like a freakin' tree."

I've always suspected that disease has played a key role in my ability to shop for clothes in the Sears' Kids section and my squeaky high voice. The doctor ran tests confirming I had low testosterone. It was like a weight had been lifted from my shoulders, then fell and hit me in the gut.

"At least you're alive," the doctor told me with the perkiness of Kelly Ripa, which didn't make me feel better. "It's bad enough I had to deal with cancer," I snapped. "Now I have to deal with feeling like less of a man." We tried a patch, but it didn't do much, except for giving me a horrible rash. So, I went to Plan B: perpetual hopelessness.

My voice has been especially challenging when it comes to dating. I've always liked masculine men but they seem to go for other masculine men. I met a guy online who seemed interested. We'd exchanged photos and texts, and I thought we had a connection, but when we met, he bluntly said, "You'd be much cuter with a deeper voice."

I thought I'd found the solution when I met a guy with a hearing impairment. Surely, my voice wouldn't matter. The date started off well. We got coffee, walked through Prospect Park, and talked about his job as a nurse. His voice was slurred, high-pitched, and monotone, but he spoke with confidence and I admired that.

"So, where do you work?" I asked.

"Harlem, but I don't like it," he said. "Too many black people."

Now I had the speech disability, as in: I didn't know what to say. I decided to cut it short, so I lied and told him I wasn't feeling well and we walked back to the subway. He dropped his cup on the sidewalk and didn't pick it up, which made me hate him more.

"Do you want to go out again?" he asked.

"I don't think so."

"Because I'm deaf?"

"No, because you're racist and a litter bug."

I needed a vacation. I went home and researched Florida hotels. I chose an all-male resort based on photos of attractive, naked men basking in the sunshine, and called to make a reservation.

"Hi. I'm inquiring about booking a room."

"Sorry," he said. "This is a hotel for men only."

I slammed down the phone and booked a room at the Hilton, but it didn't lessen the sting. Later in the evening, I was checking my email when I received a message from the director of my latest play. The subject line read: New Review In. I hesitated clicking the link—I couldn't take another letdown—but curiosity took over. I scanned the first few lines, my heart thumping in my chest, and they read: "Mark Jason Williams has a strong, courageous voice that's urgently needed in contemporary theater." At last: The world was really hearing me, and it had nothing to do with speaking.

WHAT I LEARNED FROM HAVING VITILIGO

By India Garcia, Teen Vogue, November 29, 2016

They appeared pretty quickly, without warning. Strange speckles and splotches of white formed on my knees, arms, and feet in fascinating arrangements. I was 13, tan-skinned, not religious, approaching high school, and not particularly insecure when I began to notice the patches, and the way their unfamiliarity challenged my physical security. After constant research and a significant dose of confusion, I made a single trip to the dermatologist with my parents. It was a plain beige building, much like every other building in Scottsdale, Arizona—unmistakably the desert. When I walked inside, there was a children's play area surrounded by various chairs and magazines, and a library of brochures and pamphlets urging patients to seek help and information about their medical concerns. But wasn't that why I was here?

My name was called. I rolled up my blue jeans so the doctor could examine my knees with a flashlight. Plain white patches, small, in shapes that you would see on a cow, not a human. I was uncomfortable, on the verge of learning something about myself that I would probably try to reject. A few minutes passed, and I was told I had Vitiligo. The dermatologist couldn't tell us much more about the condition, however. He scratched his head.

"Eh, could be an autoimmune disease, causes are still uncertain," he said.

Courtesy of Google, the only somewhat scientific explanation I later found was that altered pigmentation of the skin is usually brought about by our melanocytes destroying themselves within the comfort of our own bodies. For now, the doctor fidgeted with his ball point pen and spoke to us about topical creams, casually slipping in that there was currently no cure for the disorder—the last words I wanted to hear. Yet I was more concerned about the $300 check my parents were writing for the appointment, than my initial distaste with the doctor. During the moment when I needed the person with the degree to speak to me in a balance of scientific syntax and plain language, he was relatively mute and uneducated, as if this was the first time he spoke to someone "spotted." I politely thanked him when the appointment was over and left the rubber-smelling cubicle.

Unfortunately, the spots grew more noticeable over the years. After further research and personal analysis, I learned that the disorder did have one consistent trait: symmetry. The imperfections mimicked one another on each half of my body. Elbows, knees, underarms, feet, inner thighs, wrists were now invaded with the abnormality. My olive skin was tarnished. The splotches were pure white and resembled kaleidoscopic images. They were delicate in appearance, popping up without warning or consent, choosing the specific place in which they would like to exist. Every night, I searched online for an explanation. I became a victim to the columns of questions with response boxes left unanswered. There wasn't an explanation for my condition; there were suggested treatments—treatments like topical creams and PUVA laser. Medical sources encouraged me to stay out

of the sun completely, ironic because I lived in the sunniest state in the country. As the blemishes grew more noticeable, I was more susceptible to telling white lies. People would ask constantly, "What is that on your elbow?" "You have something on your arm." I would reply with "birthmark," which made much more sense to me then than it does now. With every new confrontation, I crawled sheepishly back inside myself, losing a bit of my identity each time.

I resented the disorder for the way it hindered my potential experiences and opportunities as a young girl. I wanted to play volleyball, but I never did. I didn't wear dresses in fear of unsolicited comments about my legs. I was disappointed in my situation, and in myself for being disappointed in the first place. During the second semester of my junior year of high school, I joined the girls lacrosse team. I was automatically expected to wear the white and blue miniskirt and matching tank top, exposing the imperfections that lived on the surface of my skin. This was the first jab I took at my skin insecurity.

Over time, I became less self-conscious, but when I *was* uncomfortable, I felt guilty and wrong, like I was ungrateful. After all, there were people who endured physical pain everyday, patients who truly suffered. My situation was only skin-deep. It was merely an external flaw that stung internally, but it never caused me actual harm. I felt ashamed to talk about the low self-esteem I developed and the experiences I missed out on, so I didn't. I didn't want to be the girl who asked herself, "Why me?" It took four years to finally breathe the words, "Why not me?"

This was around the same time

THE BYLINE BIBLE

that I saw Winnie Harlow on the 21st season of *America's Next Top Model*. The black American model lives with Vitiligo as well, but radiates a level of poise I didn't know was possible among those with the disorder we shared. More recently, Harlow was seen in Beyoncé's music video, *Lemonade*, as a symbol of strength and beauty. I read article after article about her, finding inspiration in the way she held herself, in the way she accepted the condition while not seeing the discolorations as something to be fixed. It was the first time I had been exposed to another person who made me feel less alone. It was the first time I felt confident enough to reveal myself and the flawed parts of my body, without feeling like I owed the world an explanation.

As an 18 year-old college freshman living in New York, I continue to search for more answers about the condition. However, I am no longer seeking a way to fix it. The past year has forced me to grow, along with Winnie Harlow and the 50 million bodies actively exhibiting the disorder. I now throw myself into new experiences as much as I can and choose to view my insecurity and discomfort with my body as only a segment of the self I used to cover up. I have been with my boyfriend for over a year and owe a good part of my self-assurance to the confidence he instills in me. He loves the marks. To others, my condition may be seen as an unfortunate abnormality, but it isn't up to me to prove them wrong. It is up to me to accept myself, spotted or not.

I STOLE A WHITE GIRL AND TOOK HER TO PROM

BY VICTOR VARNADO, SALON.COM, SEPTEMBER 30, 2017

My prom date's parents had no idea their white daughter would spend the evening with a black man.

For starters, they didn't know I was black. As an African-American man born with albinism, I have seen the look of awareness creep across faces when people set aside their initial assessment, based on my light skin and hair, and finally figure out that I am black. As they come to terms with this realization, their silent reactions range from harmless ("Well, I'll be. I had no idea you even existed!") to the irrational ("I've been betrayed! Why did you trick me?"). Moments like these have plagued my life.

For me, high school began with ostracism. I was teased about my very light hair and skin, lazy eye and Coke-bottle glasses. But as I matured from a terrified freshman to a more confident senior, my classmates' attitude toward me transformed dramatically. The most important change for me was that suddenly women didn't find me revolting.

The first thing I wanted to do with my newly acceptable level of attractiveness was ask my friend Kate to prom. Kate had dark hair, a great sense of humor, boobs and combat boots—everything that at 18 I felt was important. Although she listened to better music than I did—she liked The Replacements while I liked A-ha—Kate did think I was cool enough to hang out with intermittently. Sometimes we met for lunch in the concrete commons area separating the two buildings comprising Minneapolis North High School's campus. We would slowly chew breaded chicken breasts while criticizing everyone else's clothes.

Before asking Kate out, I watched her from inside the glass double doors of the southern building until I could slow down my breathing enough to feel normal. I left the safety of the doorway and asked, "Will you go to prom with me?" She paused, looked surprised, smiled and then agreed to the date.

The next day, every time I saw her she smiled or blushed. I wondered if this was what dating felt like. Then the following afternoon, Kate greeted me in the lunchroom with tears in her eyes.

"I'm sorry," she said.

Although we were surrounded by cafeteria commotion, it felt like she and I were alone.

"My—my parents won't let me go to prom with you," she stammered.

"Why?" I was so confused.

"Because you're black." She said it like I maybe should have known.

I was genuinely surprised. My whole life people shunned me for looking different, but never for my race.

Apparently, when Kate told her parents she had been asked to prom, she pointed me out in the yearbook to her mother, who thought I was "different looking" but nice enough.

Her father, on the other hand, took one look at my photo and had questions.

"What is he?" he asked.

Kate said that I was black, that both my parents were black. Through a genetic anomaly, they produced a child like me.

The look on Kate's face filled in the rest of the story. She turned around and left the lunchroom as quickly as she could. I was left standing alone, surrounded by everyone I knew.

That evening, I broke the news to my friends Dave and Pete. The three of us had planned to triple date to the prom. We were renting a limo together. Now, with Kate pulling out of our date, our entire evening was harpooned.

But I'd always been a fan of John Hughes' movies, especially his romantic comedies like *Sixteen Candles*. Molly Ringwald took an incredible risk before landing her true love. So why couldn't I come up with my own madcap scheme to win Kate's heart?

What would happen if I sent one of my incredibly white friends to Kate's house on prom night? Maybe I could fool her parents into thinking she was going to the dance with a safe Caucasian male.

Pete and Dave were in—I just had to pick my proxy.

Pete was my hunkiest buddy. His father was an ex-Marine, and his brother was a fireman. He came from Nordic stock. Every time a new attractive girl moved to our school district, it was inevitable that he would end up in bed with her. Was I handing Kate over to him? Pete was definitely not the guy for the job.

Dave was a tall and nerdy German kid with blonde hair and thick glasses. I would find out later that Dave got more action than anybody, but at the time he made me feel safe.

The next day I presented the idea to Kate over lunch. She was flabbergasted at the plan for Dave to be our ethnic beard, but she agreed to play along.

On the night of the dance, Dave, Pete, their dates and I all arrived outside of Kate's house in a limo. I had picked a cumberbund and bow tie to match Kate's blue dress, so Dave and I switched our tuxedo accessories to avoid any suspicion.

Pete and I watched from the limousine as Kate's father greeted Dave and ushered him into their living room for pictures. It was surreal. Part of me felt so smart that I had come up with a way to trick Kate's parents. I also felt like a creep hiding in the car while a white guy posed with my prom date.

Eventually, Kate and Dave emerged and jumped into the limo. I stayed hidden until the car door closed, and we were all safe behind privacy glass. Once Dave and I switched our accessories back, Kate and I sat next to each other, awkwardly, not touching at all.

That evening we danced, we bowled, and we held hands. By the end of the night, as the limo dropped other kids off, one by one, Kate and I had grown bold. We pulled up outside of Kate's house. We stood on her sidewalk. If Kate's mother had looked out of her window right then, she would have seen us. Kate and I leaned in for a kiss. We may have been too excited because we bumped teeth. We were both too embarrassed to correct our mistake, so the fumbled kiss was all we had.

Years later, when Kate was in her early twenties and sitting in the back of her parents' station wagon on a family trip, she decided it was time to tell them that she spent prom with that black kid who didn't really look black.

Her father kept driving but screamed "WHAT?!" in an exaggerated cartoon fashion. He wasn't a fan.

Kate's mother responded just the way a movie mom might. "I knew it!" she said, laughing.

Kate and I didn't end up together, but the part of our short relationship that I kept has affected my dealings with intimacy since. Life rewarded me for taking a chance. My experience with Kate became a seminal moment. Risk became my blueprint for how relationships that were worth it began.

Most of the time, seizing the moment *has* led to something exceptional. When I started a conversation on Facebook with a woman I'd never met, she asked if I would meet her in New Orleans after she finished her stint rebuilding houses shortly after Hurricane Katrina. I agreed. We met for the first time at a boutique hotel on Bourbon Street and enjoyed three days of dancing, jazz, gumbo and gambling. We toured an almost empty aquarium as it was being restocked after the storm. Since the rules were relaxed, I even got to pet my first penguin.

Taking chances has sometimes led to terrible things, too. But even though I woke up to an empty wallet and a missing phone after almost a week of hanging out with a poet from Kansas—who to this day swears she will pay me back—I still enjoyed the conversation, the affection, and joy she gave me before she robbed me blind.

MY MOM'S VISION, MY INHERITANCE

By Enma Elias, Wall Street Journal, May 11, 2017

"Hola mija, how are you?" my mom, Rosa, texted me last month. I hesitated before replying that I had woken up again to that sharp pain behind my eyelids. Like her, I was born with granular dystrophy, a rare eye condition that occasionally causes "eruptions" and leaves scar tissue on my corneas. Whenever I mentioned it, my usually chirpy mom would wilt. "I gave you all that is bad," she would sigh. She felt responsible for my affliction. For a long time, I blamed her too.

My mom was diagnosed in 1991, long after her vision had begun to fail. She was 27, and I was 4; we had arrived in the U.S. after fleeing Guatemala's civil war. Back home proper health care had been rare and expensive. We came to California to live with my dad, Hernan, a cook who worked 16 hours a day to bring us to America.

My mom eventually learned to drive, but often, especially at night, she depended on my dad, and later my brother and me. Since I also had the disease, I joked that it was the blind leading the blind when we would try to find our way, driving slowly and squinting at road signs while cars behind us honked.

When my eruptions came, the loss of vision and pain were debilitating to the point of depression. Light was excruciating, and I retreated to a darkened room for days at a time. My mom soothed me and blamed herself. I stewed in silent agreement.

After she turned 50, she was referred to an ophthalmologist who specialized in rare diseases. He was fascinated by her condition. Soon the room was filled with excited young physicians who'd never seen a real-life case. She needed surgery, and the doctor battled her insurance company for months until it approved two corneal transplants. I had been so concerned with my own struggle that I hadn't noticed hers. But I felt a pang of anxiety as I imagined her driving home from her housekeeping job during the winter, when the sun set before she left.

After the first surgery I picked her up from outpatient care. A week later, her other cornea was replaced. "Colors are brighter," she said. My congratulatory smile hid more than a touch of sadness. My roommates and boyfriend worried that they sometimes found me hanging out in the dark. How had I not realized all the lights were off? A selfie revealed a trail of faint freckles across my cheeks, which I had not noticed. My friends laughed and said, "Yes, you've always had those."

I asked my doctor about surgery, but he said I didn't need it yet. This was infuriating, but I was no longer angry with my mom. I realized that my parents had left their country and sacrificed every day to give me and my brother a better life. They made sure I got checkups, glasses, braces, shots. I've earned a college degree in English and am now studying journalism at the New School.

When I told my mom that I had inherited her freckles, she inspected my face proudly. "Mija, your vision is fine. Your life is good!" She was right. She'd bequeathed to me not only her freckles and deteriorating eye disease, but also everything good in my life that she'd never had growing up.

THE RECKONING

By Kenan Trebincevic,
New York Times "Lives,"
December 2, 2011

After reading an article on Bosnia's tourism boom, my brother, Eldin, and I decided it was time to face down our past. We reasoned that we were really doing this for our 72-year-old father, Senahid. If he didn't see the country of his birth or his childhood friends soon, he never would. Yet within days I became obsessed with creating a to-do list for our trip: 1) Take a picture of the concentration camp my brother and father survived; 2) visit the cemetery where the karate coach who betrayed us was buried; 3) confront Petra, the neighbor who stole from my mother.

The minute we stepped out of the car in front of our old apartment building, my hands began to sweat. We fled 18 years ago, one year into the Bosnian war, and had not been back since. My father's friend Truly bought our apartment as a summer home in 2006, the year my mom died of cancer. (We were living in Connecticut by then.) Truly and my father both worked with the city's sports clubs and were close friends for 30 years. "You and your brother should know what your father did for this city and its people," Truly said when he greeted me. "That's why he stayed alive."

As we approached the building, I could see Truly's two pretty teenage daughters staring down at us from the third-floor balcony. I was reminded of what it was like to be 12, shouting to my friends below as I rushed to get to karate practice. It still shocked me to recall that it was my coach who, put in charge of the city's special-police unit, arrived with the army van to cleanse the building of its Muslims. They marched to our door and told my father, "You have an hour to leave or you will be killed." We left and went to stay with my aunt. My father and brother were picked up a month later and put into a camp. My mother and I eventually made it back to the apartment, where we were all reunited three months later. We were the only Muslim family who didn't flee the building when the war began. But we lived in fear that someone would come back for us.

Inside, the building hadn't changed—the same impossibly high steps, the same brown mailboxes. Only the tenants' names were different. After the war, this side of town came to be populated by Serbs. Bosnians like us were now a minority.

As I walked into the apartment, I headed for my old bedroom. I used to lie on the floor peeping through the tiny holes in the shades that were drawn all day and night so soldiers couldn't see you and spray the windows with bullets.

Coming up to our apartment, I passed Petra, our old neighbor. She was in her late 60s now. When she caught sight of me, she put down her grocery bags and sat on the stairs to smoke a cigarette, hoping to avoid me.

I flashed back to the night she barged into our dining room and told my mother to give her the skirt she was wearing. The next day it was the dining-room rug Petra wanted. A week later, she invited my mother for coffee, and they sat with their feet resting on the stolen rug. Truly's wife promised my mother that she would never acknowledge Petra. "All summer long I walk by her as if I'm walking by a grave," she said.

Petra liked to tell the paramilitaries where Muslims were living so they could come and cart them away in meat trucks. Her husband, Obren, worked as a guard in the concentration camp. (It was the same one from which my brother and father were miraculously released, as prisoners were being transferred, hours before CNN arrived to show the world the atrocities.) While Petra requisitioned my mother's things, Obren brought me canned beans and plum jam. He remembered the time my father stood up for him during a tenants' meeting just before the fighting began. Years later, we learned he died of esophageal cancer. His wife has lasted almost as long as a Galápagos tortoise. The monsters always live.

As she approached our floor, her footsteps became halting, her breathing heavy. She fumbled for her key. Her eyes didn't meet mine. "No one has forgotten," I said. She put her head down. The door opened with a long sigh, then closed. There was silence.

I heard laughter coming from our old living room and joined my friends inside. Truly turned to his daughters and said, "If the two of you were only a few years older, you could marry one of the boys." They blushed, smiling. "Once they turn 18," I said to make them less uncomfortable.

Later that night, I reached into my pocket for my to-do list and crossed off item No. 3.

SEND IN THE CLOWN SHARE

By Robert Markowitz,
Purple Clover, September 24, 2016

In 1994, when I was 37, I traded in my lawyer suit-and-tie for colorful clown gear, and returned to my Jewish mother's attic bedroom in the suburbs. Within a couple of months, she hauled me to her therapist.

As Mom and I drove up Old White Plains Road to her Scarsdale psychotherapist, she singled out every field of law that she could identify in hope that one would resonate and bring me back to my senses. But I had come home 3,000 miles from California to seek work that didn't make me cry in the morning. I told my mother that I wanted to be an entertainer.

"Over my dead body," she replied.

We entered a seven-gabled Tudor building in Scarsdale where Mom's analyst had his office. Ten minutes later, he fetched us from the waiting room.

The doctor's office was a reassuring blend of mahogany woodwork and a classic Persian rug. He was a slight, bespectacled man with thinning dark hair and a beard. Although he shook hands with me and smiled, I felt edgy, as if meeting my mother's collaborator. A diploma on the wall showed that he was a Columbia Ph.D., and I recognized the name as Jewish.

"Doctor," my 63 year-old mother said before we even sat down, "This is Robert. I'm afraid that he would be on the street if it wasn't for me." She slipped him a folded check.

I wondered if Mom would be so agitated about my career change if Dad were still alive. He had died suddenly from a stroke on the town tennis courts eight years before. Mom held onto her job teaching remedial reading for the full pension.

The doctor smiled and shook my hand. He motioned for us to sit. "Your mother believes that if she did not let you live at her house, you would be forced to support yourself."

"He would have to get a job if he didn't live with me," my mother said.

Her analyst steepled his fingers. "Is that true?"

Forcing myself to remain seated, my temples grew uncomfortably hot. I felt embarrassed in front of the doctor, who, I was certain, invited his mom to a fancy brunch on Mother's Day and whisked her off to Belize with his family on Spring Break. Indeed, his forehead was tanned.

"I want to love my work," I said, almost inaudibly.

"What do you think that might be?" he asked.

"I don't know," I said. "So far, working as a clown at parties."

"He's very convincing," my mother said, as if this were part of my disease.

She turned to me. "A wife and a baby would make you figure it out." Mom looked expectantly at the doctor.

"I wouldn't recommend marriage and children as a way to resolve a life crisis," he said, nervously rotating his gold wedding ring. My mother had told me in the car that she consulted him only in times of crisis, not weekly, which went against his psychoanalytic training. He didn't appear much older than me.

"So you think Robert is having a life crisis?" Mom said, her eyes widening.

The doctor grimaced. Just when he thought that he'd settled one issue, my mother had opened another, using his phrase.

He glanced at me. "I suppose so," he said, "but it's not my place to diagnose your son, Mrs. Markowitz."

"So you think I was foolish to bring him in?"

"I didn't say that."

"But it puts you in a difficult situation," she said.

Now the analyst was the beleaguered party. He slouched forward. "Mrs. Markowitz," he said, "are you truly asking your son to move out?"

"No, I would never do that!" She thought a moment. "Maybe never is too strong."

"So what is it that you really want?" Mom's therapist asked her.

"I want my son to be happy being a lawyer."

"Your choice is limited to whether you let him stay in your house," he said.

Blood flowed to my face along with a shot of victory adrenalin. My mother's shoulders shrunk and her face narrowed. Did only I notice her chair growing bigger around a pinched and frail body?

There was no pleasure in defeating her. But it was important for me to stand my ground. I had been the second child out of her womb. Mom blamed herself for my older brother's death from Riley-Day, a congenital disease, and her self-contempt surfaced in stressful moments. For me, leaving law was a step out from that shadow of shame. I was done with compensating for it.

When we left the doctor's office, we both knew that things had changed between us, even if I would still live under her roof and eat her food for months to come. I needed to get my bearings before I could move on and eventually build a career playing music for children—doing what makes me happy.

VALENTINE'S DAY LETTER TO MY BODY PARTS

By Lexie Bean, Teen Vogue, February 13, 2017

I sent myself the only Valentine that made me cry. Days alone in a hospital bed tucked between dim lights and a thick language barrier, I could no longer deny how far I tried to run from my own body. I originally admitted myself seeking a diagnosis to understand the hurt I had collected over the years. I was seeking a cure to overcome feeling, as I made the assumption that healing meant every day got better. It just wasn't working out for me.

For years I went in and out of the hospital without a diagnosis. I was simply afraid of my body—heavy with the question, "Will anyone believe me?" I closed the notebook onto my lap, IV dripping into my tired veins, it is from there I started writing letters to my body parts. I had to make it better by carving out a place for myself instead of carving into my own skin.

I am trans. From a young age I was sexually and emotionally abused. I rarely place these sentences next to each other because I don't want anyone to confuse my trauma with my liberation. Forced into someone else's destination, nothing about rape taught me to be honest with myself. I grew from a place where telling my body's truth would uproot everything. Language was used to manipulate my boundaries. Silence was better. The hurt said it was best to become a see-through version of myself so I don't have to keep falling into the trauma of fallen toys.

Yet I am often asked when coming out as LGBTQ is "Do you feel that way because someone did that to you? Because you still have healing to do?" Who I am has no root. Feeling seen is nothing to recover from.

I thought for too long that if identities and dreams were compartmentalized, I would be safer. I would be more valuable if I were easier to understand. Stumbling over my pronouns, sending me back home, people didn't always know what to do with me. I could be a sweet girl, I could have a safe suburban family, ignoring everything that didn't fit into their fantasy. I tried to beat them to the punch by pre-maturely erasing myself through dissociation, self-diag-

THE BYLINE BIBLE

nosing with anything that fit into one word, and attempting suicide. There is that subtle yet persistent feeling of being out of place that cuts and cuts and cuts. I didn't understand until I moved out of my Michigan hometown why almost all of my Gay-Straight Alliance friends covered their arms with wristbands from Claire's.

The last year I went to the hospital I wrote three letters to my body parts: one to my leg hair, one to the space between my hips, and another to the baby teeth that now live in my mother's night stand. I only wrote to the pieces of myself that I have tried to detach from while seeking safety. I was learning to stay one piece at a time. I was learning how to find a safe space to meet myself with honesty. I had not yet come out as trans.

I had sent to my leg hair, "I sometimes pretend you are fields of restless wheat that outline my home." I held my knees as I recalled the space between my hips, "I feel responsible—you lost a body that you can never grow back. You are now unsealed, and bore with holes for nightmares to sink into your folds ... There is only evidence of that someone else was here pushing, pushing, pushing. I catch my breath." I told my estranged baby teeth, "Looking into her nightstand, there's evidence of bodies that were never whole. Children who had never known what it meant to have these baby teeth. Each and all teeth shed served as evidence of he who abused his duties as the tooth fairy."

None of my early letters ended with the word "love." Sometimes they still don't, and that's OK. Like healing, relationships are never linear. I wanted every part of me to survive whether or not they were perfect. As in any connection, there are days it seemed as if the tenderness will last forever, some days are more like playing hard to get, or it's a fight. Sometimes I can't look at the other without seeing the men who hurt me and kicked me out of my own house.

Sometimes peace looks more like conflict. Sometimes positivity looks more like moving and feeling in every direction. Sometimes love looks more like letting the seemingly unlovable parts of me survive. Love is trusting I will never be just one thing. This Valentine's Day, I'm going to return to all the parts of myself I tried to cut off for the convenience of others. I'm going to write to my body parts difficult to hold as I seek wholeness, in a shape that no one has ever seen before.

For the record, I haven't been in the hospital since 2012, the same year I sent my first letters.

DREAM ME A RIVER

By Carlos Saavedra Vélez,
New York Times, May 24, 2016

My schedule was packed with therapy patients back to back until 7 p.m. I wanted to make sure that everyone was seen and everything was taken care of before I left for vacation: medications refilled, phone calls returned, medical documentation completed. I was in a state of flow. Then I got a call from a former patient's wife, informing me he had died. It stopped me.

Andrew had been an athletic and charismatic civil engineer in his early 40s, married with two young children. He came to see me for a drug addiction, which had started innocuously in his mid-30s with some occasional recreational use. Over the years his use increased until it consumed most of his life. A month before he came to see me, he had lost his job, and his wife was threatening divorce.

I started him on medication and he began attending an intensive outpatient treatment program. He stopped using, and within three weeks of treatment he accepted a job that would take him out of New York, to Maryland, half of the week. This meant he would be leaving his daily treatment program. I advised against this because it was so early in his recovery. He said he didn't think it would be a problem: He would make sure to come to his weekly sessions and he would attend 12-step meetings. I felt very uneasy. My experience had been that this sort of thing was what led people to ease out of treatment into relapse. I shared my concerns. He nodded with a gentle smile. My words had no effect on him. I felt it in my core.

Eventually he started missing our sessions. Then one day he came in to tell me that it would be his last visit. He said that he was going to follow up with a new doctor who was a better fit for him.

It was five months after that visit when I received the call from his wife. Andrew, I learned, never followed up with the other doctor, and stopped every form of treatment. Soon he relapsed, and after months of secret drug use, he overdosed. I remembered the pleasant nod he gave me when I voiced my concerns. A profound heaviness descended over me. But as the day went on, I felt better, lifted by the patients who walked into my office to share their stories. It was the best medicine for me.

A few days later, as I rested on a beautiful beach on the southern coast of Brazil, Andrew came to mind like one of the many wispy low clouds blowing into the coast—a mystery, an unarticulated question. I again felt a heaviness. I knew doctors couldn't save everyone. I had learned that a long time ago. I was sad about Andrew's death, but I thought that I was at peace with it. Soon I would learn otherwise.

Later that day, a beautiful woman who looked to be in her early 60s started casually talking to me at the beach. She told me she was a spiritual healer and believed that we were all working through the traumas and ailments of our ancestors. She asked me what was my birth order. I told her I was the first born. "The father's firstborn son comes into the world to work through the issues of his maternal grandfather," she said. That struck me. My maternal grandfather died from complications of alcoholism when he was 49, before I was born. I had long been aware of the connection between my ending up in the field of addiction treatment and my having an alcoholic grandfather, but I had never felt its emotional resonance until that moment, with the memory of my deceased patient lingering.

After a long evening walk, I found the comfort of my bed and fell into a deep sleep. I dreamed I was in medical school again. I was in a small classroom, seated by a student I did not recognize. He reminded me of an elementary school classmate whose name was also

Carlos. I could see in this student's face that something was distressing him. I had to help him so I said assertively, "We are talking."

We looked for an empty room so we could speak in private, but each room we found was filled. Eventually we found an empty classroom. As I started to walk in, another student began coming in with a group to do a project. I told her emphatically, "This room is mine." They left without question. Then my classmate walked in and I followed. When I closed the door, the wall behind him disappeared and gave onto a savage river surrounded by thick tropical vegetation. The river brimmed with gray water rushing forth with relentless force. It looked like the river behind my maternal grandmother's home in San Sebastián, Puerto Rico, except that this one was fuller and more ferocious.

As soon as the river appeared, the student threw himself in it. I jumped in terror to save him. I was able to wrap my arm around his dangling foot. I began screaming from the top of my lungs, "Ayúdenme, ayúdenme!" which means, "Help me, help me!" in Spanish. The more I screamed, the more he fought me. I could feel his foot slipping away. My screams woke me up. It took me a few moments to catch my breath and realize I was in my hotel in Brazil. I was mystified and shaken.

I eventually went back to sleep, but the dream stayed with me. I've thought about it every day since. It exposed a hidden grief for the loss of someone I was incapable of saving. That someone, most recently, was Andrew, yet the sorrow, I now realized, preceded his passing. Trying to cope with that old unconscious grief was no doubt what led me to treat addiction, and into psychiatry in the first place, the hope of having the power to change someone immutable. I thought about my mother, who had studied social work, motivated by her desire to help alcoholics like her father, whom she couldn't stop from dying.

It was all becoming clear: My mother had transmitted to me unconsciously her desire to save her father and entrusted me also with taking on his pain—just as the spiritual healer said. The figure that jumped into the river represented not only Andrew and my grandfather, but also me. I had my own pain, which had led me into my own psychoanalysis years before. The dream suggested that I was afraid that the current of my powerful feelings would sweep me away the way it did Andrew and my grandfather.

The dream was a reminder that I can't rescue anyone from his or her feelings, not myself or my patients. I can only learn to live with my own and be an instrument for my patients to do the same if they so choose.

WHY BEING A HAIRSTYLIST HONORS MY JEWISH FAMILY TRADITIONS

By Lisa J. Daniels,
The Jewish Forward, June 18, 2017

There's an off-Broadway comedy show

that has been around for several years, *My Son The Waiter: A Jewish Tragedy*. The title pokes fun at a stereotype that has Jewish parents disappointed because their child didn't become a lawyer or a doctor. Like most children of Jewish families whose forebears immigrated to the United States from Eastern Europe, I grew up assuming I would go to college, and I did. I graduated from Brandeis University in 1979. Ten years later I became a hairstylist.

To me, my work was the ultimate gig—artistic, entrepreneurial, fun. Listening to my interesting, accomplished clients in metropolitan Washington, D.C., for 23 years was as cozy and intimate as pillow talk. We told each other everything. Facing the mirror together, we sought answers about superficial appearance that were really about core identity. *Is this me? Is this my best self?* Because of my intellectual family, though, I agonized over those questions throughout most of my career.

My parents weren't the most observant Jews, but they had certainly adopted the value of using higher education as a springboard to a professional career. My mother was a second-wave feminist with a thriving psychotherapy practice. My father was an international trade lawyer/lobbyist. I was more interested in hair and make-up than in anything else.

That passion grew from dealing with my own kinky, curly hair, a frizzled mess that was completely out of style in the late 1960s, the era of smooth, straight hair.

As a teenager I tried to straighten it in the makeshift salon of our black-and-white tiled bathroom. In front of the medicine cabinet mirror, I mixed and applied smelly solutions from the home-straightening kits I bought with my babysitting earnings. In that small room reeking of pungent chemicals, I first felt the excitement of setting transformation into motion. The possibility of changing into someone different was thrilling.

Appearance seemed decidedly not feminist or intellectual. So my interest in hair remained a girly, guilty pleasure. Finally, when I was 32, 10 years after I graduated from college with a Bachelor of Arts in English, I went to Graham Webb International Academy of Hair, in Arlington, Virginia.

If my parents were appalled, they hid it well. They both quickly (and bravely) became my loyal clients while I was still in school. I told myself I would do hair "for a little while" until I figured out what I really wanted to be when I grew up. Mastering the techniques and tools of my trade felt artistic—the hair-color swatch book inspired my creativity like a freshly opened 100-pack of crayons, and my shears became an extension of my mind's eye as I deftly sculpted away extraneous hair to reveal the hidden beauty I saw in my clients.

I worked in what psychologists call flow. I was energized and fully focused, and I enjoyed what I was doing. It was gratifying to be trusted for my taste, my expertise and my counsel on everything from the important—challenges at work, with relationships and parenting—to the mundane, like what color to paint the dining room.

I owned a business, earned a six-figure income and supported my family as the major breadwinner in my marriage. But I still felt disapproval. Someone in my family spoke of her hairdresser as "my girl." Another, the first female child of my immigrant grandparents to earn a doctorate, actually rolled her eyes when my work came up in conversation. Although my mother seemed supportive and loved her hair, I noticed she was critical of her sister, who "wasted her education" by being "only" an elementary school secretary.

The first question anyone asks a new acquaintance in the D.C. area is, "What do you do?" Over the years, I had social conversations end abruptly when I answered that question. Inevitably, those same people would corner me later in the ladies' room for a free impromptu hair consultation. People asked if I had any famous clients. I did. Naming those women illuminated me with an instant reflected legitimacy that was irrelevant, but one that I still welcomed as social tender. I managed to slip Brandeis into every conversation with someone new.

The stereotype is that hairdressers are flakey, dumb, gum-popping party people. In my experience, though, most stylists are smart and perceptive. We are warm, wise listeners. We are highly skilled in the worlds of chemistry, geometry and physics.

I retired six years ago after 23 years "behind the chair." Snobbery toward the trades is real, but looking back I realize my conflict about doing hair was self-imposed. I let other people's misperceptions influence how I felt. I was lucky to do work that I loved.

My 24-year-old son recently decided not to continue with college. He is on his own "less traditional" path. As his mom I am defending his decision to my family and at the same time resisting the urge to talk him into going back to school.

We American Jews encourage our kids to get a good education as a means of having a successful life. But our heritage is actually rooted in the trades. Generations of Jews in Europe, and of immigrants to the United States, were garment workers, cigar rollers, butchers, printers, tailors, weavers, silversmiths, day laborers and bakers. In fact, the Talmud's most famous rabbinic statement about parents' obligations to children (Kiddushin 29a) includes, among other things, teaching them Torah and a trade.

It turns out that having a trade was in line with my Jewish heritage after all.

WHAT COLOR IS YOUR PRINCESS

By Doreen Oliver, New York Times, October 28, 2012

Last Halloween, my 3-year-old son wanted to be a princess. Assuming this was similar to his robot and rock star phases, I broached the subject again a few days after his initial declaration. "Bug, what do you want to be for Halloween?"

"A princess," he said, his Spider-Man backpack bobbing as we walked hand-in-hand to school.

"Sure, but you know, usually princesses are girls and princes boys." I paused. "Do you want to be a prince?"

"Noooo," he said.

I was a liberated African-American woman. When my mother wanted to buy my firstborn, Xavier, clothes every shade of blue, I insisted, "Color has no gender!" After Bug was born, I joked he was the little girl I never had, since he was really chatty for his age, and I always imagined that's how a little girl would be. Xavier's speech was limited because of his autism, so talks with a child were new for me.

Our conversations were often about his favorite color, which was usually pink, although once during yoga class, he chose blue. (Yes, we both loved Parent and Pea yoga.) I laughed when Bug came downstairs one afternoon, draped in a rose-colored sheet, exclaiming, "Mommy, I'm a princess!"

I pictured Oct. 31: my handsome, sturdy brown-skinned son in a flowing wig and poofy dress, tiara sparkling atop his head. I saw us trick-or-treating in our New Jersey suburb, going from one colonial to the next, our neighbors asking "And what are you, uh, little girl?" as they dropped candy in his bag after a curious glance at me.

I could handle that. Like Bug, I didn't mind going against the grain. Also, the simple fact that one of my sons could express himself was a blessing. If he wanted to be a princess, then darn it, he'd be a royal She.

But when I browsed for costumes, I felt uneasy. In the princess section, long wigs were the color of spun gold. Even Snow White's silky tresses glistened through the cellophane, the opposite texture of my son's coarse hair. Whether it was Cinderella or her fairy godmother, each package showed a picture of a smiling white woman who glowed. "You, too, can be me," she beckoned, "for this one special day."

I left the store in a panic. I didn't care if my son wanted to be a princess. I just didn't want him to want to be a white princess.

I thought about how Bug's preschool celebrated Black History Month, but the fairy-tale books lining the shelves featured white characters. Xavier's therapists were white and female. We avoided television, but couldn't miss the outdoor ads showcasing pale models you either wanted to kiss or emulate. Our suburb is diverse, but we happened to be the only black family on our block.

Suddenly, white women were everywhere.

I'd gone through my own identity crisis at my predominantly white middle school. I lost patches of hair trying to get a soft (albeit oily) Jheri curl. When I was slightly older than Bug, I'd wrap a towel around my head and let it hang down my back, whipping it back and forth in the mirror, feeling beautiful. While swimming at camp, the other girls rose out of the lake, bronzed, hair slick and orderly, while I stood nearby, blackened by the sun, mortified when those same girls peered into my mass of kinky natural hair, wondering why it didn't get wet underwater.

I didn't want that for my son.

After the heartbreak of Xavier's diagnosis, my husband and I were forced to define what "success" meant for our children. While we were trying to get Xavier to simply point, 1-year old Bug thrust his cup at me and said, "I'm thirsty!" Our boys were distinctly different, but we wanted to raise both to be confident and proud of who they are.

So if it turns out Bug is gay, we'd embrace his identity. But if he wanted to be white, we'd have to have a talk.

I discovered his idea of a princess had blond hair and peach-colored skin. To prepare for my intervention, I sifted through my mother's wig collection and sorted through pictures of real African queens to give him an ethnic flair and historical perspective. I was ready.

And then Bug spied the DJ Lance Rock costume from "Yo Gabba Gabba" and dumped the princess idea. So it goes with 3-year-olds.

Not so with their mothers. We plant seeds in our children, then sculpture beautiful gardens around them, believing they will flower into our creations. But our children peek beyond those bushes out into the world and decide for themselves who they will be. Thinking we can choose for them is simply a fairy tale.

WHEN I LOST MY PHONE, I LOST MY YOUNGER BROTHER ALL OVER AGAIN

By Emillio Mesa, Quartz,
July 16, 2017

I eventually erased my mother's frantic voicemail, but it still beats inside me, like a second heart.

"Your brother is dead! Please come home," she screamed.

A sudden heart attack claimed my brother's life at 30. He died in his sleep, found by his eldest son.

When I lost my iPhone, eight months after his death, I mourned him for the second time. All the childhood pictures and final texts my brother, Wesley, had sent me were on there. I had not backed any of it up in my iCloud account. I feared the phone slipped out of the back pocket of my new black skinny jeans after I crossed a crowded bar.

"They're too tight for slip-outs. You were pick pocketed," said my friend as he securely placed his iPhone in his *front* pocket.

I thought the geniuses who created the "Find My iPhone" app would be my savior if I ever misplaced my phone. But now it wasn't technology on which I desperately relied; I was at the mercy of whomever snatched my phone and was reading my frantic pleas.

"Life or death situation. No joke. Please contact me. I WILL PAY YOU," I texted, from a friend's iPhone to my stolen one.

I wasn't yet freaking out because I could track my phone's whereabouts. The dot that represented my phone was still on the move. But after one hour, it disappeared for good, along with my hope of any reconnection. My guilt kicked into overdrive. Not only did I lose my brother, but also the relationship we'd just restarted.

A year after I was born in the Dominican Republic, my mother divorced my father. She left me in the care of my grandparents and left for New York City. Five years later she returned to me, with a new husband and child. That's when I first met my brother, Wesley. I was introspective; Wesley was hyperactive. From identical outfits to forced playdates, our mother pushed a bond.

A year after we were all united, our mother divorced Wesley's father. Newly single, in a one-bedroom apartment in the Bronx, she doted on Wesley and depended on me. I became my brother's guardian and my mother's spokesperson at school. Several times each month

I faced the principal, in her office, due to Wesley's disruptive behavior. At home, I complained to Mom about being pulled out of class, to receive yet another lecture on his disobedience.

"I know it's hard, but you are his big brother, and I'm at work," our mom explained.

"He is my HALF-brother," I responded.

"You are full brothers because you both came from me," she replied, as she placed both my hands, firmly, on her stomach.

Throughout the rest of our childhood, we fought for attention with our fists and words. While Wesley and our mother danced to merengue in the living room, I'd lock myself in my room, with Madonna in my earphones, ruminating on a plan to move out the day after high school graduation.

It took ten years of distance to change my relationship with my brother. After college, I immersed myself in my career. I also sought therapy for my maternal deprivation. My brother stayed by my mother's side and helped her grow the child daycare learning center she founded. He also got married and had four kids. His last two sons, Xavier and Agustin, shared the exact age difference we did, four years apart. Unlike us, his wife, Sasha, had a close relationship with her older sister.

"This is our new family. I want them to love you, from the beginning," Wesley said to me.

When I moved to San Francisco, and he stayed in New York, we texted countless times a week, with the "family plan" and two iPhones I bought for us. Though we managed to establish a connection, we were still total opposites.

I was an orthorexic neat freak. Wesley was carefree and over-nourished. But we managed to stay in touch.

The hope that whoever had my phone would return it had vanished. I wished there was an app available to reach that thief's heart. I got a replacement through my insurance after a $200 copay. Two weeks later, at work, I received a text from an unknown number. It was the person who had "purchased" my old phone through Craigslist, in Indiana.

"Can you remove your iCloud account so I have a usable phone?" texted the stranger.

"Contact the thief you bought it from, if it isn't you," I replied.

"Could I pay you to remove it? I have tried to contact the person with no luck."

"My brother is dead! His last texts to me and family pictures are on that phone," I explained.

"I do repair phones, and I think I could get them for you. But I need access," extended the person.

I was tempted to take the offer. But it could have been a scam. I did not want to risk getting burned while feeling so vulnerable.

"Stop this NOW, or I will contact the authorities," I texted. "Deal with it. I still am," I demanded.

So, I permanently blocked the stranger's number. In the palm of my hand I stared at the cold, shiny screen of my smartphone, and remembered how eight months before, I had to shut down Wesley's Facebook account. Though my brother was beloved by many, my mother and I did not want to be bombarded with messages while we mourned.

Facebook does offer an option for remembrance. For centuries, people have searched for the secret of eternal life, and now the social networking site offered to convert deceased users' pages into permanent memorials. But, if I couldn't restore his physical being, keeping his digital presence alive wasn't the solution. For some, their program is a great comfort. For us, it was a reminder of the pain of loss. We'd prefer a drive to the cemetery for a "visit," instead of a website.

Given that we passed on the memorial, there are two ways to take a Facebook profile offline—deletion or deactivation, which hides a user's page, but allows for reactivation later. We decided to delete it permanently—but I didn't have my brother's password. I Googled "how to permanently close an account for a deceased person." I needed to submit a special request form, which required copies of the dead person's birth and death certificates, in addition to proof of authority under local law that I was the legitimate representative of my brother or his estate. I was all the things the requirements asked for. But Wesley and I had different last names, and proof of that would have been needed as well. I still had to help my mother plan and co-host the funeral, clear all belongings from his apartment, and settle his finances.

To delete his account without providing the documentation, I had to figure out his password. It took five hours and multiple name combinations, but I cracked it, with Sasha's help. It was the first two letters of the names of each of his two sons—and me.

"Your brother always called the three of you his boys," Sasha shared with me.

The day before Wesley's burial, I deleted his profile. He loathed social media, calling it "the blabbermouth." He only started a Facebook page after I moved away. I reexamined its content and pondered the irony that I would erase the very presence I'd urged him to create. On his profile page were countless posts asking if he was dead.

The private messages section contained demands for him to prove his death, along with cries for him to watch over them from heaven. I sent a note to everyone in his contact list:

"It is with great sadness and heavy hearts that we inform you that Wesley has died. This message comes from his brother and mother. We thank you for your condolences. This will be the final message from his account."

I found the picture of the first time we met when he and our mother picked me up from the Dominican Republic. He smiled; I wrapped an arm around his shoulders. I burned that image into my mind to access the following day, at his open-casket funeral. I could replace most of the lost pictures from our childhood, thanks to our mother's archives.

When scanning the old photos, I noticed how, in times before digital, the people and environments captured faded along with the paper quality. Now we can remaster memories through Photoshop and reverse the aging process via specialized filters. But there are no back-ups for the ones we love. It's been three years since Wesley died.

The records of our digital connection are lost to me, but I still remember his last text to me by heart: "Hey how r u? Just want to let u know I miss u and I love u. Wish u were here, I really need my big brother."

WHEN MY GIRLFRIEND WAS GROPED RIGHT IN FRONT OF ME, I DIDN'T BELIEVE HER

By Jay Deitcher, Washington Post Solo-ish, November 29, 2017

I met Annie at the NAACP in Albany, N.Y., where we both volunteered. We're from different backgrounds. I'm Jewish; she's Nigerian, Jamaican and had been spiritually searching. She wanted to learn to drive, and I wanted to teach her. With Annie behind the wheel, we discussed liberal politics and our mutual love of Toni Morrison's novels.

She got her license, and soon we were dating. Four years into our relationship, while on a weekend trip, she made a wisecrack about marriage. She was 24 and thinking about commitment, and I was 31 and thinking about comic books. I got upset. She stopped talking to me.

"You can't go changing everything," I said, storming off the bus onto the moonlit Manhattan street. My last girlfriend and I had broken up because I couldn't commit. Desperately autonomous, I needed more time.

I reached for her bags from under the bus, but she beat me to it. She didn't want my help.

She walked so far ahead of me I only saw the blur of her purple sundress as she marched up West 33rd Street. I watched as a short, brown-haired man staggered toward Annie, bumping into her before stumbling off. I saw her turn and scream obscenities at him.

"Stop him, Jay," she shouted, as he walked past me. "He grabbed my crotch."

I was still fuming over the bus dispute, and her causing drama on the street upset me more. Annie had never lied to me, but I figured it must have been an accident and that she was overreacting.

Another man stopped to ask Annie if she was all right. He looked directly in my eyes and said: "That guy walked up and put his hands on her." I saw no reason he would lie. With a male stranger looking at me to do something, I raced after the groper. He bolted but was so intoxicated, his pants fell, causing him to trip over his feet. I had a burst of confidence and blocked him off, nodding to my girlfriend to call the police.

"You gonna fight me?" he asked, with boozy breath.

"No," I said. My strategy was to keep his mouth running until the police came. "That's my girlfriend you just touched."

"I'm sorry, man," he said, smiling, apologizing to me and not Annie. "Listen, I'm sorry. Okay?"

"No, it's not okay," I said. "You can't touch women without their permission."

I demanded he sit down and sober up.

"Where are you coming from?" I asked.

He said he was on a tourist visa from Ecuador, staying at his cousin's apartment and trying to find work. Annie told him to pose for a picture—not mentioning it was for the police. He smiled in the shot.

For 45 minutes, we waited. Annie made numerous 911 calls, eventually walking to 34th Street to get two officers' attention. "It's been happening a lot lately," one of the officers explained.

No one had responded to our call, they said, because "normally by the time we get there, the creep's gone." The officers were amazed I'd restrained the assailant without touching him. They said I had the right to physically apprehend him. My girlfriend glared at me, upset I hadn't punched the guy.

The officers cuffed the groper, and we went to the station to give our story. "He won't be visiting America for long," the officer said. Two weeks later, an assistant district attorney asked Annie to come to her office. The prosecutor mentioned possible deportation and asked Annie if she'd prefer the groper went to rehab or jail. Although Annie was an advocate for restorative justice and rehabilitation, in the moment, she chose jail. When the prosecutor asked why, Annie was firm: "He had no right to touch me." Annie walked out of the office and never contacted the assistant DA again, never looking into what happened to the man who had grabbed her. She didn't want to know.

Annie made me promise not to talk about what happened, yet once the #MeToo movement began, she said it was time for me to publicly take responsibility for not believing her.

So many brave women have been sharing their experiences as survivors of sexual harassment and assault, things I've never had to deal with. Recently, Annie told me about other traumatic experiences she'd never shared. I was speechless. I'd looked at Annie as a woman who would knock a dude out if he stepped to her wrong. Yet at points in her life she was powerless against abuse.

While dating Annie, I've received points for not being a monster. Because I'd never cursed her out or raised my fist, I've been seen as a good guy. However, after the incident, I felt ashamed of my behavior and saw a therapist to work on why I hadn't trusted Annie, why it took a man to make me believe her.

I realized that my denial that Annie had been assaulted perpetuated the violence against her. Working to better myself meant having many conversations with Annie about commitment and realizing that she had plans, and I wanted to be a part of them. Although I valued my independence, I made it *my* choice to fulfill her needs and to share decisions. (We eventually got married under a chuppah and jumped the broom.)

When I asked Annie why she stayed with me after that incident on the street, she said it was because I was willing to learn.

FINDING FORGIVENESS AFTER DECADES OF GUILT

By Gail Eisenberg, New York Times Well Family, August 25, 2017

Visceral congestion, pending chemical examination.

Decades later, those five words on a mustard-yellow death certificate were the only explanation I'd had for my mother's demise in May of 1980, when I was 14. The question remained: Had my mother killed herself? Without proof, I would allow myself to waver. I convinced myself that uncertainty was better than having to say goodbye. But about 10 years ago, as I approached 40—the age Mom was when she died—

I needed resolution. I was determined to ground myself in facts. I dialed New York City's chief medical examiner to request a copy of her autopsy report.

Within two weeks, I held the legal-size pages folded tightly in thirds. As I read, I imagined my mother's toe-tagged body draped in a crisp white sheet as it slid out from the metal chamber, the glint of the scalpel, the snap of latex gloves. The pages of the report included terms I didn't understand, quantities I couldn't comprehend, body parts I didn't know existed. My mother described à la carte.

Then: Final cause of death: Acute propoxyphene and diazepam toxicity. Suicide.

My list of socially marginalized affiliations grew—motherless, gay, only child, suicide survivor. I thanked God I wasn't left-handed. I felt sad, yet satisfied. Until I saw something on the document I'd somehow missed:

Notes found at scene to be brought to mortuary.

"Did Mom kill herself?" I'd asked my father many times over the years, wondering if he'd protected me from the truth at 14, hoping he'd tell me at 40.

"I don't think Mama meant to do it that day," he'd reply. "All the medications she was on caught up to her."

Her unfortunately named shrink, Dr. Dye, had dispensed the psychotropics of the time, the pill for every ill: Thorazine, the antipsychotic; Nardil, the antidepressant; Lithium, the mood stabilizer; Valium, the sedative. And she had had shock therapy; there was a lot going on in her head.

Still, I needed to know what happened, and I repeatedly asked my dad whether there was a note.

"Your mother wrote a lot of notes," he always said.

She did. There were "Drink your V-8!" messages left in my brown bag lunches and "Gail looks like a fresh devil! (ha-ha)" on the backs of photographs. There were letters about what we'd do together one day, words that gave me hope. But what kind of note awaited me? I contacted the medical examiner's office again. Six months passed before I received an answer.

"Ms. Eisenberg," the man said, "I'm calling to let you know that the suicide note is ready for pick up."

I'm calling to let you know your dog is groomed, and ready for pick up.

I'm calling to let you know your picture is framed, and ready for pick up.

Your dry cleaning is done, and ready for pick up.

The odds were against it: A majority of those who commit suicide do not leave a note. Still, I knew how much she'd yearned for a chance to explain herself to the son she felt she had abandoned when she'd given him up for adoption in the 1950s. I hoped she wanted to leave me a note as much as I needed to find one.

The last time I saw my mother alive, she stood before me in our apartment in Rockaway Beach, Queens, with her wrists wrapped tightly in white bandages. In full makeup and a teased strawberry-blond wig, she looked like Charo. I worried she'd succeed at what she'd twice attempted and continued to threaten. It haunted me. I cared, I loved her, I wanted her to live, to get better, to be happy. But I was also embarrassed by her and sick of her.

"Go ahead and do it already," I

THE BYLINE BIBLE

yelled.

At least, that's the way I remember it. We were fighting, and I left the apartment. For decades, I'd wondered how my mother died and whether, by daring her, I was an accomplice in her death.

Anticipation gave way to amazement when I saw my mother's familiar handwriting—the triple-underlined words, errant dashes and exclamations, a circled phrase and an equal sign—her death sentences.

My Angel, I tried so hard not to do this.

Those words assured me of my mother's love. Mom had forgiven me. And now I was free to forgive myself.

HOT HUMILIATION ESSAYS BY MY STUDENTS

As with each assignment, the more pieces you read and study, the better your own attempt will be. Here are some links to "humiliation essays" my students have published over the years.

- www.nytimes.com/2016/11/25/well/family/becoming-the-sports-parent
  -i-wished-id-had.html
- www.nytimes.com/2017/10/20/style/modern-love-single-unemployed-
  and-suddenly-myself.html
- opinionator.blogs.nytimes.com/2013/12/25/eczema-and-holy
  -water/#more-151151
- www.nytimes.com/2010/01/10/sports/football/10cheer.html
- opinionator.blogs.nytimes.com/author/adane-byron/
- mobile.nytimes.com/2007/04/22/magazine/22lives.t.html
- opinionator.blogs.nytimes.com/2015/10/07/the-end-isnt-near/
- opinionator.blogs.nytimes.com/2012/10/01/from-hunger/
- www.nytimes.com/2007/10/07/fashion/07love.html
- www.washingtonpost.com/news/parenting/wp/2017/05/24/mom
  -i-gotta-go-theres-a-gunshot-dealing-with-my-daughters-job-as-a
  -cop/?utm_term=.650dd5224557
- www.washingtonpost.com/news/soloish/wp/2016/10/17/when-i
  -was-accused-of-groping-a-woman-i-was-mad-like-trump-then-i
  -repented/?utm_term=.a840e9fa0dd1
- www.washingtonpost.com/news/parenting/wp/2015/03/30/i-may-be-a
  -single-mom-but-im-not-doing-it-alone/?utm_term=.ae66f078b7ee
- www.washingtonpost.com/wp-dyn/content/article/2009/02/06/
  AR2009020602087.html

- www.washingtonpost.com/posteverything/wp/2015/10/06/im-60-my-boss-is-a-20-something-its-awkward/?utm_term=.ef82c1ed39c6
- www.washingtonpost.com/news/soloish/wp/2017/06/23/i-loved-traveling-abroad-and-he-would-follow-but-how-far-was-too-far/?utm_term=.e73284897c0f
- www.newsweek.com/my-turn-escaping-my-mothers-shadow-78161
- www.salon.com/2017/09/10/my-playboy-club-education/
- www.salon.com/2014/09/01/i_never_should_have_followed_my_dreams/
- www.salon.com/2012/07/20/my_husband_the_criminal/
- www.brainchildmag.com/tag/helen-chernikoff/
- www.salon.com/2012/05/11/their_moms_were_crazy_about_me/
- www.salon.com/2013/08/18/the_facebook_reunion_i_never_saw_coming/
- www.salon.com/2013/01/23/i_married_my_sorority_sister/
- www.salon.com/2008/02/13/removable_tattoo_ink/
- www.slate.com/blogs/xx_factor/2009/10/14/i_tried_to_become_a_spy_to_get_away_from_my_parents.html
- www.newsweek.com/new-dads-postpartum-depression-77109
- www.newsweek.com/my-turn-how-spinal-injury-united-my-family-89587
- www.newsweek.com/my-turn-how-i-became-legal-citizen-91679
- www.highbeam.com/doc/1G1-148913463.html
- www.newsweek.com/my-turn-dog-made-us-family-76339
- qz.com/583979/as-a-dog-walker-pack-mentality-has-taught-me-everything-i-know-about-working-with-humans/
- qz.com/489226/confessions-of-a-life-coach-when-my-clients-succeed-im-left-with-nothing/
- qz.com/454975/ten-years-after-breaking-my-engagement-i-made-good-on-the-ring-i-never-returned/
- qz.com/893632/im-a-psychotherapist-but-the-craziest-job-i-ever-had-was-driving-escorts-to-meet-their-clients/
- opinionator.blogs.nytimes.com/2011/10/05/years-of-atonement/#more-107167
- www.psychologytoday.com/articles/201305/two-minute-memoir-the-newlywed-examination
- www.psychologytoday.com/articles/200711/unlawfully-wedded-wife
- www.oprah.com/style/chris-edwards-transgender-identity-and-clothing

- www.marieclaire.com/sex-love/a22310/boyfriend-sex-addiction-porn/
- www.marieclaire.com/sex-love/advice/a4291/my-boyfriends-ex-oscar
  -win/
- www.cosmopolitan.com/sex-love/a60034/how-i-told-my-father-that-i
  -did-porn/
- www.cosmopolitan.com/sex-love/news/a30825/what-its-like-to-date-a
  -celebrity/
- beverlywillett.com/articles/family-circle
- www.self.com/story/cheating-with-food
- www.self.com/story/enemy-within
- www.elle.com/beauty/health-fitness/advice/a12170/giving-in-to
  -rhinoplasty-442923/
- "The Mystery of M.S." by Stacey Kramer, June 2007, *Self* Magazine
- www.damemagazine.com/2015/10/07/i-donated-my-dead-body-give
  -my-life-purpose
- www.essence.com/2016/04/01/day-i-realized-my-son-has-autism
- observer.com/2014/10/roofied-at-50-youre-never-too-old-for-date-rape
  -drugs/
- forward.com/sisterhood/210866/life-love-and-the-proverbs-of-judge
  -judy/?attribution=tag-article-listing-6-headline
- forward.com/sisterhood/210627/learning-to-conquer-my-daughters
  -ocd-and-my-own/?attribution=author-article-listing-2-headline
- forward.com/opinion/13127/freed-from-the-slavery-of-illness-01641/
- www.vice.com/en_us/article/mg5mv4/my-boyfriend-tried-to-kill-
  me-412
- www.thefrisky.com/2013-01-16/girl-talk-why-im-leaving-my-gun
  -behind/
- www.thefrisky.com/2011-11-21/girl-talk-my-paranoia-led-me-astray/
- www.purpleclover.com/relationships/7501-truth-about-where-came-/
- tinhouse.com/the-birthmark/
- www.nytimes.com/2016/11/06/fashion/modern-love-children
  -cuddling-physical-intimacy.html
- www.nytimes.com/2008/07/13/fashion/13love.html
- entropymag.org/name-tags-5-how-naming-my-familys-white
  -supremacy-led-me-to-change-my-own-name/

CHAPTER 2

The Joy of Getting Killed

After you've written and revised your piece several times, you are not ready for fame, fun, or fortune. You are ready for feedback. This response can come from a teacher, classmate, critic, mentor, colleague, writing group, or ghost editor—in person or online. But do not proceed without it.

I've been writing professionally every day for thirty-five years, yet I still have no idea whether my early drafts are dazzling or disastrous. The only rule seems to be: If I think my pages are brilliant, they stink. If I'm embarrassed by how badly a piece turned out, it's usually decent and on its way. I've found this to be true of most writers in the world.

Immersed in the middle of a literary project, you often can see only what's in front of you, not the broader picture. You're too close to the material to have an unbiased perspective or recognize where it may fit in a larger context. It's almost impossible to evaluate your own work. Experienced editors look at your creation objectively, from the outside, to catch problems you can't, the way a doctor can read an X-ray that you couldn't interpret yourself.

Luckily, while writing is a solitary art, publishing is collaborative. Once you write and sell your piece, it's not over. There are newspaper, magazine, webzine, and book house staffs whose tasks are to polish your prose, fix your punctuation, and mend your mistakes. Even after struggling through several drafts, most aspiring authors I know are not capable of doing this well on their own. If you don't believe me, compare a personal blog or website rant to essays that get into *The Wash-*

ington Post. The difference is having expert elves behind the scenes improving your work versus being a lone scribe, myopically struggling with no overview.

Newspaper and magazine editors know their readers and their publication's style better than you do, and they are worthy of your trust. To compete in the marketplace, you can't be a control freak. Not every word sprouting from your brain is a keeper. Chances are, many phrases are boring, repetitive, clichéd, or unclear. New writers might "bury the lede" by hiding their best line in the fifth paragraph. You must rely on someone else's judgment and, as William Faulkner instructed, "Kill your darlings." The favorite clever lines that you're convinced show your eloquence may not be the treasures you imagine. To a more cynical eye, they may be obscuring your bigger point.

Every term, when I try to determine why half of my students get published and the other half don't, I find that the successful ones show up with pieces, listen carefully to the critique they get in class, and revise (sometimes many times) before they send out work. The ability to hear, accept, and incorporate criticism is the most important element to moving forward. Professionals know that writing is really rewriting. The stubborn divas who sniff, "You can't touch a comma," usually get stuck in oblivion, alienating people they need to get ahead.

You know the famous best-selling authors who pen a masterpiece, then publish trash or vanish? I think it's because they decide they no longer need anyone's help or approval. Of all the writers I know, very few sit at home alone, complete a piece, then submit and sell it to a major publication without a thorough overhaul. One reason I wouldn't quickly post anything on a personal blog or free website (along with not getting paid) is that you won't get a kind editor to tell you, "Sorry, this is nonsensical."

Of course, whose advice you take is essential and can make all the difference. The reason that I sell almost every word I write to the places I aim for is that I've developed methods for getting comments on every page from seriously smart critics I trust. I do this *before* I submit my work. The fastest way to kick a piece into shape is to take classes with teachers who are good critics, or hire a professional ghost editor to work with one-on-one. Yet those methods can also be expensive on an ongoing basis. Needing a way to continually get feedback, I started a weekly writing workshop with people who had published work I admired, which is why they were invited to my home to drink my wine and trash my pages. This is where I present my roughest drafts.

Part of the secret to being prolific is not being afraid to suck. I write every single day, whether or not I'm feeling the flow. When I once told a best-selling mentor I had writer's block, he said, "Plumbers don't get plumber's block. Don't be self-indulgent. Just get to work." He added, "A page a day is a book a year." Since then, I've written at least one page a day—300 words—before I eat breakfast, answer my e-mail, read the newspaper, or take a shower. The way I see it, it's my job to get at least 300 words on the page every day. Once I do, it's the task of my writing group, teacher, critics, or ghost editor to tell me what's worth keeping and what I should throw out. I ask for comments and revise accordingly. A week, month, or year after my piece runs, I still find sentences that can be improved.

Yes, hearing criticism can hurt. Especially with first-person writing, when someone will say, "She's so whiny and unlikable," and the "she" being dissed is you. The first time I read my work aloud in a writing class, I felt outraged, offended, and emotionally destroyed by the harsh assessments. But then something wonderful happened: I went home, muttering how stupid my professor and fellow students were. Then I looked over their critiques and begrudgingly tried the changes to see if any made sense, just as an experiment. Voilà! My creation was instantly, insanely better. It felt like magic. My ambition outweighed my vanity, so I grew a thicker skin and became addicted to this process. After I graduated, I formed two writers' groups to kill me twice a week that I still schedule my deadlines around.

The way it works: Participants make hard copies and read a short section of their work aloud (like a 900-word essay) while the others take notes. Then the writer has to be silent to really hear their colleagues' critiques. If the writer talks back or argues, he isn't listening because he's too busy being defensive. One time, a workshopper named Joel listened carefully to his story getting slaughtered. Afterwards he responded, "You're all assholes." Everybody cracked up, including Joel, since we all feel like that when our "darlings" are judged to be lacking.

Most Common Essay Feedback

1. "The beginning didn't grab me so maybe start with the stronger scene on page two."
2. "There's not enough drama, conflict, tension."
3. "This is a typical story I've heard before with no new timely lede or spin. Why should I care now?"
4. "You didn't reveal enough that's fascinating, provocative, or surprising about yourself. I can't see you and don't like you yet."
5. "There's not enough change/emotional arc/wisdom/surprise/cathartic revelation at the end."
6. "This is just a screed about how much you hate your mother/ex/boss/creepy co-worker/sibling/former shrink/roommate."
7. "Your essay doesn't work in present tense/third person/second person/switching back-and-forth from French to English/in 7,000 words of rhyming iambic pentameter/filled with footnotes."

How You Want to Respond to Critiques

1. "You just don't get it, you totally missed my entire artistic motivation!"
2. "I can't believe you don't see how brilliant and important that first paragraph is!"
3. "If I took all your suggestions, it would completely ruin my voice and my piece."
4. "If you're so smart, why aren't you a rich and famous writer?"
5. "You're too old/young/white/female/male/straight/poor/privileged/urban/rural to understand."
6. "This is why it's impossible to get published. I give up."
7. "You're an asshole."

How You Should Respond to Critiques

1. Take deep breaths and stay silent.
2. Nod and scrawl notes to hide your tears.
3. Say "Thank you. That's interesting. I'll think about it."
4. Try the suggestion and see how it plays out.
5. Go back to your original draft, skeptical of the new criticism, but not ruling anything out.
6. Reread both again carefully and reluctantly swallow your pride, admitting the revision is better.
7. Get more criticism on your new draft!

When anyone says something negative about your work, it's common to feel vulnerable, naked, stupid, ashamed, and shut down. Being judged and assessed can be hard and confusing. Once a critic advised me to switch the past tense in my then novel-in-progress *Speed Shrinking*[1] to present tense. "How absurd," I thought. "You're so off base. Don't you know that I've always detested present tense!" But when I looked it up, I saw that the critic's own acclaimed fiction—which I admired—was in present tense. So I tried it—just for the first page, as an experiment—to appease this misguided person. I brought in the new version to my writing workshop.

"Amazing! This really pops now," said a tough critic. "I can't believe how much better it is."

It turned out, in this rare instance with fiction, everyone agreed present tense was better, including the St. Martin's editor who bought that book.

Yet even with my esteemed professors, workshop members, and ghost editors, I've never taken every single suggestion to heart. I knew the backgrounds of the people whose opinion I was begging for, and that scribes and editors tend to steer you into their style. So when a talented poet urged me to make my themes darker, like hers, I saw she

---

1. St. Martin's Press, 2009

was sharp, yet probably too serious for light humor pieces I was aiming at *Funny Times* or *National Lampoon*. A sophisticated former *New York Times* editor was right about my need for more facts. Yet he might have been too conservative to appreciate the profanity and provocative sexual references in my pieces aimed at *Salon*, *Cosmopolitan*, and *Tin House*. I took into account their talents and biases. Sometimes I didn't understand or agree with a specific recommendation to reorder paragraphs or substitute one adjective for another. Yet, I reasoned, if my readers targeted a section for revision, there was probably something that needed to be addressed. So I'd painstakingly go over my original to see if it could be improved, though not necessarily in the way they recommended.

Since there were usually a dozen of us, happily there was often a consensus as to what lines should be nixed and which expressions garnered multiple stars (our code for excellence). There's a good reason that this atmosphere is re-created in many writing classes and workshops: Criticism and editing work wonders. After penning the 900-word essay, the secret weapon for publishing success is: Get criticism from a professional who writes or edits this kind of piece.

Don't Show Your Essay To ...

1. A friend in a completely different field who would have zero idea of the market you are aiming for.
2. A colleague who might be competitive and trash your idea or try to steal it.
3. Your boss who does not need to know such personal details about you or that you're moonlighting.
4. A well-known writer you've never met.
5. A professional ghost editor you don't offer to pay.
6. The partner, roommate, or relative who will say, "This is perfect. Send it out right now."

Here's Who You Should Ask

1. Teachers or classmates in an essay or journalism course or seminar. If you haven't taken one, do. You're not allowed to complain, "It's too hard to get published," if you've never taken any kind of formal writing instruction. Would you expect to be a doctor, lawyer, or accountant without any training?
2. Members of your writing workshop. If you're not in one, join a group you've heard about in person or online, or form your own.
3. Your favorite mentor, former teacher, or critic whose opinion you find reliable.
4. A close colleague who has published pieces you admire in places you want to break into. (Though if you're not going to offer payment, this is an imposition. So if she agrees, make sure you treat for breakfast, lunch, dinner, or drinks, buy her book if she has one out, and/or show gratitude and grace if she says she's too busy.)
5. A ghost editor you can hire who is well known in this particular genre. If you e-mail me, I will be happy to recommend one.

Note: If anyone e-mails me, "Would you read and critique my piece?" I answer, "Take my class or seminar." If someone responds, "I love your work and wish I could, but I'm in Alaska/have twelve infants/work ninety-nine hours a week putting food on the table," I say, "Okay, here's a great ghost editor I recommend." If you haven't read my work, Google me, or lie and say you have.

WHOM SHOULD I HIRE?

Don't Google "ghost editor" and hire the first result to pop up, handing over your credit card number without getting a recommendation from someone you trust. Ghost editors vary greatly with experience, cost, style, expertise, and focus. I make sure, in advance, that the one I hire can line edit, fix my mistakes and punctuation, as well as give me overall comments as to whether she thinks my pages are publishable. If not, I want specific suggestions on what to fix.

There are people calling themselves "ghost editor," "book doctor," "proofreader," "line editor," "copyeditor," "rewrite person," "script editor," "reviser," "teacher," "manuscript analyst," "ghost writer," "developmental editor," "acquisitions editor," and "writing coach." The glossary at the end of the book defines most of these terms. But each type of editor works differently, at varied rates. Before you commit to working with someone, clarify what he is offering, including whether he will look at a revision or be available for questions by phone or e-mail. (Some will give you only written feedback.)

None of the professionals you contact will be available that day, happy to read your one-hundred-line e-mail and the essay you've attached, rewrite it all, make it brilliant, refer you to their *New Yorker* editor friend, and hold your hand until your piece is published and paid for. That's not how it works. Instead, be polite and patient, and approach a ghost editor with a three-line e-mail, the way you'd work with any business contact. Many ghost editors will be busy for days or weeks. Once they give you notes and line edits on how to improve your piece, they will offer zero recommendations of where it might be published. They usually will not look at a revision without added payment.

A former newspaper editor I admire gets a hundred dollars an hour to do this, while an academic who is an excellent line editor charges five dollars a page. When in doubt about whether to hire someone you've never met, here are ways to decide.

1. Has he published anything? If so, read to see if you like it and want to emulate his style.

2. If she has only worked as an editor or agent with no bylines, will she share testimonials of former clients you can check with? If not, try someone who can. The best ghost editors have this information on their websites. For example, if you Google Sally Arteseros, the ghost editor I hired to help me sell my first memoir to Random House, you'll find her picture, bio, phone, and e-mail on a site called "Independent Editors Group." She lists her résumé highlights (twenty-five years at Doubleday), education, areas of interest, and her successful clients.

3. Check his résumé or LinkedIn profile to get a better sense of his background.
4. Get a referral from someone in the field, like me. The benefit of e-mailing me two lines (not twenty or two hundred) mentioning your project is that I'll share details of the terrific editors I use. I know if they've published themselves, their fees, locations, time frames, expertise, and what to expect. (And if you start by telling me how much you like *The Byline Bible* I'll probably get back to you faster.)
5. Budget carefully. The ghost editor I work with gets one hundred dollars an hour, and I once paid Sally, the former book editor I mentioned, twenty-two hundred dollars to line edit my 250-page memoir manuscript. Though that book sold for fifty thousand dollars, and prices for ghost editing have risen, that was my limit. Some ghost editors get ten thousand dollars for a book—just not from me (especially since there's no predicting what will sell). On the other hand, it seemed smart when someone nervous about her debut spent some of her $100,000 book advance to work with a professional ghost editor first. That way the pages she handed into her agent or publisher were more impressive and helped her publish faster and get a second book deal.
6. If an editor has little experience, but she's nice and inexpensive, consider taking a chance on a small job, deciding a fee in advance. A colleague with good clips charged my student fifty dollars to edit 900 words. It went so well, they continued working together for two years.
7. Be realistic. While in my classes and seminars, I sometimes suggest a specific column and share my editors' names and e-mails, but most teachers, ghost editors, and coaches don't help with this kind of marketing. There is never a guarantee that hiring a particular ghost editor behind the scenes will get you published and paid. If you have no luck after a few tries, move on to someone else. Don't forget you can always take a class or seminar (which might be cheaper) or start your own writing/critique group for free. Check

out the credentials of all instructors and colleagues to make sure you're working with editors and fellow authors you admire.

There isn't one way to triumph in any field, and I often quote my main rule with writing and love: "You can do anything as long as it works." That said, I've never known anyone who sat alone in their home and, without getting any feedback, became successful in publishing. Every writer has to find her own method and support system. I had many beloved teachers, mentors, and editors who saved my life and career. Of course, I wrote a book about it, *Only as Good as Your Word*.[2] I'm glad I took my shrink's smart advice, to "Hang out with people you want to be."

---

2. Seal Press, 2007

CHAPTER 3

Finding Your Essay a Home

Many people harbor the illusion that a writer sits alone, toiling in her garret, then somehow miraculously gets discovered by a teacher, agent, manager, or big publisher. In actuality, the fastest road to selling your work is to proactively get the right name and address of the editor at your target publication. Then you submit your entire piece with a short cover letter, mostly electronically, though sometimes still by snail mail or fax. But how do you figure out the right person to send it to?

HOW NOT TO FIND AN EDITOR

1. **SHAMELESS SELF-PROMOTION.** Don't go to a weekend literary conference, evening reading, or publishing panel, rush up to an editor afterwards, shove a hard copy of your pages in his face, saying, "This is right up your alley." Unless it's specifically billed as "a pitch slam," nobody wants to be bombarded with paper or unsolicited pitches at a public event. Better to politely introduce yourself, ask for or share a business card, and try to connect online the next day, during regular business hours.

2. **CHASING WRITERS.** Don't e-mail a freelancer you've never met to say, "I just saw your byline in *The New Yorker*. I have a perfect piece to pitch there. What's your editor's name?" (That's the equivalent of saying, "Hey, you have a great job. I'd like to steal it. Will you help me?") Staff writers might be nicer since you are not their direct competition. But in general look for senior, assigning, or assistant editors, not fellow scribes you've never met.

3. **FLOGGING YOUR BLOGGING.** Don't show off your piece on your personal blog, LinkedIn, Facebook, and HuffPost, then send the links to an editor with the note, "I just posted this piece that got tons of likes everywhere. You should publish it, too." If it's already out there, most editors won't buy it. They want exclusive material. In a line about yourself, you could say that you have fifty thousand Instagram or Twitter followers and include your tag or link. But very few publications will pay for reprints.

4. **SOCIAL MEDIA STALKING.** Unless an editor has specifically sent out a call for pitches to be DM'd, don't direct message anyone on Facebook, Twitter, or Instagram with an attachment saying, "Here's my piece." Some kind editors include their e-mail in their bios. If not, you may get away with saying, "I'm a fan of yours. Could I trouble you for your work e-mail?"

5. **FAKE FRIENDSHIP.** Be aware that sending a friend request on Facebook or LinkedIn's "Invitation to Connect" to an editor you've never met, hoping to become a freelancer or staff writer, could be alienating. There are better ways to connect (like getting his e-mail and pitching directly).

6. **DEAR ANONYMOUS.** Don't submit your piece to "Editor" or "To whom it may concern" at a generic address without trying to find the name of the right person in the right section.

7. **MASS E-MAILING.** Don't send your essay to every editor whose e-mail you've found simultaneously, planning to go with the highest bidder. Most editors hate multiple submissions. So try one at a time, then follow up. There is a special place in hell reserved for freelancers who submit a piece to several editors working at the same publication. When they find out (as they often do, since they sit together forty hours a week) the aspiring writer can be ghosted and blacklisted. So: Pick one.

8. **COLD-CALLING STRANGERS.** Every editor is different and has her own preferences about how she prefers to be reached. But even if you find the right telephone number, I would not call someone you don't know to pitch anything over the phone or in a message.

BETTER WAYS TO LOCATE AN EDITOR

1. **MASTHEADS.** Most newspapers and magazines have a public list of everyone who works on each section. While *The New Yorker* and *The New York Times* don't share this inside information, many others do, including webzines with an "about this publication" page that shares the names of their editors. If you buy *Poets & Writers*, for example, page 3 has a breakdown of everyone employed there, from the editor-in-chief, associate editor, assistant editor, and editorial assistants to the publisher, frequently with their e-mail addresses. Unless you have a personal connection, editor-in-chief is too high. I usually aim for an associate editor or one who handles a particular section, like Daniel Jones at "Modern Love" or Lisa Bonos at *The Washington Post*'s "Solo-ish" column.

2. **RESEARCH.** If there's no masthead or you can't find editor e-mails, search the publication's name, the section you want, and "editor," and the right name may pop up. A tech-savvy student found the names and e-mails of every employee at *The New York Times*, so it is doable. A friend says she searches "Call for pitches" and "Pitch Me" on Twitter and has connected with multiple editors that way.

3. **TELEPHONE.** You know that box with numbers on it, referred to as a landline? Most major newspaper and magazine companies still have them with human operators who aren't named Siri. So you can politely ask the receptionist, "I'd like to submit an essay and wondered if I can have the name and e-mail of the editor?" The worst that happened to me was when the person unexpectedly put me through to the editor. I nervously hung up. Then I called back, calmly introduced myself and asked for his e-mail, which he shared; he later bought my piece.

4. **FIND CONNECTIONS.** It may be worth it to pay for online services like Mediabistro.com or LinkedIn Premium, which offer resources in all areas of the media to help you get names and e-mails of editors, as well as specifics about which editors are looking for what kind of work from whom. Also check out FreelanceSuccess.com, Ed2010.com, and WritersDigest.com.

5. **GET ONLINE SUPPORT.** If you can't afford classes, seminars, or services, you can join free in-person or online writing groups where like-minded members share information. I am a member of multiple Facebook circles for writers who share triumphs and traumas and where editors post calls for specific pieces they are looking for. That recently led me to getting published in *The Washington Post's* op-ed page and Atlantic.com's education verticals.

6. **LISTEN CAREFULLY.** There are many popular podcasts for writers, including Grammar Girl: Quick and Dirty Tips, The Writer Files, A Way With Words (NPR) , Longform, I Should be Writing, The Dead Robots' Society, Beautiful Writers Podcast, and my former student Keysha Whitaker's terrific Behind the Prose, where she interviews authors—including me.

7. **FIND HUMAN PEERS.** Meeting other professionals is a good way to ease the chaos and confusion of freelancing. Join unions or organizations you are eligible for and can afford, where you'll meet editors, agents, and fellow writers for relatively small fees. Over the years my husband and I have been involved with PEN American Center, National Book Critics Circle (NBCC), American Society of Journalists and Authors (ASJA), The Authors Guild, and the Writers Guild of America. Colleagues have also spoken highly of the National Writers Union, Society of Children's Book Writers and Illustrators, National Writers Association, Sisters in Crime, Romance Writers of America, and The International Women's Writing Guild. While some have strict requirements or high initiation fees, others allow newcomers to participate. PEN America and NBCC have low student rates while ASJA, the Association of Writers & Writing Programs, and Tin House's Portland summer workshops give out scholarships based on merit and need.

8. **GO TO CONFERENCES.** You can meet top-level agents, editors, and fascinating authors by getting involved with PEN American Center's International Festival, *The New Yorker* Festival, NBCC, Writer's Digest, and ASJA's annual symposia, as well as book festivals in Brooklyn, Los Angeles, Miami, Detroit, Columbus, and other

places. They are listed toward the end of *Poets & Writers*. Or Google your town and "book festival." Even if it's not in your city, it might be worth it to fly, train, or bus in to meet one hundred editors in one day. Sometimes purchasing a ten-dollar ticket to one event will enable you to meet multiple luminaries in a room, while supporting an important arts group at the same time. At a free NBCC award ceremony, I'd never been as starstruck as when I got to sit next to Joan Didion and speak with her.

9. **FOLLOW THE MONEY.** You can use Twitter, Facebook, Instagram, and LinkedIn to locate editors you want to be following, a smart way to find out what their age, town, background, interests, and tastes are—though I'd wait until you get their direct work e-mail addresses to submit anything, keeping careful boundaries. A student told me about a free Firefox add-on called Hunter (http://hunter.io), and the Web services anymailfinder.com and verify -email.org are designed to help you find someone's e-mail address.

10. **FIGURE OUT E-MAIL FORMATS.** Some publications use a standard format for all their staff e-mails, for example: first initial, period, last name before Hearst.com, newyorker.com, wsj.com, or conde-nast.com, though each company is different and they are subject to change. You can guess, then try verify-email.org to see if you've nailed it or not.

11. **GET A LITTLE HELP FROM YOUR FRIENDS.** Ask anyone you know who works for the publication you are aiming for or has a freelance byline there that you admire. Make sure to be humble and charming, not entitled. If someone I didn't know contacted me and said only, "I want to publish a piece in *The Washington Post.* What's your editor's name?" I would probably ignore the request. Yet if someone tried, "I admired your latest op-ed for *The Washington Post.* I'm a struggling writer who wonders whether you'd consider sharing the editor's e-mail," I might be willing to pass it on.

12. **DOUBLE-CHECK BEFORE SENDING.** The only thing certain in freelance writing is uncertainty. Editors are fired, rehired, and switch jobs. Well-known magazines fold at the last second. Beloved

columns are killed. Webzines go out of business daily. So even if I've worked with an editor a few weeks earlier, I go online to confirm she remains at the same place. When someone has a new job, he'll often announce it on social media and/or update his brief bio on Twitter, Facebook, and LinkedIn fairly quickly. So Googling not only makes good business sense, it's also fun to learn publishing news before anyone else.

13. **ADULT EDUCATION.** Of course, as a feature journalism teacher, I'm not unbiased when I recommend taking a writing course. In my fifteen-week New School classes (which cost about $750 if you don't take it for college credit), I bring in twenty different editors to speak annually, which is how so many of my students wind up published. Several students made enough freelancing to cover the price of the class. I hand out a list of editors I work with that I update every term. Many teaching colleagues around the country also bring in speakers and share their contacts. I would help the people who take my classes and seminars over strangers asking for assistance any day, and do.

CHAPTER 4

Under Cover

My journalism students are shocked by my belief that sending short, perfect cover letters to introduce mediocre pages will sell their piece faster than submitting a stellar essay with a lousy missive. Of course, I'm not advocating sending out pages that are less than superb. But here's why a great initial presentation is essential: Making mistakes or revealing a bad attitude can lead an editor to delete your e-mail or toss your envelope in the garbage without reading what's attached. On the other hand, if you manage to charm someone on staff into giving your piece a serious look, that editor may work with you to make it publishable even if it's not ready for press yet. Here are steps to ensure your first impression isn't your last.

1. **BE BRIEF.** Three to five lines are usually sufficient.
2. **BE PROFESSIONAL.** A cover letter needs to explain only the piece you've already written and are attaching. That's different than a longer query letter, where you summarize what you haven't written yet but plan to in the future. Either way, "Hey Sarah, how's it going?" is not how I'd start a business correspondence, even if the editor is twenty-two, looks cool on Instagram, or is a friend of a friend. "Dear Ms. Smith" is more respectful.
3. **SAVE WACKY AND WITTY FOR LATER.** Self-deprecation can be hilarious when it comes from Margaret Cho, Chris Rock, Amy Schumer, or David Sedaris. It can work wonders in a well-crafted essay. But humor is subjective, and it's hard for novices to pull off in a very short introduction letter. So don't yuck it up too quickly for the wrong editor. In three-line e-mails and texts, irony, sarcasm,

and playfulness can be easily misunderstood, especially when coming from strangers who might not get your personality or appreciate your familiarity. After one class, a student wanting my help e-mailed me, "You're an exceptional critic and teacher, though maybe a pain in the butt sometimes." Instead of funny, I found this off-putting and kept my distance.

Rob Spillman, editor of the acclaimed literary magazine *Tin House*, once instructed my class: "Don't act crazy." Or at least keep the craziness in your pages, not in your letter. There can be a fine line when you're pitching a piece about your schizophrenia, addictions, manic depression, obsessive-compulsive disorder, or anxiety disorder. Someone I didn't know once introduced himself as "wildly neurotic alcoholic and chain-smoker." Not wanting a headache, I told him I was too busy and recommended he work with another teacher.

4. **EMULATE THE VOICE YOU WANT TO PUBLISH YOU.** When describing my piece, I often use the tone of the publication I'm aiming for. I once sent *Cosmopolitan* a story on "how I just met the man I wanted to father the children I didn't want to have." I would not have described a piece that way to an editor at *The Nation*. Make sure you read several issues of the publication before throwing your writer's cap in the ring.

5. **GET A NAME.** Although many columns will instruct you to just send your work to generic e-mail addresses (like "op-ed submission"), I never send anything without a specific name on my letter. Otherwise, I can't follow up with anyone and I fear my piece will get lost in a huge folder of unsolicited material. If you must use these addresses, first try to figure out the right editor for the section you're aiming for. You can usually find this information on mastheads or websites, in an Internet search, or with a quick phone call. When submitting an essay to *The New York Times'* "Modern Love" column, I use their standard address, modernlove@nytimes.com, which the editor Daniel Jones prefers, but I begin "Dear Mr. Jones."

6. **SPELL THAT NAME CORRECTLY.** Sounds easy. Yet tons of editors tell me that when they see their named misspelled, they feel they can't trust the author to be accurate or fact-check anything else. So they say no.

7. **BE ACCESSIBLE.** Make sure to put your name, full address, phone number, and e-mail address on top of your letter, your submission, and all correspondence, even if it's electronic. Many editors will send cyber rejections but would rather pick up the phone to say "yes" or ask if you're willing to rewrite pronto. If they can't reach you, they might just call someone else. Do not send your piece out then go off the grid, backpacking in Thailand for six weeks. Look up whether your target publication runs daily, weekly, monthly, bi-monthly, annually, or is updated on the web 24/7. Many magazines and newspapers now have both a paper and a Web division that operate separately. The paper version of *Tin House* comes out four times a year, offers more remuneration, and can often take six months to reply. TinHouse.com doesn't pay as well, but it takes more pieces, which translates to more chances. Be conscious of which editor and section you've sent your work to and how long they take to respond, info that many post on their submission guidelines.

8. **PAY RESPECT.** Don't begin a missive by launching into your accomplishments, ideas, or needs. Do your homework and spend time researching so you can offer homage to the higher-up you want help from by saying you're a fan of something she's recently run or written. (Many editors also write.) Don't pick the first thing that comes up on Google or something from ten years ago. To submit to the "Modern Love" editor Daniel Jones, I'd start with something like:

> Dear Mr. Jones, I love your column ("You May Want to Marry My Husband" made me cry), the new podcast (Colin Farrell's was awesome), and your insightful book *Love Illuminated*. I hope you'll consider my piece about how, after thirteen years of marriage, my husband decided to move in with me.

(That was my exact 15-word essay description that worked.)

THE BYLINE BIBLE

Editors are sharp and can smell phony praise. Don't vaguely mention that you adored a piece or a book you didn't read (or at least skimmed). A *New York Times* editor friend recalled being impressed with a cover letter by a new writer who told him, "I thought your section's handling of the recent mayoral scandal was much smarter than *The New Yorker*'s version."

9. **EMPHASIZE CONNECTIONS.** If you're lucky enough to have a go-between or insider's link to the publication you're querying, don't wait until the end of your letter to mention it. Many readers won't get that far. When someone starts an e-mail to me, "My friend Gerry Jonas gave me your name," I immediately think: *Damn, I have to be nice to this person.* Why? Because I trust Gerry's judgment, he helped me, and I return the favor every time, even if I'm busy. Another person made the mistake of e-mailing me "Marla recommended I call you. I guess she's too busy and important now to work with me." I contacted Marla, who (not surprisingly) reported that this aspiring writer was needy and inappropriate. So I didn't work with her either. Lavishly praising your mutual acquaintance is common sense. Anything negative is self-destructive. If you don't know anyone, look up the editors' bios to see if you can find common ground. Throwing in "as your Midwest neighbor," "as a fellow Yalie," or "I'm another working mom from Montclair" might establish a bond.

10. **THE HARDER YOU WORK, THE LUCKIER YOU'LL GET.** Planning a book publishing charity panel, my fantasy panelist was former *New Yorker* and Random House Editor-in-Chief Daniel Menaker. Although I'd met him years before, it was an ambitious choice. I could have started by saying how much I'd enjoyed his novel *The Treatment* (which I did). Yet on a quick Internet search for an update, I discovered the film version of his book was opening that night at a nearby theater. I waited twenty-four hours until I could see his movie. Then I wrote a fresh, timely letter that received an immediate affirmative response. He may have said "yes" regardless, but why chance it? I prefer to work at lightning speed, but sometimes it's better to be patient and better prepared.

11. **SAY WHY YOU.** Make sure to mention any expertise or experience you have in a short bio that might make the editor more likely to take your work. "As an Iranian expat who speaks Farsi, I hope you'll consider my essay on the personal stakes of the Iran missile crisis" will get attention. "I majored in philosophy and minored in English at NYU, worked in banking for three years until I married, had two children, and moved to New Jersey," not so much. Only include information that is relevant and may sell your essay, not your entire résumé. If you have clips, you could say, "My writing has appeared in the *Daily News* and *Post*," but don't list a dozen small zines nobody has heard of, or letters to the editor, which don't count as clips. You could include one or two related links you're proud of, if they are recent, but not ten. A colleague once told me the most confident, successful writers do the shortest cover letters. Understate, don't overstate.

12. **FIGURE OUT THE LEAD TIME.** Since *Psychology Today* comes out only four times a year, they plan way ahead. In March, they are closing their fall issue. A monthly like *Esquire* often closes each issue four to five months in advance. A weekly like *The Village Voice* may need only ten days' notice to rush a piece through. A webzine like *Slate*, which is updated daily, could take a piece on Tuesday that goes live Wednesday morning. Be conscious of the math because it could determine the numbers in your bank account.

13. **SAY WHY NOW.** If there is anything in your essay that is timely, exclusive, or in the news, make that clear up front. When my student Darnycya Smith sent her piece "My Molotov Christmas in Brooklyn" to an editor at *The Frisky* webzine, she wrote in her cover letter and subject heading "Timely Christmas piece/December 25," which was the day it ran. When another student, Danielle Gelfand, sent her essay "Years of Atonement," about her father's death on Yom Kippur, to *The New York Times'* Opinion section, she told the editor, "I hope this might work for Yom Kippur, on October 7 this year." She mentioned her topical hook in the subject heading ("Yom Kippur pitch, October 7.") It went live on October 5. My colleague

Amy Klein submitted "Looking for a Blessing to Marry," about her rabbi's prediction that she'd meet her husband on Hanukkah, to *The New York Times'* "Modern Love" editor, saying, "I thought this may work for the upcoming Jewish Festival of Lights." It ran that December. It doesn't just have to be a holiday. My student Stephanie Siu tagged her *New York Times* essay to Donald Trump's presidency; the essay ran on the day of his inauguration. I submitted an essay to *Salon* called "My Personal Michigan Recount" about the presidential recount on December 9, 2016, the day it was posted. A topical peg will always run faster than a generic timeless piece that editors call "an evergreen."

14. **BE HUMBLE.** Despite your conviction that you're a genius worthy of instant attention, be careful not to come across as presumptuous, self-involved, flippant, demanding, or delusional. I'm not an editor who buys or sells anything. Yet I get many requests to read unsolicited manuscripts and proposals in emphatic language that certain publishing guides mistakenly promote. After the release of my first memoir, *Five Men Who Broke My Heart*, my bemused editor mailed me the thick copy of a five-hundred-page manuscript from a male stranger in Texas. His letter bragged, "Hey there, I'm enclosing *my* great memoir, about the five *women* who broke my heart. I hoped you'd plug it to your editor and agent." He'd sent the male equivalent of my memoir—which he neglected to mention he'd bought, skimmed through, or even liked. He was sure I'd want to read his project cloning mine to help him get published. He wasted postage and killed trees, since I put his pages in the trash.

While it's good to sound confident, I wouldn't start with "Here's my fantastic work that I know your readers will relate to." Instead of "I'm sure you'll love this," try to pay respect (see #8), or at least tone down your self-importance to "I hope you will consider this."

15. **PERFECTING YOUR HOLLYWOOD MOVIE PITCH MAY LEAD TO A MOVIE.** Along with including what exactly you want, a good cover letter will entice an editor or agent into reading your submission. So describe the story you send in a very short, engaging way. I often

quote my former student Katie Naylon's pithy, successful cover letter to Jerry Portwood, who at the time was the editor of *New York Press*, a small out-there Manhattan weekly newspaper. She wrote, "Dear Mr. Portwood, I love your recent theatre reviews. Attached please find my essay on how I ran a phone sex operation in college when I was still a virgin. I hope it might work for your '8 Million Stories' column." It did! Portwood told me he wanted the piece from the description alone. (Naylon later recycled the comic premise for her hilarious 2012 rom-com *For a Good Time, Call...*)

16. **BE ARTFUL.** I am much better at writing than I am at "pitching," which is writing about what I am going to be writing. Since I recommend completing an entire essay before starting your cover letter, here's a trick I learned: You can use the best lines of your piece to describe it to the editor. When I submitted my *New York Times* piece "The Bride Wore White—and Black," I began my explanation, "I was married twice last summer. I wore two different dresses in two different colors in two different cities ..." Those were the first two lines of the essay I'd spent months completing.

17. **BE A LITTLE MYSTERIOUS.** In that letter, I didn't share the next part of the sentence: "... where I said 'I do' to the same man. The first wedding was for me. The second was for my mother." I left it out so the editor would be more intrigued. If you map out every single twist and turn in your short recap, there's no incentive to read on. Some editors prefer to see pitches, not the entire piece. In that case, if I'm describing an original story, I keep it vague. Sharing all details, addresses, and sources will make my exclusive newsflash easier to steal. For my *Time Out New York* piece on kooky ways New Yorkers like me tried to quit smoking, I mentioned a nameless addiction specialist, hypnotherapist, and Smokenders and Nicotine Anonymous groups without providing names or e-mails. Instead of overstuffing, whet the editor's appetite.

18. **STICK TO E-MAIL AND SNAIL MAIL.** Don't phone publishing staff you don't know. I wasn't surprised to learn a student was hung up on

when an editor was on deadline and had no time for an unsolicited call. Some editors accept faxes, especially if they are overseas. Try to suss out which way a publication wants to be pitched. Otherwise mail is usually the way to go.

19. **HAVE A SMART HEADING.** Try to see the world from an editor's point of view and make his life easier. If you are sending a piece to a *Salon* editor, in the line for "Subject" do not write "*Salon* submission" (as five million others will). Also don't use the editor's name. Instead I use the topical reminder and my own title. "Michigan Recount essay Dec. 9" worked quickly for *Salon*. If your piece has no timely reference, say something fun or unusual. "My Best Friend Married My Brother essay submission" worked. But don't swear, be sexual, or sound like an advertisement—or it could get caught in the spam filter. Editors get bombarded by PR e-mails, so make sure yours makes it clear it's from an author, not a public relations firm.

20. **DON'T TELL THE CO-OP BOARD ABOUT YOUR TWO ABORTIONS.** This is a euphemism I use for: Don't offer unrelated facts about yourself that could sabotage your chances. Mentioning that you are going through a lousy divorce will be relevant only if you submit a piece about relationships. Sharing that you used to be an alcoholic or drug addict is only necessary if that's what your essay is about. Even saying that you have a Harvard M.F.A. might be a turnoff if you are trying a literary editor with an unrelated story about an illness you lived through. Editors aren't shrinks; keep your personal shares to a minimum with people you don't yet know.

21. **START SMALL.** When making initial contact, I ask the editor to read one short piece, nothing more. Not two pieces attached, or five ideas, or three versions of the same essay. Suggesting a weekly column to an editor you've never met is like asking a cute stranger, "Will you go out with me every Saturday night for the next three years?" Coming off desperate or demanding is a losing strategy. Like a first date, if all goes well, you'll get another chance.

CliffNotes Version: What Not to Do

1. Don't address your letter "Dear Editor" without Googling to find the right name and e-mail.
2. Don't start with yourself and what you want without a reference to the editor or publication first.
3. Don't send your letter without proofreading, triple-checking the spelling of all names, and/or having someone else check that there are no typos or mistakes.
4. Don't write an unsolicited cover letter that's longer than six lines.
5. Don't arrogantly tell the editor that his readers will surely love your brilliant piece.
6. Don't submit your essay to multiple publications at the same time. Many newspapers and magazines will consider a piece only if you've sent it to them exclusively.
7. Do not attach your résumé, photos, and a bevy of links that nobody requested.
8. Don't criticize something the editor has run in the past, offering your piece as the antidote.
9. Don't send your piece to an editor you read about without checking to see that she is still alive, with the publication, and in the same position she was in the 2012 article you found on LinkedIn (since editors move around constantly).
10. Don't find an editor on Facebook, Instagram, or Twitter and bombard them with friend requests or pitches. (Though you can send one direct message saying "I'm a fan of your publication. I have an idea I'd like to pitch you. May I trouble you for a work e-mail?")
11. Don't ignore explicit requests to only submit work (by e-mail, snail mail, fax, or through the electronic submission form on their website), deciding those rules don't apply to you.
12. Never offer lots of irrelevant details about your life, background, and opinions in the first paragraph before letting the editor know why you are contacting him and what you want.
13. Don't guess at the gender pronoun of an editor if you can't tell from their name, picture, or work. Instead of trying "Ms. Jerry Smith" just write "Dear Jerry Smith," which is safer.
14. Don't submit a piece on Monday then phone the editor on Tuesday morning to ask, "Did you read it yet?"

15. Don't phone the editor at all, unless you have an extremely timely important piece you already sent, followed up on, and didn't yet hear back about, or are returning her call.
16. Don't post "I sent my piece to this arrogant *New York Times* editor who rejected it in five minutes. I bet he didn't even read it," or anything else negative on the Internet, even if you think you're in a private chatroom or Facebook group.

Cover Letters We Never Finished Reading

Every editor I've asked over the years has a list of letters from new writers that started so badly, they didn't finish reading the rest. Some were so funny, I started taking notes.

1. Though I've never heard of your magazine before …
2. While I haven't published anything in my whole life and only get rejections …
3. To whom it may concern …
4. Excuse the typos, misspellings, and mistakes, I'm sending this on the jitney to the Hamptons from my iPhone …
5. I read about your promotion to editor-in-chief and wondered what kind of stuff you buy.
6. I'm going to Japan, need anything?
7. I just graduated college Phi Beta Kappa and my journalism professor found my work brilliant, so I thought you would too.
8. Although you already ran four pieces on this topic last month …
9. I'm giving you twenty-four hours to be the first to publish my exclusive piece on …
10. Hey Dude, wassup?
11. I already published this on my website, blog, and HuffPost, but hope you'll re-run it.
12. As a student who detests the media and agrees with the president that it's unfair and elitist …
13. I hated the right-wing screed you ran by your staff writer last week, so I'm sure you'll want my essay, telling the true story.
14. You don't know me, but I'll phone you later to discuss my important piece.

15. I've just completed 100,000 words of my debut novel, which I'm sure you'll want to read, even though your website says you publish only nonfiction.
16. Before submitting my piece, I want to find out what you pay and if I'll be able to keep the rights for the book this is excerpted from ...
17. My shrink encouraged me to send this out, despite my fear of success and suicidal feelings when it comes to failure ...
18. The other editors you work with said no to this piece, but they didn't get it ...
19. My name is Lisa, I'm a freshman from Ohio, taking music and journalism classes although my parents wanted me to study business ...
20. My teacher Susan Shapiro told me to send this to you since you've paid a lot of money to her other students in the past ...

(Rule: Please say only that a contact "Gave me your name," never "Told me to send this to you" which makes you—and your connection—look bad.)

Successful Cover Letters by Students

Note: Several of the editors in these letters have since left their jobs and some of the columns have ended, so I updated some of the names. Double-check before sending your own piece.

....

Dear Mr. Greenman,

My professor Sue Shapiro gave me your e-mail. I'm an avid *Daily News* op-ed reader and really enjoyed your column on the Cathie Black debacle back in April. Please find my essay on my experience as an almost failed Pakistani immigrant student in the NYC public school system attached and pasted below. I hoped it might be timely since Chancellor Dennis Walcott just announced his plans for a much-needed English learning program in the New York City schools.

Gratefully,

Miral Sattar

www.nydailynews.com/opinion/foes-standardized-tests
-students-wrong-article-1.968369

···

Hi Emma Allen,

Thank you for the nice words on my *McSweeney's* piece. I love
Shouts & Murmurs.

I hope you'll consider my timely piece "The Angry Electorate,"
which I have attached and pasted below. I'd be honored if you'd
consider it. Thank you!

Keysha Whitaker

www.newyorker.com/humor/daily-shouts/how-to-deal-with-an
-angry-electorate

···

Dear Erin Keane,

My teacher Susan Shapiro shared your e-mail. I adore *Salon*. I loved
recent pieces you've published by Jess Henriquez and Tiffanie Drayton and I was moved by the vulnerability and insight of your recent
piece "Never Show Them Your Back." Thank you for putting a spot-
light on body image issues in your new series.

If you're open to it, I have an original essay, "My Man Boobs," about
my experience of gynecomastia and male breast reduction surgery. I
hoped it would be timely as there is a current lawsuit against a phar-
maceutical company whose medication is causing the development
of breast tissue in adolescent boys. Thanks for your time.

Zack Valenti

www.salon.com/2014/01/02/man_boobs_and_my_decade_of_
shame/

···

Dear Ms. Dell'Antonia,

I'm a fan of Motherlode and enjoyed Kate Hass's enlightening "The Case For Bribing Kids to Memorize Poetry." I hope you'll consider my timely essay "The Magic of Belonging," about celebrating the Hindu New Year at my daughter's secular preschool, attached and pasted below. Diwali will be observed this year on October 23.

Gratefully,

Swati Khurana

parenting.blogs.nytimes.com/2014/10/22/diwali-once-hidden-now-lit-large/

Dear Mr. Catapano,

You were great at the recent Strand Bookstore panel and I love the pieces you've run by Gabrielle Selz and Liza Monroy.

Attached and pasted below please find "My Mother's Shadow," my essay about how, after the Bosnian war, my mother rescued a Pomeranian from Connecticut's Humane Society. As Muslims who'd barely survived the ethnic cleansing campaign against us, we knew what it meant to be saved.

My work has appeared in *The New York Times* before, as well as *The Wall Street Journal* and *Salon*.

Sincerely,

Kenan Trebincevic

opinionator.blogs.nytimes.com/2015/03/09/my-mothers-shadow/?mcubz=0

Five Cover Letters of Mine That Worked

Dear Ms. Bolonik,

I love *DAME* magazine and really enjoyed Amy Klein's recent fertility piece. I hoped my new essay "Women Problems" might work for you. It's about how—in my most vulnerable moment with a cancer scare—this raging feminist only wanted to see a male doctor. I thought tying in Roxane Gay's book *Bad Feminist* might make it timely and it's also breast cancer awareness month.

I've written for *The New York Times*, *The Nation*, and *The Washington Post*. Thanks for your time.

Sue Shapiro

www.damemagazine.com/2014/11/18/can-feminist-also-be-sexist

Dear Ms. Kern,

I love *New York* magazine's "Love & War" and enjoyed your recent piece on the sex lives of college students. Given the recent sexual discrimination and harassment lawsuits at Boston, UCLA, and Columbia, I hoped you'd find my essay "Professor or Predator"—about my own illicit affair with my professor—timely and provocative (since it's not the opinion you'd expect for a feminist). I attached and pasted the piece below.

I've written for *The New York Times*, *The Wall Street Journal*, *Newsweek*, *Marie Claire*, and Oprah.com. Thanks.

Susan Shapiro

www.thecut.com/2016/04/professor-predator-line-isnt-always-clear.html

Dear Ms. Keane,

I've had the honor of writing for *Salon* in the past and I love the recent work you've run by Gigi Blanchard, Court Stroud, and Laura Zam.

I hope you'll consider my essay "The Forgiveness Tour," which I thought could be timely for Yom Kippur, coming up this week (October 12). I've attached and pasted it below.

I'm an author who has written for *The New York Times*, *New York* magazine, *Newsday*, *Elle*, *Marie Claire*, and Oprah.com.

Sincerely,

Susan Shapiro

www.salon.com/2016/10/11/the-forgiveness-tour-when-the-only
-thing-better-than-hearing-im-sorry-is-saying-it/

Hi Adam Kushner,

Thanks for your kind response to my last piece. I hoped you'd consider "Smokeout," about what happens to a tenant who smokes when their building votes to abolish smoking. My building's co-op board has called an April meeting to vote in a ban. It's happening across the country, with the U.S. Department of Housing and Urban Development encouraging no-smoking policies in private and public housing. As a former two-pack-a-day smoker, I offer better solutions than shaming and eviction threats. (Echoing the real-estate-mogul-in-chief?)

I've written for *The Washington Post*, *The New York Times*, and *New York* magazine and I'm the author of two addiction books. Thank you!

Susan Shapiro

www.washingtonpost.com/posteverything/wp/2017/04/18/
dont-evict-tenants-who-smoke-people-cant-quit-at-will/?utm_
term=.80f7e84d7959

Dear Ms. Schama,

Sharisse Tracey gave me your e-mail. I enjoyed her piece on her military marriage and your pieces on equal parenting and *Transparent* (just watched the four amazing new episodes). And I've been in love with *Elle* forever.

I hoped you'd consider my new essay "Caught in the Web," about my illicit link to my first lover's wife. I hoped Adele's song "Hello" and the "Crazy Ex-Girlfriend" references make it timely.

I write for *The New York Times*, *The Washington Post*, and *Marie Claire*, and have upcoming work in Oprah.com. I've pasted and attached the essay below.

Thank you for your time.

Susan Shapiro

www.marieclaire.com/sex-love/a17762/i-was-the-secret -confidante-of-my-exs-wife/

www.esquire.com/lifestyle/sex/a40280/facebook-friends-ex -boyfriend-wife/

Perk: this piece ran in five digital Hearst publications—*Elle*, *Esquire*, *Cosmopolitan*, *Good Housekeeping*, and *Redbook* (for no extra fee, but great exposure).

HOW TO SUBMIT YOUR PIECE

Obviously, the most common way to submit writing these days is by e-mail. To use this method, type your short cover letter, then paste your entire essay below, as well as attaching it in a Word document. Yes, I advocate *both* attaching and pasting. Some editors avoid attachments, having caught a virus after opening a file from a server they didn't recognize. They prefer to scroll down to read a few lines, to gauge their interest. Others click on a file fast and hate scrolling.

Still, every publication is different, and five editors at the same newspaper may have five different preferences for how they receive work. That's why smart writers first get a copy of the paper or magazine to research the place where they want to be published and follow submission guidelines. *The Sun*, an award-winning North Carolina magazine that pays up to three thousand dollars for a personal essay, still accepts submissions through the mail. If you want to sell your work there, go to Barnes & Noble or an indie bookstore to buy current issues of *The Sun*, contact them directly to purchase back copies, and/or Google to read samples of what they've recently run. Then you can e-mail your piece or snail mail a typed, double-spaced submission to their editorial department in an envelope with a stamp, the old-fashioned way. It may take months to get a response, but if they say yes, it will be worth it.

Some newspaper editors at *The New York Times'* op-ed page, for example, will take e-mail but also still read hard copy submissions and accept faxes, especially for international transmissions. I even know aspiring writers in New York who have had luck dropping off a hard copy of their work in an envelope at the front desk. Don't assume you know how an editorial board works unless you've asked, looked it up, or had success selling work there.

In the subject heading, don't put "*Salon* submission" like thousands of others do. I used my title and my timely angle. When submitting to *Salon*, I tried: "The Forgiveness Tour essay submission/Yom Kippur Oct. 11." That worked. My piece was posted twenty-four hours later.

Once you have sent in your essay, nothing is guaranteed. Of course you hope an editor will read it immediately and call you to say "this is brilliant, we'll run it as a cover story tomorrow." Yet except for the few places that send a bounce-back e-mail saying, "We have received your submission, we'll let you know if we want it," you won't even know if they received it. I recommend starting on another piece five minutes after sending the first one so you don't drive yourself—or the editor—crazy. Otherwise you'll have to wait to hear back and that could take ten minutes or ten months.

WHAT MIGHT HAPPEN

1. **REJECTION.** Within minutes, hours, days, or months after submission, many editors e-mail writers some variation of "Sorry this isn't right for us." That means they don't want what you sent and they're not interested in seeing another draft. Don't revise it and resubmit to another editor there. Do not respond negatively. "Modern Love" editor Daniel Jones told stories that cracked up my class: one about the guy he said no to, who then revised the piece and tried again. When he was rejected a second time, he responded by e-mailing Jones one word: "Lame." Another time a young woman (mistakenly?) sent Jones her mother's response to the rejection: "Well, fuck *The New York Times*." Not surprisingly, neither of these writers has broken into his column.

   I never bother thanking an editor for rejecting me. Everyone gets too many e-mails and calls, and they usually don't want to hear anything more from someone they just turned down. I prefer to wait until I'm ready to try that same editor with a different idea a month later, saying, "Thanks for your prompt response last time. I hope this new piece works better." I wouldn't write back that day or the next with your second try, though. *Tin House* editor Rob Spillman told my class to consider a dating metaphor. If you ask someone out for Friday night and she says "No," a person who wants to be successful will not follow up with "Then will you go out with me Saturday night? No? How about Sunday?" A better reaction would be to give yourself credit for trying and getting out there. Congratulations, you're in the game! Now back off and re-strategize so next time you'll win.

2. **INVITATION TO RESUBMIT.** Sometimes an editor will say something flattering such as, "This is well-written and interesting, but we've already covered the topic. Try again." That doesn't mean try again with a revision of what she just rejected. It means wait, chill out, then figure out a different piece to submit a month or two later. Spillman noticed that if he told a male author, "Sorry not right for us," the author would often quickly submit again and again with

entitled expectations. If he told a female writer, "This is close, try me with something else," he may never hear from her a second time. Or it could take a year. Male or female, waiting a month until you have something ready is laudable. Yet I wouldn't wait twelve months, since the kind editor may have moved elsewhere.

3. **SUGGESTIONS TO REVISE.** Many times a student will tell me, "Darn, the editor hated it." When I ask to see the rejection, I find that the editor did not hate the work at all. He responded with something like, "This isn't bad, but we'd need it shorter and more topical." Sometimes you'll get an opinion that is longer and complex. Editor Paul Smalera recently told a colleague, "I liked reading this story, but I'm not sure it's for us at *Quartz*. There's too much dialogue. It's not our style. If you're willing to rework it with the main aspects of the story told in narrative, it may be a better fit." My colleague revised and sold it. When an editor takes time to make specific requests, I rewrite quickly, trying to take the editor's suggestions, though there are no guarantees. Everything is "on spec," which means you do the work on speculation without a contract, then they decide if they will buy it.

4. **AN UNEQUIVOCAL YES.** My favorite recent acceptance read: "I love this. It will work for our next issue. Thanks. I'm attaching a W-2." Some editors like to pick up the phone to say yes and also to ask if the writer will be willing to revise based on notes. My answer is almost always, "Yes, of course" since "No, you can't change a comma" will usually forfeit your clip. Recently an Atlantic.com editor of a section called CityLab told me she liked my opinion piece about how expensive graduate writing programs should be more practical and help their students career-wise. She was more interested in a third-person reported piece on this topic. Because I wanted my first byline in Atlantic.com, I did an about-face and revised it, with quotes and statistics. Here it is: www.citylab.com/life/2017/01/finally-writing-programs-take-a-practical-turn/512168/

After an editor says yes, now is the time to discuss edits and for you to briefly and politely ask, "How much do you pay?" and "Do you need me to revise it, send you an invoice, or sign a contract?" No long gushy lines of gratitude, as if you've won an Academy Award, or hysterical announcements on social media. Your byline hasn't appeared yet and you haven't been paid. Until it's out and the check clears, contain yourself.

5. **A CONFUSING MAYBE.** Sometimes an editor will tell a writer, "I really like this, but we're backed up for six months" without adding, "If you wait, I'll buy it." In a recent case with a top newspaper, my student wasn't sure if the editor was saying no, perhaps in the future, or try me again. I recommended he write, "Thank you. I'm willing to wait for you." Eight months later his story ran, for six hundred dollars. In another case, an editor told my pupil Sarah, who submitted an essay involving a yoga class she taught, "We just covered yoga classes. Maybe try me in a few months?" She resubmitted two months later and he published her.

6. **RADIO SILENCE.** Unfortunately, with editors you don't know, this often happens. Don't assume they read your pages, thought you were stupid, and will never buy your work. They probably have a thousand e-mails in their inbox and haven't gotten to it. Having fancy software like HubStop might let you know if your e-mail has been opened. But that does not mean the editor has read it all or decided yet. She may have skimmed the lede, looking for something on the upcoming holiday, then closed the file without finishing. If you don't hear anything, you should check back in a few weeks so it doesn't get lost or forgotten. My student Victor Varnado recently sold two "humiliation essays" to *Salon* and *VICE*. Both times he followed up and the editors told him they'd missed his original submission.

THE ART OF FOLLOWING UP

I determine when to check back with an editor by how often the publication comes out. For a daily newspaper or webzine that updates 24/7, I try within a week, especially if my essay is very timely. If I send it

Monday, I follow up Thursday. (I never bother editors on Friday afternoon or weekends unless they specifically say it's okay.) For a weekly, I wait two weeks. For a monthly, I come back in four weeks. For quarterly journals or magazines that come out only one to six times a year (like *Psychology Today* or *Tin House*), I wait months. Here are ways that worked for me in the past.

1. **BUTTER UP THE BOSS.** Most people working on staff at a newspaper or magazine also write and publish their own work. So I research the editor, find something he has recently written, and e-mail, "I love what you wrote on the hurricane. Congrats. I wondered if you had a chance to look at 'My Email Crisis,' attached and pasted again, for your convenience."

2. **DO YOUR HOMEWORK.** If that doesn't work and the editor isn't a writer with bylines I can find, I Google her column or section, find something she's just published by someone else, and e-mail, "I love Sally Smith's story about the hurricane. How poignant. I wondered if you had a chance to look at 'My Email Crisis' yet, attached and pasted below, for your convenience."

3. **SEND A SECRET SECOND ROUND.** Instead of officially following up, I sometimes wait a week and pretend I never sent anything. I e-mail it again, deleting the "forward" so you can't tell it's been sent before. I do not add a note asking, "Did you miss this the first time?" I don't know if editors missed it or felt guilty they ignored it the last try, but I've sold many pieces this way.

4. **MAZEL TOV TO THE MAGAZINE.** I look up the publication on social media, find something significant happening, and mention their good news, e-mailing "Congratulations on the expansion of your section. How awesome. I hoped this might give you room for my essay 'My Email Crisis,' which I've attached and pasted below for your convenience."

5. **BE A NEWS HOUND.** I check Google Updates for something on my topic in the news. If what happened to me just happened to a famous person, it might make my story more relevant. When I find it, I update my opening, then e-mail the editor, "The front page

of *The Wall Street Journal* just ran an article about Hillary Clinton's e-mail crisis, which coincidently mirrors what I've written. I hoped this new timelier lede might work for my essay 'My Email Crisis.' I've attached and pasted it below for your convenience." In this case, mine ran that week in *The New York Observer* under the headline the editor wrote: "Storage Wars: My Hillary-Like Email Crisis." My e-mail story ended happier than Hillary's, though she did get a much bigger book advance. observer.com/2015/04/my-mid-cyber-life-crisis/

6. **DOUBLE-CHECK.** Several times after radio silence, I assumed it meant the editor hated my work. Then I found out the real reason: *The Village Voice* editor was on maternity leave for four months. Another time, a *VICE* editor was fired. The staffer at *Mademoiselle* I worked with watched her entire publication fold. A *New York* magazine bigwig I'd loved working with took a bigger job elsewhere. When you look up submission guidelines, the editors at *The New York Times'* "Modern Love" and *Tin House* let you know they can take up to six months to get back to you. So now, if I don't hear back, I check Facebook, Twitter, LinkedIn, and publication websites. Editors will often tell you their freelance requirements and update their professional status. This is a good way to make sure they are still where they were and learn their rules and time frame.

7. **GO AWAY.** After checking the editor is still in place, I usually follow up three times. If I don't hear anything at all, I give up trying that piece with that section. Yes, it's frustrating when I'm sure my latest political theory is perfect for *The Wall Street Journal*, as do one thousand other aspiring politicos each month. Now is the perfect time to send this essay elsewhere and write something new.

8. **PULL THE E-MAIL CHAIN.** If an editor has said something nice in the past or encouraged me to try again, I find our old correspondence. (Part of the reason I had the aforementioned e-mail problem is that I never delete anything.) I include the last encouraging note she sent, with an updated cover letter to submit my new piece, along with a new subject heading mentioning my title to subtly remind the editor we are not complete strangers and she liked my previous work.

9. **CLIP HANGER.** Once, *Cosmopolitan* rejected my essay "Between Love and Ambition: A Daughter and Mother Find Each Other," saying, "Well done, but not quite right for us." Luckily, a publisher friend at a small regional magazine called *Michigan Woman* (thank you, Glenda Greenwald) bought that piece for one hundred dollars. After it came out, I sent a new piece to my *Cosmo* editor with a nice note starting, "Thank you for your prompt, kind response to my last piece. It finally did find a home," and I also linked the clip. The *Cosmo* editor shocked me by offering five hundred dollars to run "Between Love and Ambition" again. I said yes! I guess it looked better in print, with artwork. It reminded me of when I was single and went to parties alone and no guys would check me out. When I walked in with a date, all of a sudden I was hotter. It never hurts to keep in touch with an editor who is being generous. Don't ever be bitchy and imply, "Ha ha somebody else published what you rejected." Instead, sincerely thanking the editor for his time and consideration might give you more to be thankful for.

How Not to Follow Up

1. Don't e-mail the editor the next day asking, "Did you read it yet?" and don't phone, text, or instant message an editor you don't know.
2. Don't e-mail the next day saying, "I revised it overnight. Here's the newest version."
3. While waiting to hear, don't e-mail the editor, "Since I didn't hear back from you yet, I'll also send my essay elsewhere," and simultaneously send it to five other publications.
4. Don't apologize or waste lines overexplaining yourself, as in "I'm so sorry to bother you again while I'm sure you're very busy covering 9/11, but I wasn't sure if you received my piece because ..."
5. Don't get impatient and submit the same story to another editor at the same place. An exception can be made only if you are

positive they're in completely different sections. *The New York Times* editors from the op-ed page, "Modern Love," Well Family, the *Book Review* and *Sunday Magazine* do not work together, so you could try them all—one at a time. On the other hand, ten editors from the *New York Times'* op-ed page, Sunday Review section, Opinionator blog, and "The Stone" and "On Campus" columns sit next to each other in the newsroom. If you send the same story to a bunch of editors in the same office, you risk them all passing around your piece, saying, "Look what this impatient jerk just did."

HOW NOT TO DEAL WITH REJECTION

Getting shot down is part of the publishing process for everyone. When I finish an essay, I try to have low expectations and assume I'll get blown off several times before it finds a home. In fact, I sometimes write a list of seven potential publications where I can submit my piece and methodically go down the list. I tell myself I haven't *really* tried until I've hit all seven. (And then I write another list of seven more.) Getting a bunch of thumbs down means nothing. There are many stories of famed manuscripts that were first rejected. George Orwell's classic *Animal Farm* was allegedly called "a stupid and pointless fable" by the Knopf editor who hated it. (It went on to sell twenty million copies.)

I used to have "rejection slip parties" for my students where the cost of admission was a letter or e-mail printout from an editor saying, "No." Taped to the walls were tons of my previous brush-offs. My favorite ones were from editors who later wound up buying my work. While turndowns can feel terrible, here's how not to react.

1. Don't get manically depressed, drunk, and stoned (as I used to), which will make everything worse.
2. Don't post nasty notes on social media about the editors who said no, even if you think it's in a private group or chat page. (I know tons of editors on private groups and chat pages.)

3. Don't drop out of your journalism class, writing workshop, college, or graduate school, claiming "it's just too hard" and "there's no way for someone new to break in."
4. Don't resent every writer you read who gets in the publication you wanted to, or assume they all have more brains, balls, money, moxie, and/or connections than you do.
5. Don't catastrophize and assume one no means nothing you write in the future will see print.

HOW TO HANDLE REJECTION BETTER

1. **DISCUSS WITH YOUR TEACHER/MENTOR/SHRINK/OLDER COLLEAGUES.** Seek out someone more seasoned in the field to identify what you may be doing wrong and how to fix it. When students have asked me this over the years, my most common responses have been, "You're being impatient," "Why did you submit 5,000 words to a short column?" "Starting with 'When I was six in 1994' is the opposite of timely," and "You've never taken a writing class before in your life and you're surprised *The New Yorker* editor said no to your first submission?"

2. **KEEP TRYING NEW EDITORS.** While it's very disappointing to get negative responses, just because a few people say no doesn't mean you won't sell what you've written. I once sold an essay on my fourteenth try that led to a Random House book. My former student Teresa Fazio published her story—about an affair she had while serving as a U.S. Marine—in *The New York Times'* At War blog, after getting rejected by eight other *New York Times* editors from different sections. (atwar.blogs.nytimes.com/author/teresa-fazio/?mcubz=0) Sometimes it's a numbers game, so remember the adage: "The harder I work, the luckier I get."

3. **GET TOUGHER CRITICISM.** Often if ten editors don't like something I've written, I bring it back into my writing group to try and figure out what can be improved. If my usual critics can't tell me what's wrong with it, I'll hire a tougher ghost editor. I can't tell you how

many times a student has told me, "My other teacher loved this," or "My weekly workshop said this was my most brilliant piece," and I find it still needs tons of work.

4. **REVISE AND UPDATE.** If I love a piece, I will often listen carefully to criticism then give it an overhaul. That could mean a much timelier lede, a different focus, a younger angle, additional research, or a more dramatic ending. Before resubmitting, I first change the lede and rework the piece in the voice of each publication I'm trying.

5. **DEVELOP A WISER WORK STRATEGY.** Many writers sit alone at their computer, revise their piece a few times, then send it in. If that's not working for you, take a class. If bringing in your piece and getting it critiqued by a teacher once a week isn't leading to success, try other methods. My favorite advice for writing and love: "You can do anything as long as it works." Even after six years of writing classes, I still needed a weekly writing workshop and ghost editors I hired to kill my "darlings" again, along with a smart shrink to talk out my career frustrations and help me recover from rejections faster.

6. **PUT IT AWAY FOR A WHILE.** If you can't make a specific piece sing, taking a break from it might do the trick. Sometimes I go away, work on something else, and six months or a year later, reread it from a different perspective. Then revise.

7. **TRY SWITCHING GENRES.** Often a student will show me a personal essay that I'll suggest turning into an op-ed, humor, or service piece. I'm open to rethinking my own work, too. What I once saw as a first-person op-ed on the lack of professional instruction in writing programs became the third-person reported story I linked for Atlantic .com. This flexibility and willingness to compromise extends to my longer projects as well. I once wrote an entire nonfiction book that didn't sell—until I fictionalized it to make it my comic novel *Speed Shrinking.* A co-authored memoir turned into the best-selling self-help book *Unhooked.* In fact, all of my published books started out as something else. I asked for criticism, reshrunk, rethought, revised, rewrote, and had much more success with the reinvention. And if I can redraft an entire book, you can certainly redo three pages.

CHAPTER 5

After Yes: Now What?

If an editor says he wants to publish the essay you submitted, don't jump up and down and respond: "Fucking amazing, dude, go for it!" You might not realize he could be asking you to give away all rights to your piece forever, for no money, and may not even plan to use it for two years. Whether it's by e-mail or phone, pay careful attention to his words. If you aren't sent an official contract, this could be your only legal agreement. So before posting all over social media, "I am now officially a published writer," consider what the editor is telling you. Then, very politely, ask these five brief questions.

1. **WHAT DO YOU PAY?**

While it is still possible to get five thousand dollars for an essay, these days the average amount for a first piece is one to two hundred dollars. You should do research before submitting to find out if the publication pays, how much, and whether your piece will be running in print, online, or both. That said, prices, budgets, and priorities change, each editor and section is different, and many new online variations of old magazines have evolving rates.

If the answer to your question about payment is some variation of "no," or "we don't have money to financially compensate our writers at this time," or "we pay in exposure," you have a few choices. You can respond, "That's okay. Take my piece anyway." Sometimes it's worth it to get a good clip. I've encouraged students to say yes to university newspapers and prestigious literary publications like TinHouse.com, *The Brooklyn Rail*, *Honeysuckle Magazine*, and *The Millions*, which generally don't have much dough and thus don't offer you any.

Sometimes clips in small places can lead you to be paid and reprinted by the *Best American Essay* series and lead to books and *Chicken Soup for the Soul* anthologies. Roxane Gay, Stephen Elliott, and Cheryl Strayed got their start at *The Rumpus*, an online magazine that doesn't usually pay. Also, a few times pupils had topical op-ed pieces in bigger places (like *Newsday*, *The Philadelphia Inquirer*, and *The Detroit News*) that editors wanted but didn't offer money for. In some cases, it would be a shame to let a topical piece expire before finding an audience. Good things can happen later. After I let my colleague Jerry Portwood print a humorous essay of mine for free in the *New York Press*, my mentor Ian Frazier reprinted it in his great HarperCollins anthology *Humor Me*, where I was honored to be right next to David Sedaris.

Conversely, it enrages me that *HuffPost* was started by a millionaire who decided, as a rule, not to pay freelance writers, perpetuating a horrible trend for our industry. So I never give them original material. (Though I was happy to hear that one of their essay sections now pays one hundred dollars a piece.) The only time I let a piece of mine be posted there for free is when it's a reprint and I want a bigger audience, or when I want more exposure for short excerpts or visuals from a book I've already been paid for, to help sell copies.

If you want to be financially compensated for your writing, now is the time for you to tell the editor, "Oh, I'm sorry, I thought you paid writers. I can't work for free," and withdraw your submission. Once in a while, when I've stated that, the editor will then say, "Okay, we can give you fifty dollars" (or one hundred dollars) and then I say yes. A few times, when an editor offered me one hundred dollars, I've said, "My usual fee is five hundred dollars" (or one thousand dollars), and he upped the payment. But I have been doing this for thirty-five years, and I usually play hardball only when I have a connection or feel confident that I can sell my piece for the higher amount to another editor.

Most places pay after publication and can take as long as six months to get you in their system. So don't go on a shopping spree until the check clears or the direct deposit is in your account. A few big magazines may give you a contract and pay in advance, but don't count on it.

I've had checks that bounced and been owed money I never saw by editors who were fired or publications that went out of business.

Publications will often send you a tax form you need to fill out before they can pay you, and a few places might first need you to mail or scan a signed invoice. If you don't know how to do this, ask to see another invoice or find a template online to emulate. Be sure to save your invoices as PDF files so they can't be altered. Mine look like this:

January 10, 2018 INVOICE

To: Editor of Magazine Who Owes Me Money I Need Right Now/ address/phone/e-mail

From: Broke Freelance Writer's name/address/phone/e-mail/social security #

For: Freelance essay called "You Owe Me Money" with link (if it has already run online)

Fee: $150 by check (or say direct deposit and give your bank name, account & routing numbers)

Writer signature.

Some publications will mail your check. Others pay only with direct deposit so they'll ask for your bank information. I didn't like the idea of giving my account data out, but sometimes I had no choice; many publications only pay this way these days. The faster you get them what they need, the quicker the money will leave their account and enter yours.

2. **IF YOU MAKE CHANGES, WILL YOU SHOW ME AN EDITED VERSION BEFORE IT RUNS?**

Sometimes there will be queries and questions about your piece they need you to answer. A few editors will pick up the phone and want to work with you on a new draft. It is not uncommon for an editor to accept your piece, give you radio silence for four months, then call or e-mail several times in a row at the last second, when the publication is ready to go to press. You should respond to an editor's messages immediately. If you are not willing to compromise or revise fast, she will probably say "forget it" and instead take the work of someone who is less high maintenance. So now is the time to be charming, gracious, and quick on your feet. Don't dawdle if he is on a tight deadline. Answer as briefly as possible.

Unfortunately, other times they will put their big fat fingers all over your work of art, adding nonsensical phrases and screwing up facts without your input. There is not much you can do about it except to have a courteous discussion or else ruin your chances for future clips. An editor who is taking your essay has every right to cut, revise, or rewrite it to fit her publication better. She knows her audience intimately, better than you do. She doesn't, however, have a right to be inaccurate. Sometimes an editor in a hurry will not show you her version, or will send it to you quickly and get annoyed if you push back. In those cases, I usually suck it up. (If you expand into books, you'll have more say about every single comma.)

There is no situation where "You screwed up my whole piece and ruined it!" is an appropriate reaction, even if it's true or how you feel. (As my shrink often reminds me, "Feelings misinform.") If you are shown a version you don't like, or one that has errors, a better way to play it is to say calmly, "Thank you so much for your smart edits. I went over it again to fix the mistakes and added back a few lines I couldn't live without." It is not unusual to go back and forth several times.

I was recently arguing with an editor on my cell phone *during* my class, over a piece he'd bought six weeks before. Suddenly on a tight deadline, a copyeditor had just made changes that took out my jokes and specific word phrasings. The new lines added were sloppy, clichéd, incorrect, not the way I would say it, and basically sucked. I tried to make corrections and resurrect my voice. But I was so depressed and worried the piece was destroyed that I couldn't sleep all night. ("Everything is too important to you," my shrink also tells me.) Shockingly, when my essay ran the next day, I saw that my editor had heeded most of my last-minute requests, returned the piece to its original Shapiro-esque language, and I wound up happy with it. It was worth the stressed out—but polite—last-second argument.

While I always write my own title, subtitle, and nut graf (which summarizes what I think my piece is about), they will often be changed by my editor. Unfortunately, writers have little say over their own head-lines, which these days can be sensationalized for clickbait. My former student Judy Batalion complained that a piece she'd called "The Mess of Motherhood" for *Salon* was given the long title: "I've Become My Hoarder Mother: How My Kids Turned Me Into a Pathological Pack-rat." It was not only silly sounding, but amiss since she was a minimal-ist. I once named a piece about selling back rainbow-colored clothes my mother sent me "Second Chance," and the *New York Times* editor changed it to "Er, Thanks Mom." My only recourse was to pay a Web de-signer one hundred dollars to redo it with my title (for a paper clip and a JPEG) that I was prouder to show off on my website and in my clip folder.

3. DO YOU KNOW WHEN IT WILL RUN?

An editor might say, "I have no idea," (since he doesn't control his whole paper or section), or "hopefully tomorrow," and your piece will run immediately and you'll feel famous within a week. Other times he will tell you, "I'm overbooked for six months" and you just have to wait. *The New Yorker* once infamously bought and paid for a piece in advance that they held for fourteen years before running. It depends on how timely your piece is, how much you are paid and when, and how often the publication runs—which can be daily for a webzine to four to six times a year for *Tin House* or *Psychology Today*. The only thing you can do to hasten the process: Be very responsive and easy to work with, and make your piece timely and update it if there's anything fresh in the news cycle. I usually advise extreme patience and to start another piece right away.

If they haven't paid you and keep telling you that your piece will run—over several months—to no avail, and you haven't signed a con-tract, you can sell your piece elsewhere, as long as you let the editor know. But beware. A student who felt impatient with a *New York Times* editor who wouldn't give her a firm publication date gave up and sold her piece to *The Washington Post* for one hundred dollars. Then the *Times* editor e-mailed her, ready to pay six hundred dollars—but it was too late because the piece was already taken.

THE BYLINE BIBLE

4. DO YOU NEED ANYTHING ELSE FROM ME?

Some editors, like Daniel Jones at *The New York Times'* "Modern Love" column, will insist on contacting the main people mentioned in an essay to get their approval. You may have to provide phone numbers or e-mails and/or proof that you did not change names or facts. Unfortunately, if these characters don't want the piece to run, you might have to cut them out of it or your piece could be killed. *The New Yorker* staff is known for fact-checking everything—even first-person stories. They may ask you to provide printouts, photographs, videos, audiotapes, diary entries, and other proof that what you wrote is true. For reported pieces, keep careful notes and transcriptions to provide evidence if someone accuses you of inaccuracy, fictionalizing, or plagiarism.

5. WILL YOU RUN A PHOTO OF ME OR A BIO?

They might. So think carefully before sending in a picture and boring description of yourself. Make sure it's a high-resolution photograph that you like and wouldn't mind going viral. If you don't have a good one, get one taken ASAP. Also don't waste your bio line saying, "Joe Smith is a college student" or "Lisa Cohen is an accountant." What good will *that* do you? If the piece does well, lots of other editors, agents, and employers might click on it and want to contact you. So visualize the bigger picture and try something like, "Joe Smith, a college student from Ohio, writes about the intersection between education and art," or "Lisa Cohen, a New Jersey accountant, is working on a book about finance. You can follow her on Twitter at @lisacohen."

That editor I was recently arguing with wanted my bio to read: "Susan Shapiro is a writing professor." Instead I was able to change it to: "Susan Shapiro (@susanshapiro.net), a writing professor at The New School, is the author of *Five Men Who Broke My Heart* and the forthcoming *The Byline Bible*." With the new version, I garnered a thousand more Twitter followers, inquiries from students who wanted to take my class, and pleased two book editors with my plugs, along with my New School boss, just because I asked. And now I love the editor and can't wait to do another piece for her.

AFTER YOUR PIECE RUNS

Before posting it on Facebook and Twitter, and taking a screenshot for Instagram (as my students taught me), read your piece over first. If it's online and there are mistakes, they can often be repaired. If you want something fixed, e-mail the editor, "Thank you so much for taking my essay, it came out beautiful. Unfortunately there was a typo on line four and my name was spelled incorrectly." Hate to say it, but it happens. Wait until she responds. If it's in the hard copy of a newspaper or magazine, they can't redo the print run. But sometimes a piece first runs online and they can often fix it before it's in the paper. Other times they can remedy the mistake in the online version that will live forever.

If you're pleased with the way your story came out, post it and tweet it everywhere. I sometimes ask an editor if he would mind if I thank him when posting the link. Some enjoy the attention, so when I say, "Thanks to awesome editor Peter Catapano for taking my essay," he "likes" it. Other editors want to remain private. If that's the case, you can say, "Thanks to the *Daily News* for taking my latest work." You can also ask your friends, relatives, and classmates to repost and retweet. Many publications count the shares, likes, and comments. *The New York Times* actually lists the "most popular" and "most e-mailed" daily, which could cause you to web-stalk yourself for hours (as I did after my last piece ran).

Now get to work on something else. If you're sending it to the same editor, of course thank her first, though some publications don't want to keep using the same authors or have rules that you have to wait six months. When you have a new submission ready, give yourself a promotion to a better publication that pays more. If you just broke into a small webzine, aim for a major paper magazine next. For the rest of your life, you can end your cover letter by saying, "Here's a link to an essay I published," which will make it more likely that you'll get another one.

THE SIX WORST OUTCOMES

1. YOUR PIECE IS KILLED.

Sometimes, through no fault of your own or your editor, something slotted won't run. It can happen because the news has taken over the publication. I'm sure there were thousands of light essays and op-eds all set to run the week of September 11, 2001, that never saw print or went live because the World Trade Center attacks changed the entire American literary landscape for a while. Other reasons can be your editor leaves, focuses shift, something similar by someone more famous comes in, or your work is no longer timely or feels appropriate. If it's in your contract, you can get a kill fee. Most often you can try to sell your story elsewhere.

2. IT RUNS WITH MISTAKES.

Publications issue corrections all the time, so don't freak out if you see errors. Often you're not to blame for typos or changes that are inaccurate. Sometimes people you quote share misinformation that gets repeated. Other times, errors are totally your fault. My rule is: Never lie to your editor or your shrink. If you realize something in your published piece is amiss, tell your editor right away. Mistaken lines can be fixed fast online. To paraphrase Maya Angelou, "When you know better, do better."

3. SERIOUS TROUBLE.

If you reveal something illegal you've done, the police, Internal Revenue Service, or creditors can come after you, whether it's mentioning you didn't pay child support, traffic tickets, or student loans. Make sure the statute of limitations on your crime or debt has run out, delete that part of your piece, or use an alias if you can. When you publish anything libelous using someone's name or identifying characteristics that damage their reputation, you can be sued. (In 2016, *Rolling Stone* magazine paid a University of Virginia administrator three million dollars because an article they ran on college rape unfairly portrayed her as a villain.) You can be publicly accused of plagiarism, especially if you put your name on work not your own. It could be inadvertent, as it was with an editor I know who used anonymous bios from Wikipedia in something she wrote, without credit. (She remedied the problem.) Sometimes you can be falsely accused of stealing an idea, as I once was by the writers Elizabeth Cohen and Jenny Lyn Bader, who still owe me an apology. Luckily, I'd kept a trail of evidence that completely exonerated me.

4. COMMENTS CAN BE CRUEL.

Unfortunately, there are angry people who hate everything everyone else publishes (perhaps because they can't get published themselves?). And these rage-balls share horrible barbs in the commentary section after your piece. Also, in case you haven't noticed, some Americans, with different political views than you, are no longer civil when they disagree. I advise people not to read the comments. If you're curious, have a friend or loved one peruse them first, to warn you whether or not to read them. You are usually not encouraged to say thanks to every nice reaction you get. Never, ever answer a negative commenter. It will make you look bad and defensive to your editor, readers, and the world. You're a published professional; let your piece speak for itself. You can calmly tell your editor since he can cut off the comments or monitor them better. When it comes to my own work, I ignore this advice, read all the bitchy responses, get fired up, answer way too many, look foolish, and then promise I'll never do it again.

5. YOU CAN GET TROLLED.

I've had students tell me that nasty anonymous "trolls" found or followed them on Twitter, Instagram, and Facebook and used their regular e-mail, sometimes to flirt or taunt or trash their work. A male student who penned a piece on his special banana bread recipe had a few females phone him who wanted to see him cook. After my anti-marijuana piece ran in the *Los Angeles Times* (about how, as a former pothead, I disagreed with people who said pot wasn't addictive), hysterical readers found the number of my landline and called me to yell, as if I were personally stealing their stash. "My mother's dying of cancer and you want to take away her medicine!" one guy screamed.

"Actually I had a line saying I have no problem with medicinal marijuana, but the editor cut it for space reasons," I told him, and he chilled out.

That same day a grandmother from Texas phoned me crying to tell me that she admired what I wrote and feared her granddaughter was addicted to marijuana like I was. I stayed on the phone with her for a half hour, gratified to think my issues and opinion might have helped a reader.

Alas, that's not always what happens. A student had a horrific experience publishing an anti-noise op-ed, which mentioned rap music blaring in her new multicultural neighborhood. She was so upset when some readers found it racist coming from a white person and hassled her that she stopped writing op-eds. If the reaction to your work gets extreme, let your editor know. Sometimes they can take down an offensive post or the piece itself, or you could delete a Tweet or a Facebook post. Once an older student penned an opinion piece about her enlisted son's political affiliation, and *he* was the troll who hated what she'd written. He insisted she take it down or he could lose his job, and the editor complied. This is why you sometimes need to check with people you write about before you submit your work. You don't want to cause a loved one to lose a job or military posting or put anyone in danger.

6. RADIO SILENCE.

Sometimes the worst reaction is none at all. This can happen when you work for very small publications few people read, or when you've covered a mild-mannered trivial topic (like quitting your ice cream addiction) on a busy political news day, when Republicans and Democrats are fighting over a crucial healthcare vote. My colleague Amy Klein recalls getting no comments whatsoever for an infertility essay she sold to *Narratively* that posted on the same day as Hurricane Sandy. I've published pieces where there were so few comments that I've freaked out and begged my students or friends to pipe up for me. This is a good argument for aiming higher and being timely and provocative (though see #2, #3, and #4 for the risks).

THE SIX BEST OUTCOMES

1. GOING VIRAL.

Once in a while, a piece will be reposted and tweeted so often it will wind up trending and zooming into the zeitgeist. Often these are timely political screeds, for example, the now-famous piece "Donald Trump is Gaslighting America" by Lauren Duca in *Teen Vogue*, which led her to many more clips, bigger titles, and job offers. Sometimes, when my topics have involved quitting addictions or healing from mental health problems, I've had lots of e-mails, calls, and letters from people asking advice. Remembering the word *authority* starts with *author*, I try to respond nicely to everyone sane who contacts me. I've also pointed out that I'm not a shrink, though I've been happy to recommend therapists and addiction specialists I admire.

2. MORE PAID WORK.

If you publish a popular piece, your editor may want to continue working with you. Ryan Stewart's essay for *Quartz* magazine on earning six figures as a dog walker was so popular that the editor commissioned an encore that further explored the same topic. That was also the case with *The New York Times*, who asked Sarah Gerard for a return engagement (though sometimes a different editor may come calling). When Rich Prior sold an essay on how running helped him cope with his father's death to the *Hartford Courant*, an editor from *Runner's World* contacted him to do more personal pieces. Likewise, the *Daily Beast* commissioned my former student Leora Yashari, offering her a similar assignment to the one they'd admired in TeenVogue.com. Sometimes good work begets more good work.

3. TV/RADIO INTERVIEWS.

Several times, after a piece has run, I've received phone calls and e-mails from producers of news shows asking me to appear. Once, when I mentioned in *Woman's Own* magazine that my old roommate Susan Rosenberg met her husband on the subway when she admired his fancy leather shoes, they flew her and her husband out to New York and paid for their hotel. He wore the infamous shoes on the show. This has happened to many of my students as well. In some cases, producers will provide transportation and a hair and makeup artist, too. Not only can you get the word out on important subjects, you can often get a video or audio clip to post on your website, social media, and online portfolio. Though I always ask myself: Will this benefit me? Once, when *Bloomberg News* asked me to schlep uptown to discuss an Amazon petition I'd signed, I didn't want to waste a day being a free talking head to further someone else's agenda. So I said, "Only if you'll hold up my last book on screen and read the bio I wrote." They did and so did I.

4. STAFF WRITER AND EDITOR JOBS.

Once, as I finished my fifth book review assignment for a *Newsday* editor, he offered me my own paperback column, which I did for several years. After publishing short *New York Times* pieces as a freelancer, my former student Seth Kugel became a steady contract writer there, for several sections, most recently as their "Frugal Traveler." Though remember, it's presumptuous to pitch a column to an editor you've never worked with.

5. TV/FILM OPTIONS.

After publishing a provocative piece, several students have received offers from filmmakers, documentarians, and producers to take their work from stage to screen. I've had a few essays optioned myself. In my case, I was paid a few thousand dollars, though so far nothing has been made. On the other hand, my former student Judy Batalion, author of the memoir *White Walls*, (which began with a *New York Times* essay), recently sold her new short book proposal "Daughters of the Resistance: Valor, Fury, and the Untold Story of Women Resistance Fighters in Hitler's Ghettos" to DreamWorks Pictures for six figures. Batalion, the granddaughter of Holocaust survivors, had discovered firsthand accounts of young women written in Yiddish.

6. LITERARY AGENTS, ANTHOLOGIES, AND BOOK EDITORS WANT YOU.

After Kenan Trebincevic sold his first *New York Times Magazine* piece about surviving the ethnic cleansing campaign against Muslims in the Balkan war, the piece was taken by William T. Vollmann for *The Best American Travel Writing* series. Kenan was asked to be on a radio show and received offers from several agents, including one from the William Morris Agency, who sold his book (which I co-authored). See, one new short piece can change your life and launch a whole new sideline or career.

If you don't get lucky right away, try writing something bigger and better. As my late, great, 105-year-old mentor Ruth Gruber told me when I was feeling impatient, "Just keep doing it well, someone will notice." She was right, they did.

CHAPTER 6

Writing Regional

ASSIGNMENT #2

Given the widespread audience potential of the Internet, many websites are national and even international. Yet most newspapers and magazines are still divided by region. Think of the names: *Milwaukee Journal Sentinel*, the *Toronto Star*, or *Los Angeles* magazine. In my adopted state of New York, where realtors love the mantra "location, location, location," we take geographical perspective to extremes. The city is partitioned into such pages as *The Brooklyn Rail*, *Park Slope Reader*, *Long Island Press*, *Tribeca Trib*, *Queens Ledger*, *The Village Voice*, and *Chelsea Now*. It's as if every town, borough, and subdivision has its own idiosyncratic voice and readership to be reckoned with. You'd think that knowing where your audience lives would provide a framework for freelancers. Not necessarily. Here are tips to help you understand the significance of setting and learn how to use a geographical angle to write a regional essay that sells.

1. **PROXIMITY CAN DETERMINE IMPORTANCE.** The 2004 tsunami that left 186,983 people dead in India and Indonesia received far less press in the United States than the 9/11 World Trade Center attacks, which killed fewer than 3,000. As a rule, the closer an event is to home, the more newsworthy it will be to editors in that area—and to readers who may know the people or places involved. Henry Coble, a former Greensboro, North Carolina, *News & Record* editor, evaluated whether a piece would run in his newspaper based on the story's proximity to Haw River, which flows through central North Carolina. According to the incisive *Reporting for the Media* text I

used when teaching at New York University's journalism school, when a specific occurrence happened elsewhere, Coble would say, "It's a long way from the Haw," which meant that the *News & Record* audience would be less interested. Remember, a profile of an unknown hometown author from St. Louis may be more desirable to a *St. Louis Post-Dispatch* editor than a piece on best-selling author Stephen King or a London-born New York-living luminary like Zadie Smith (unless they are passing through Missouri for a book event to provide a local occasion for coverage). Editors I know are particularly interested if the celebrity or author still resides in the community, went to school there—or writes about it—the way, say, Elmore Leonard characterized his hometown of Birmingham, Michigan, in several of his great mysteries.

2. **READ EACH PUBLICATION CAREFULLY.** Shared proximity isn't enough to automatically explain a publication's slant. Growing up outside Detroit, I found a vast variance in the politics, styles, and sensibilities of *The Detroit News*, the *Detroit Free Press*, the *Detroit Jewish News*, the Birmingham *Eccentric*, *The Ann Arbor News*, *The Michigan Daily*, and my alma mater's old humor magazine, *Michegas* (Yiddish for "madness"). Almost everything can be found online these days, so there's no excuse not to research, read, and learn to delineate the differences in each demographic. If a newspaper or magazine is only in print, I'd never pitch without finding a way to get hard copies of several issues and reading them first. How? Remember that pre-Internet building called a library? If not, call their office, using a telephone to speak to a human, and ask if you can purchase back copies. While tiny papers will pay less, they may respond to your ideas faster and give you more space.

3. **PINPOINT WHAT'S UNIQUE ABOUT THE PLACE.** Just because the person you're profiling lives in Washington doesn't mean he's perfect for *The Washington Times*. What if he hates the District of Columbia or just moved there? What if your subject's left-wing views contrast with those of right-leaning readers? For a prompt, I tell my students to explore a region's personality with a piece called "This

could only happen in Greenwich Village" (or "Greenwich, Connecticut," "Greenwich, England," "Staten Island," or "West Bloomfield, Michigan"). Ask yourself why this could only occur here, analyzing what is particular to the population. A Manhattan list might include the Giants, Knicks, Yankees, Broadway, Wall Street, Chinatown, expensive housing, and the subway. When the Detroit area was my target, I'd consider car culture, the Renaissance Center, Pistons, Tigers, Red Wings, Sanders hot fudge, and Vernors soda. If you can't answer why your story could happen only here, pick a subject that's more localized and specialized.

4. **OFFER VERY SPECIFIC CREDENTIALS.** When pitching my neighborhood newspapers, *The Village Voice, The Villager*, the *East Villager*, or *Downtown Express*, I don't merely say, "I'm a Greenwich Village resident" in my query, cover letter, bio, and in the piece itself. I detail living at Eighth Street and Broadway, in the least charming high-rise on the block. I add that I've spent three decades in the area and teach at The New School and NYU, two nearby institutions. Approaching Michigan editors, I mention that I grew up on Long Lake and Middlebelt—and that my parents still live there, my dad was a doctor at Beaumont Hospital, my brother is a surgeon in Grand Blanc, I attended Shaarey Zedek Hebrew School, I graduated from the University of Michigan, and often visit home. The last time I published a newspaper article mentioning an upcoming trip and soon-to-be-published book, a local TV producer saw it and asked me to be a guest on a local program, promoting my book. (Embarrassingly, since I no longer have my driver's license, I asked my mother for a ride. When the station workers heard, they teased me for being the only one in Motor City without wheels.)

5. **BE TIMELY.** Regional stories sold by my students over the years include an October essay on Halloween parties in Summit, New Jersey, an August exposé on women sunbathing topless in public parks, and a Connecticut Democrat who witnessed President Bush's helicopter landing in her backyard for a Republican Party fundraiser (which made the cover of *Fairfield County Weekly*). My student Patricia

Crowley's Westchester *Journal News* piece recalled the summer she worked at Playland amusement park in Rye, New York. There had been a recent fatality there, so Crowley—who lived in nearby Rye Brook—made her lede topical and personal as well as geographically desirable.

6. **OFFER TO FIX PROBLEMS OF THE PLACE.** A clever, helpful idea published in *Time Out New York* by my student on how to "de-New York" your apartment, suggested ocean recordings, sunset shades, and beach-scented candles to ease urban noise and angst. Another urbanite aware of local housing limitations penned a piece on plants New Yorkers can grow with no sunlight in *The New York Times'* Metro section. An L.A. colleague sent me her story on how to navigate the West Coast without wheels, which listed subways, buses, taxis, and carpooling services like Uber which, at the time, I didn't know about.

7. **CULTIVATE A NEW REGIONAL RÉSUMÉ.** You don't have to occupy a community to cover it. If you've travelled there, become an expert. My colleague Kate Walter has summered on the Jersey shore since childhood, so she chronicled the area for the *Asbury Park Press* and *Offshore* magazine. Because Seth Kugel worked in the Bronx and spoke Spanish, his original *New York Times* beat (before cheap travel) became the surrounding Latino community. This led to his fun book *Nueva York: The Complete Guide to Latino Life in the Five Boroughs*[1]—even though Kugel is a Jewish boy with no Hispanic connections. That is, except for his co-author Carolina Gonzalez, his second language, and his passion for Mama's empanadas.

8. **CHRONICLE A QUIRKY LOCAL CHARACTER.** Editors often like to cover fascinating humans in their midst. I enjoyed reading about the shoeshine guy in Grand Central Station, the Naked Cowboy in New York's Times Square, and Shaky Jake, the late street musician and storyteller who hung out in Ann Arbor's Diagonal when I was in college. My student Jeff interviewed a man who put his four sons through graduate school by making a success of his tiny hardware store. A writer/editor I know did an investigative piece

---

1. St. Martin's Press, 2006

about a doctor with cancer who was trying to cure his own disease. I wrote about a performance artist billing herself as "a feminist clown who strips on roller skates while playing the saxophone." She said she likes to "create obstacles for myself." I found out about her through arts listings, so I made sure I'm on all the mailing lists for local theaters.

9. **STEER CLEAR OF SLANDER.** Before you write or pitch an article on someone, introduce yourself and make sure the subject wants to be written about and photographed, agrees to use his real name, and has a phone where he can be reached. If not, move on. Editors often need to fact-check a story and nobody wants to get sued. If, for example, you write a piece about a seemingly homeless man who lives in a nearby park, using his name without his permission, you could be sued for defamation. If he can prove he has a home, he might win. Luckily there are enough people in the world who want press. So find someone who wants to see her face in the paper and make sure the details you run are factual. Proof could be a printed-out e-mail, text, or letter; a tape recording; photographs; leases; birth certificates; police reports; passports; and other official documents.

10. **PROFILE AN UNUSUAL BUSINESS IN YOUR CITY.** I published several pieces on the secrets of the Strand bookstore's rare books room (where everyone from Sophia Loren to Michael Jackson have purchased ten-thousand-dollar first editions), as well as a book machine that turned computer manuscripts into a bound book in minutes. Students have sold pieces on the owner of the only cookbook store in Manhattan, a reading series called "Dirty Laundry: Loads of Prose" that took place in Laundromats in the area, the last record shop in the East Village, and a typewriter repair shop still thriving in the digital age. Editors might appreciate anything that seems out of time, out of touch, retro, or reviving.

11. **COVER A CONTROVERSY.** When Seth Kugel was walking in Washington Heights, he saw Spanish writing on bedsheets hanging outside of windows. Translating, he realized there was a fight going on between tenants and landlords. He took a picture, and the piece "Tenant Dispute Becomes Battle of Bedsheets" ran in *The New York Times'*

Metro section. You can learn about conflicts by going to local board meetings, being nosy when you see something odd, or asking around. Sometimes a local story can also have national appeal if there are larger implications for us all. The lead in water crisis in Flint, Michigan, for example, wound up on the front pages of many newspapers.

12. **ONLY REPORT ON STRANGERS.** If you pitch a third-person story, make sure you don't have a relationship with the subject and aren't involved in the problem being disputed. For any kind of reporting, news story, or profile, you have to be unbiased. If you're not sure whether your link is too close, mention it in the cover letter upfront, even if it's just "this was my hometown restaurant," "he's my old shoeshine guy," or "we went to the same college." To write about people you know well, consider a first-person essay or op-ed, making your bias and connection clear.

Regional Article Mistakes to Avoid

1. **Don't tell an editor** "Hey, I'll be in Chicago. You need anything?" Take the time to craft an unusual, idiosyncratic pitch or story.
2. **Don't submit work** to a local editor before first reading several issues of his publication.
3. **Don't guess.** If you don't know the geographical range of a publication, ask or do research. Never pitch a piece that's pegged to an area the publication doesn't cover—even if it's nearby and you think they should. "We used to get pitches about Yonkers and Woodstock all the time," recalls Frank Flaherty who, as an editor at *The New York Times'* City section, was not the least bit interested in those areas—or the writers who didn't do their homework.
4. **Try not to write about a place you've never been.** If you must, use the Internet to research the area first, fact-check, and get quotes from natives before handing in your piece.
5. **Beware of your coastal bias.** If you're aiming for national or Web editors, don't overuse references to New York or Los Angeles. I've heard many editors complain that they get too much press already, maybe because so many scribes live in those two

cities. For webzines (which are international) and big publications sold across the nation, it's better to "play in Peoria," as they say.

6. **Never lie to your shrink or your editor.** Unless you're writing a first-person essay or op-ed, many editors would consider it unethical for you to write about family members, friends, colleagues, or someone you dated or have done business with. Though once in a while, if you have a juicy story and tell an editor your connection, she will say yes and add a line of full disclosure. *The Forward* allowed me to do a piece on my second cousin Molly Jong-Fast, mentioning that her mother was the famous *Fear of Flying* author Erica Jong, her grandfather the best-selling novelist Howard Fast, and even the reporter was related by marriage. My colleague Judith Newman penned a long profile for *Vanity Fair* on Viacom chairman Sumner Redstone, her mother's cousin-in-law, making it clear her family was "the poor relation," a connection that actually gave her more credibility.

Exercises

1. **Find your places.** List four locations in the world you could be considered an expert on, including why. (Start where you were born, where you live now, where you vacation, and where you went to school.)

2. **Mine your own geography.** Instead of a sweeping generality such as "I'm from Maine," be explicit or tell a story about your place of origin. The piece I penned about how other transplanted West Bloomfield friends transported Michigan delicacies from home (like Sanders hot fudge and Vernors soda) ran in *The Detroit News'* Sunday magazine.

3. **Research potential pages.** Do a Google search to see how many recent publications you can find in the area you are targeting. Yes, the *Los Angeles Times* would be my most coveted clip on the West Coast. Yet I uncovered more than thirty publications in that area including *Korea Central Daily News*, *La Opinión*, *LA Weekly*, *Jewish Journal of Greater Los Angeles*, and the *Los Angeles Review of Books*. While not all of them may use freelancers or pay, you won't know until you explore your options.

REGIONAL PIECES BY MY STUDENTS

TO BE YOUNG AND BLACK IN GREENWICH VILLAGE RIGHT NOW

By Darnell McGee, Villager,
January 14, 2016

Let me start off by saying how much I love white people. I love them just as much as I love Asian, Indian, Latino, Middle Eastern, African and any other group I forgot to mention; but white people particularly, hold a special place in my heart.

Growing up, I had a ton of white friends, and by ton, I mean one. I had white teachers, white mentors and white encouragement from everywhere. So I've certainly come to have a great deal of appreciation and respect for the white community.

Currently, I live in the whitest of communities in New York City, the West Village. It's quite white. White people are everywhere down here: in the restaurants, at the barbershops, in the pet stores. You name it, and there are white people there. Some are very kind. Some are very beautiful. And some are racist as hell.

I grew up in Newark, New Jersey. I had two parents, a dog (briefly), and an older brother who I loathed, so a pretty typical family. There weren't many white people where I grew up. There were some sprinkles of white people occasionally thrown about, some Latinos and Portuguese.

I went to private schools most of my life, so I encountered them daily, but only for eight hours at a time. I didn't experience real racism until about the seventh grade, when my mom sent me to a highfalutin camp in Princeton for the summer. I was one of two black guys in a camp of about 50 kids.

One night, one of the guys at camp went into one of the girls' cabins, threw some water on them and ran out before anyone saw them. I knew nothing of this event until one of the counselors burst into our room and demanded to know who did it.

"Why are you coming in our room?" I griped as my roommates played Supremes to my Diana and backed me up with head nods and "Yeahs?"

"Just tell us if it was you or not," the counselor said, looking directly at me and bypassing the other two adorable white boys in the room.

"If what was me?" I said, this time getting a little more indignant. He stood there and looked me up and down, and once again asked me to come clean.

Another of my bunkmates inquired about what had happened, and when he did, the counselor looked at him, and then proceeded to walk out the room.

My bunkmates and I looked around at each other, and then one of them peered out the door to see if the counselor was still around, but he had left, and it seemed, hadn't knocked on any other rooms.

"What was that about?" I asked genuinely confused.

"I don't know" said one roommate. "I could give a s—," said the other.

But the third campmate said something I'll never forget.

"Dude, you're black. Of course he asked you," he said with a smirk.

And then like Chris Brown at a Girl Scouts meeting, it hit me: I had been racially profiled.

"Me? Me?" I thought as I gazed into the blue eyes of the boy who unlocked my blissful ignorance.

"Um yeah, you," he said with no fear and unabashed confidence. And that's the moment I realized I wasn't a kid from Newark who got a scholarship to Camp Albemarle. Instead, I was just black, and that's all that mattered in this world.

Learning this at an early age helped me prepare for a future that would include an abundance of white people. I now knew not to look for racism, but to expect it. Most important, I learned that racism is here to stay and you have to learn how to live in it.

So this is how I survive the West Village. It helps me survive the police stopping me on my way home, asking me why I'm down here. This is how I survive the memo from the superintendent telling people to look out for a guy in a black baseball cap lurking around the building. This is how I survive bartenders constantly asking me am I ready to settle up after my first drink at the restaurant's bar. This is how I survive living in the Village.

Now, I realize that the community is slightly older than my young, cool, hip self, and when I say slightly, I mean much older. Most of the residents are upper-class white couples who have lived here since it was the ghetto in the '70s. Some are new to the area, but still feel like they relocated from a suburb in Alabama—the kind of suburb that still doesn't let kids off for Dr. Martin Luther King Day. And then there are the gays, but they never hurt anybody, except of course when they're old and racist.

This is the Village in a nutshell: the nut, a small affluent suburb in New York City; the shell, a shroud of racist ideas and presumptions.

I really like the Village. I've met some cool people and awesome bartenders. I've run into some of the friendliest dogs with even friendlier owners. There is beautiful architecture and history paves the streets.

I often think maybe people would look at me differently if I had a wife and kids. Maybe being a young, single black man who likes to dress urban and roam the streets makes people uncomfortable.

Maybe if I fit more of the "norm" when it comes to living in the Village, I would draw less attention and fit in a little better. But then I think, maybe I shouldn't have to. And then that maybe turns into an "I sure as hell am not going to, so screw you."

MY MOM WAS MY ROOMMATE

By Giselle Perez, New York Times,
May 3, 2012

The last time I slept alone, it was in a crib. Ever since then, I shared a bed with my mother. And this was in Washington Heights, a Manhattan neighborhood known for its relatively affordable and spacious apartments.

I guess our place, with its four bedrooms, is considered big by many standards. But with only one bathroom, it definitely wasn't meant for eight people.

There's my mother, 61, and my father, 82, and my Uncle Ramon, who has lived with us since he got his green card back in January 2000. Then there are the twins, Elaine and Rosemary, my 30-year-old sisters. And last year my 27-year-old sister, Vanessa, was laid off from her job in Virginia Beach and wound up moving back home with her 3-year-old daughter. She is pregnant, due this August. We're like the Dominican Kardashians, with all of the drama, but none of the wealth.

According to 2011 census data, 10 percent of women (and 19 percent of men) age 25 to 34 live in their parents' homes. I'm 24, and for women in my age bracket the figure is 50 percent—though that includes college students living in dorms, something that wasn't an affordable option for me. Demographers say that the trend is rising—that it started going up before the recession, and has only continued since.

But I don't feel like part of a new trend. It just seems normal to me. Since the age of 13, I have been waking up early to prepare breakfast for my family, anything from farina—basically Cream of Wheat—to eggs, bacon and mangu, a plantain mash. My father never went to school and my mother only went to third grade, so reading and translating were also my responsibility. I wore hand-me-down clothes from my sisters. There were times we slept on the couch because there weren't enough mattresses. Our lives were based on traditional values about the importance of family, values many of our neighbors shared. I love my parents, but it was hard taking care of them when I was still a child myself. I got really stressed and cried at times.

Later, it was hard to date, because I didn't want to bring a guy to my house where he could see how crowded it was. Most of all, I didn't want anyone to find out that I had to share a bed with my mother. Because she was a noisy and restless sleeper, my father refused to share a bed or even a room with her. He had his own room, and so did my uncle. Since I was the youngest girl, I had to bunk with my mother, while my sisters shared the last room. It meant that, even at 3 a.m., when everyone was asleep, I still didn't have any privacy.

In the last few years, I've been taking night classes, which means I have some quiet time at home during the day and also that I can take a long shower in the afternoon, instead of fighting everyone for bathroom time in the morning. But a few months ago, I found out that our apartment was going to get even more crowded. Uncle Ramon's wife and his five adult children, who all have kids of their own, have always lived in the Dominican Republic. In October he was finally able to get visas for them. We were their only immediate relatives in the United States, which meant they were going to move into our overcrowded apartment. With 13 new people arriving, our apartment would soon look like an urban soup kitchen, like a clown car where people just keep popping out.

Just when I was about to reach my breaking point, my mother came to me with the news that Uncle Ramon's family wasn't moving in after all, that they'd found a place in New Jersey. Even more surprising: my uncle was moving there with them. Suddenly, for the first time ever, there was a vacant room in our apartment. I was sure my sisters and I were going to fight for the available space, and that it would probably go to Vanessa, her daughter and the new baby. But Elaine, who has always been a thoughtful sister, convinced my mother to give it to me, saying it was finally time for me to have my own space. Everyone else agreed.

I immediately decided to mark my territory. I painted one wall pink and the rest a pale silver to make the room look bigger. I bought a television and a new mattress, all my own. But my first night in the new room, I kept waking up every hour, nervous and sweating. After all this time, I didn't know how to sleep without my mother! It felt like I was going through withdrawal.

It took a month before I could sleep the full night, but now that I'm used to it, I feel like I'll never be able to share a bed with someone else again. When I graduate this month, I'll be the first person in my family with a four-year college degree. I'm trying to line up a full-time job, and I have already started applying for apartments in Chelsea, Hell's Kitchen and the Bronx—anywhere but Washington Heights. Until then, every night in my own bed, I find peace, stretching my arms and legs out as far as I like.

FROM THE LAND OF SAMBA, A STEW OF MEMORIES

By Camila Santos, New York Times, May 21, 2006

The facade lacks the bright green, yellow and blue of the flag, a common clue that Brazilians use to identify supermarkets selling the products they grew up with. But navigating the tight shelves stocked with curries, Turkish grape leaves and baklava, tucked away among bottles of Croatian jam and Georgian seltzer water,

they find the coveted aisle, marked by the globe inside a diamond that is part of the Brazilian flag.

For these customers, that is the only identification necessary for the Brazilian section of the Trade Fair supermarket on 30th Avenue at 30th Street in Astoria, Queens. The store sells products from more than 50 nations. According to Frank Jaber, the owner of the Trade Fair chain, sales of Brazilian goods at that market average $40,000 a month, making them the third most popular line of ethnic products.

In these aisles, taste and memory intertwine. Those who can't afford to visit their homeland, and those who are in the United States illegally and fear they would never be able to visit home and return, can at least savor a flavor of the land of their birth.

Small packets of coconut water become an invitation to reminisce about the beach. The cans of condensed milk, or leite moça provide the main ingredient for brigadeiro, a homemade candy served at children's birthday parties back home. Requeijão a velvety version of cream cheese, is eaten on salt crackers or spread on small French rolls sold in bakeries found on corners throughout the homeland.

"It's as if I've stepped into a mini-Brazil," said Isaura Lopez, 64, a housekeeper who moved to the neighborhood eight years ago and was looking for bars of Phebo soap. "Everything is so different here, even the soap. Ours have more perfume."

Brazilian-inflected products range from the homey (packs of Pilão coffee) to the exceedingly exotic (glass jars of geléia de mocotó, a tutti-frutti-flavored beef bone-marrow gelatin).

"We try to establish some sort of food communication with our clients," said Mr. Jaber, a Venezuelan who owns 11 Trade Fairs in Queens. "What they ask for is what we put on our shelves."

Habit also creates loyal customers, like Vanete da Mata, 39, an engineer who frequently makes the hour-long trip from Harlem to buy bags of farinha, roasted cassava flour. How would she feel if she couldn't find what she wanted? "Oh, no!" she replied. "Don't even think about asking me this question."

Do not ask it either of Neilson Crespo, 45, a resident of Astoria who spends his days working as a mechanic and his nights checking coats at S.O.B.'s, a Brazilian nightspot in SoHo. Having products from his country available at the local supermarket, he said, has made his immigrant lot more bearable: "It has become a solace."

GOP CONGRESSMAN HELPED ME BEAT CANCER— SHOWING HOW WE CAN AND MUST CARE FOR EACH OTHER

By Julie Charnet, Philadelphia Inquirer, October 25, 2017

Recently, I was happy to read about a bipartisan compromise on health-care laws. A lifelong liberal, I was actually saved by a Republican congressman.

When I was working at a textbook distributor in South Jersey, my employer didn't provide health insurance. As a 24-year-old temp/musician, medical care was not a concern. If I had an infection, my primary-care physician was paid in full and generic antibiotics were affordable. My parents were divorced and my mother had me on her plan, along with my younger sister, until I turned 23.

During an office visit for a bad cold, while I waited for prescription nose spray, my doctor noticed a small bump on the side of my neck.

I said: "It's nothing. It's been there awhile."

He pushed on it. "I don't like it, get a scan," he said.

My mother demanded I do it right away. As a clinical microbiologist, she understood cells. She gave me her credit card to pay for the $500 scan and I pictured a minor procedure to remove the cyst. The thought of asking for another day off scared me more than surgery.

One CAT scan and MRI later, I was referred to an oncologist. My head raced with thoughts about losing my job and my life. As my mother drove us to the consult, she looked worried. We were ushered into a large office. The doctor had my file and diagnosis:

I had cancer of the lymphatic system, Hodgkin's lymphoma. It was in Stage IIB and growing.

From that small bump on my neck were two long and wide snakelike tumors growing down the inside of my body, he explained. It was barely visible outside.

My stomach went on a roller-coaster. Confused, I focused on the doctor's words but could not process anything. I wondered if surgery was an option. The doctor read my mind. "You'll need chemotherapy and possibly radiation," he said. Numb, I leaned back on his couch.

When I got back to my apartment, I tried to figure out how to pay for my medical costs. The next day, my family researched every hospital sliding scale and private practice. No discount would be enough to pay for chemo, blood work, and the repeat bimonthly process. It almost totaled $100,000, which nobody had. We all kept looking.

At the time, my sister still lived at home and was an intern for a Republican congressman, Jim Saxton. "He's one of the good ones," she said. He cared about the environment and gun control. A lifelong Democrat, I'd been skeptical. But she went into work and asked him for any advice about my illness. I was at my mother's for dinner when my sister walked in. "Empty whatever you have left in that savings account and quit your job tomorrow," she said. "You need to go on public assistance."

I was surprised. Welfare was for other people and I didn't know anyone personally who used it. My parents had careers and my grandparents had worked from age 16.

Those "other people" now included me. Since I would be too sick to work for a few months, I left my job and went on food stamps. It was surreal. I learned which items could be purchased with that blue card. At the time, cigarettes and nonedibles were off-limits. I smoked but had no motivation to quit (I already had cancer). I bought food at the local Wawa because I was too embarrassed to shop at a supermarket.

Saxton instructed his assistant to call me and explain Medicaid. Neither he nor his assistant ever asked whom I'd voted for and I never volunteered the information.

After treatment began, I received a call from the congressman's staff every week for months. My sister no longer worked in their office, but they still wanted to check on me. I was an individual, not a constituent from his party. They were decent people who recognized a horrible situation. If he ran today, I'd vote for him.

My parents didn't discuss politics often and their affiliation changed with certain elections. My mother yelled, "Reagan's pushing us into war!" or "Carter was no saint." My father cursed every Democratic New Jersey governor over taxes. Individuals mattered.

When chemo ended and I recovered enough to work, I immediately found a job as an administrative assistant. The company handed me my first medical insurance card and I was elated. Collection agencies were calling me daily for thousands owed to the hospital. Eventually, I had to file Chapter 7 bankruptcy.

Thankfully, I found a great job and got back on my feet. For two decades, I've been in remission. I'm forever grateful to my family and Jim Saxton, a moderate Republican congressman who showed understanding, compassion, and saved me.

We need to take care of each other.

HOW BOXING MADE ME A BETTER DOCTOR

By Olaf Kroneman, MD, Quartz, October 25, 2017

I recognized Ali Haakim, the 55-year-old black man in my Royal Oak office, as one of the best professional Detroit boxers since Joe Louis. As the Michigan Heavyweight Champion, he'd ranked eighth in the world. Now he was sick. I wanted to help.

"I've heard of you. You were famous," I said.

"Back in the day," he told me.

"I fought in the Detroit Golden Gloves tournament in 1968," I told him.

"Right after the riots? Why?" he asked.

"I wanted to understand why the races couldn't get along." I said. "Muhammad Ali was my hero."

"Boxing can cure hate," he said. "Were you any good?"

"Not bad for a white guy," I admitted.

When I was in high school, boxing in downtown Detroit for four years made me more open-minded. I tried new exercises like jumping rope. It taught me how to be disciplined, to make split second decisions in the ring and not second guess myself—all traits that helped me through medical school. Now, as a 65-year-old white doctor, I wanted common ground with Ali. I told him that his kidneys were failing and soon he'd need dialysis. He didn't flinch, accepting the verdict as if he'd just lost to a hometown decision.

"Doc, I don't want to go on the machine. What about a new kidney?"

"It's difficult to go directly to kidney transplant," I said. "There's a long waiting list."

"I've seen too many brothers decline on dialysis," he said.

I nodded. "Black people have four times higher incidence of kidney failure than Caucasians because of genetics and the environment," I said. More than half of my patients were black or Latino. I explained another option. If he was willing to risk a kidney that wasn't the best quality, it might help him avoid dialysis. "But it's a risk."

"Every time I stepped into the ring I took a risk. I fought Ernie Shavers. He could kill you with either hand. This is no different," he said. "Doc what would you do?"

"I'd rather take a chance with an extended donor kidney than fight Ernie Shavers."

"You're not experimenting?" he asked.

I flashed to the Tuskegee syphilis study that ended in 1973, the year I entered medical school. The first physician who protested was Dr. Irwin Schatz of Detroit's Henry Ford Hospital, who complained to the Public Health Service, who never replied.

"No, this is not an experiment," I reassured.

"I trust you."

Three months later Ali received a kidney that worked. When he returned to my clinic, he was fit. He'd gained twenty pounds, his health robust. "Doc, I never knew how bad I felt," he said. "Funny the kidney was from a white man. We're all the same on the inside, where you can't see color."

"We have interchangeable parts. Now we need interchangeable hearts," I said.

"I've been blessed. I'm going to give back," he said. "I'll open a gym. Get the kids off the street. Teach them to box. Girls too."

I offered to donate money but he really needed a doctor for tournaments.

"A doctor as in me?" I was uneasy.

My Christian-Danish background and patient advocacy often got me in trouble. What if someone was hurt during a tournament? I'd taken an oath to do no harm. Was it too dangerous? Amateur boxing ranked the twenty-third most dangerous contact sport. Football and hockey were more dangerous. Soccer, basketball, lacrosse, track and field, wrestling, competitive swimming and diving had more reported injuries.

Still I took out a liability policy and worried about venturing into black neighborhoods that might not welcome me. Then I realized Ali took a risk in my operating room with a marginal kidney. He trusted me in a medical world that many minorities viewed with suspicion. I'd trust him in his world. At the tournament, the audience stood and sang the Star Spangled Banner, a cappella. In the bout, two ten-year-old boys boxed for one minute with a one minute rest in between. Their form was excellent, their punches made safe by the equipment, more like fencing. When it was over the crowd applauded and the boxers bowed. The headgear was removed, revealing proud smiles.

I examined the boxers. They were fine. With older fighters, when a blow landed, the fight was stopped, the fighter examined. Vigilant people at ringside could stop a match. At one point when I stopped a match, the referee told me "No kid ever died of a bloody nose," implying I was being too vigilant so I backed off a bit. Women in the ring had headgear with a face-guard, large gloves, and technique. A predator would have his hands full if he tried messing with them. With a daughter and three grand-daughters, I'd been opposed to women boxing. No longer.

In the last three years, I've taken orders from mostly black and Latino coaches, trainers and referees who were very fair and diligent committed to their sportsmanship. It was the kind of loyalty and collegiality I'd found lacking in my predominately white male medical establishment, where I'd witnessed more cheap shots out of the ring.

When Ali thanked me and offered a stipend, I told him to give it to his gym, Haakim's Boxing and Achievement Academy, to help the kids out. Recently, one of his young boxers won the World Boxing Federation Middleweight boxing title and is in line for the world WBO title. Other boxers are ducking him because he's so good. His name is Winfred Harris Jr., aka "The Hot Boy."

Ali gave me a gift one day: a navy blue beret. "This is the same kind that Jack Johnson wore in 1909," he said. "You'll be fly for a white guy." I wasn't. But I still volunteer as a fight doctor in Detroit, which makes me a better person and a better kidney doctor.

ALWAYS A BED-WETTER, NEVER A BRIDE

By Lavanya Sunkara, New York Times, December 7, 2011

As a travel writer for a luxury magazine, I get to sleep in exotic locations on top of memory-foam mattresses with 800-thread-count sheets. It is a major indulgence, since for most of my childhood and my early teens, I slept on the floor on wet sheets and a rubber mat.

I grew up in a town called Garividi, on the outskirts of Visakhapatnam, a steel port city on the eastern coast of India. Garividi was slightly more advanced than a village because it had an iron ore factory that brought businesses, schools and a hospital there when I was a kid in the 1980s. But it didn't have pharmacies selling Pull-Ups or doctors providing medication for chronic bed-wetters like me. And so, four to five nights a week, until high school, I woke up with a wet blanket under me and guilt over my head.

We lived in a small one-bedroom apartment, next to a noisy movie theater and opposite a dairy farm. My father, a college professor and the head of the household, occupied the only bed we had while my mother slept next to my little brother and me on the floor. She wanted to make sure we didn't feel neglected. But before she put me to sleep, she gave me a nightly warning,

"You better not be lazy and wet the bed again!"

Almost every morning she woke up cursing. After sending my dad off to work, she dragged the soaked linens out and washed them by hand while the neighbors watched. Everyone knew about my "condition." "Who would marry someone who wets the bed every night?" she'd ask me. As loving as she was, staying up late to help me with my homework and cooking my favorite meals, she was just as harsh about my humiliating nocturnal habit. Neither of my parents could understand that I had no control over it.

The older I got, the harder it became. My best friend, Niru, who was among the few who accepted me, had no clue why I could never sleep over. I rarely spoke up at school, never played sports, failed at singing and dancing, sat in the back of the class and hid my low grades from my parents.

Then, when I was 15, my family moved to the United States. During the weeks we spent packing our things and the long hours on the plane, I convinced myself that my condition wouldn't be a problem in America. Somehow the change in time or climate would solve it. I was eager to leave my past behind. When we moved in with my mom's older sister—my pedamma—in Astoria, Queens, my mother warned me: "Don't shame our family here. They don't know about your problem. If they find out, they could kick us out sooner than we could afford to leave."

For the first few weeks, things went smoothly—either because I was too scared of falling asleep or I was hardly drinking any water. Yet, one night, when I crashed on my aunt's lavish living room couch after a long day of exploring the Museum of Natural History, my bladder emptied itself. There was no rubber mat underneath to stop the urine from seeping through the fancy, cream-colored cushions. I woke up early and panicked, rubbed the soiled area with a wet cloth, sprayed air freshener and flipped the cushion upside down, praying no one would find out.

But that afternoon, as I was reading the latest horror by R.L. Stine in the Queens library next to my dad, who was browsing the help wanted section of the newspaper, his cellphone rang. "They found what you did and we must go home immediately," he told me.

"Who would marry someone who wets the bed every night?"

Blood rushed to my head and my cheeks burned. My secret was out. I sweated through my blouse during the 20 minute walk of shame back home. Both families sat down around the dining table to discuss my problem. My mother's gaze was hotter than the chai she poured into our cups. Then Uncle Murthy, a generous man and my only sympathizer, looked at my sorry face and broke the silence. "How come you never took her to a urologist?"

We had come from a place where it was hard enough to get a doctor to take care of the most serious health issues, let alone something as private (and embarrassing) as bed-wetting. The doctors in our extended family just told my parents to be patient until I grew up, when my bladder would be bigger. But my uncle's words gave me hope.

THE BYLINE BIBLE

The next week, I took the 7 train to a clinic near Flushing to meet with a urologist my father had found. After running tests and taking my medical history, the doctor diagnosed primary nocturnal enuresis, involuntary nightly urination that continues past the age of 5. I was one of only a few adolescents to have this condition continue into the mid-teens.

Since behavioral-based treatments like nightly wakeups failed and bedwetting alarms held little hope at this later stage, the doctor put me on a common drug used to curb bed-wetting. Within a few months, I started to wake up dry.

The relief that came with the end of my bed-wetting era afforded me a new life. I started feeling more confident; I made friends; I joined moot court. Teachers started to like me, and encouraged me to apply for college scholarships. When I got into Fordham University, my parents couldn't have been prouder. It seemed all my problems were behind me.

Upon graduation, I moved to Berkeley, worked for the Sierra Club, and eventually went back to school with hopes of becoming an environmental lawyer. Through an Indian outdoor group, I met and fell in love with an aspiring software entrepreneur. Although he came from a completely different world, growing up upper middle class in Silicon Valley, with an Indian father and a white mother, we bonded over our progressive values and love of nature.

But after we had dated for two years, he cheated on me, and then said he couldn't marry me—he had always imagined that his wife would be white as well. I was devastated. I felt like my mother's warnings had come back to haunt me. One morning, instead of waking up with a wet blanket underneath me, I woke up with a dark cloud above. The mild depression I had suffered for years turned clinical. I dropped out of law school when a mental breakdown landed me in the hospital.

This time, my family came to my rescue. They didn't criticize me for my "condition." They didn't think it was my fault. They flew out to California and brought me back to New York, to their new home on Long Island. And this time they sought medical assistance. They took me to a psychiatrist and waited patiently for my recovery. They were everything they weren't when I was growing up. My father said he believed in me when I was struggling to find a job in the tough economy. My mother listened and offered to help when I worried about my law school debt. Some nights, when I couldn't bear to fall asleep, she would get in bed beside me and tell me Indian folk tales. My favorite one was about a father who teaches his sons that a single twig is far easier to break than a bunch of them together.

Five years later, I'm happy and healthy, and still in New York—the city that became my family's home; the city that saved me twice.

RHODE ISLAND AUTHOR SEARCHES FOR FATHER'S FORGOTTEN GRAVE

By Judith Glynn, Providence Journal, April 7, 2016

I hardly knew him but he shaped my life. A thank-you was owed. But where was he? My errand that day was to purchase a kitchen countertop, not search for my father's grave. But as I drove past St. Francis Cemetery in Pawtucket, I suddenly wondered if he was buried there.

Although my memory of him had faded, I turned into the cemetery feeling an urge to honor my dad. After all, I was his only child. But after my mother left him due to his heavy drinking, we had little contact. She had to work full-time. I was 6 and alone too often, instability and poverty ruining my childhood.

The hum of traffic turned still in the hallowed ground as I entered a chapel I assumed kept burial records. A man was seated at a desk.

"I'd like to know if my father is buried here. His name is Albert Glynn," I said nonchalantly.

"We don't go by name. We need the date of death," he said.

I was ashamed to not know it. Staring at the clerk, I had a flashback to an obligatory deathbed visit at the dismal Howard state facility in Cranston where he was a welfare patient. I was a young married adult with two children. His sister, Dorothy, made me kiss my father goodbye. I was appalled. I owed him nothing. When I returned to my husband and family in their waiting car, I sobbed. Why had she done that to me?

I told the cemetery clerk I'd get the date at the department of vital records.

Instead, I went to the countertop store. A month later when I asked the vital statistics clerk about my father, she said I'd need his date of death, not just his name.

Let it go, I told myself driving to my Fox Point home. But as a divorced mother of four and grandmother to six, my family facts mattered. I had resumed my maiden name when I ended my 14-year marriage. That made me the last Glynn in an Irish Catholic family who'd emigrated from Ireland in the late 1800s to work in Vermont's quarries.

I did have a faded newspaper clip from 1907 announcing my father's premature birth in Montpelier, one that defied death. Adult photos captured his dashing looks and lively brown eyes. He lived in Rhode Island when he and Mother met as hospital employees. She said he had the gift of gab, held odd jobs, smoked Camels and "Mom" was tattooed on his bicep. He was a chronic boozer. She married him despite her father's refusal to walk her down the aisle.

When my mother went into labor for my birth, she put an Aunt Jemima pancake box in her apartment window on South Providence's Sassafras Street. That alerted her neighbor to drive Mom to the hospital. When my father awoke from a stupor, the neighbor slapped his face with a rolled-up newspaper and said he had a daughter.

Until I married at 23, my mother and I led a nomadic existence in third-floor Providence tenements, most on the East Side. She was a proud, feisty woman who worked as a medical secretary. From Dad I received not even a card. His well-off spinster sister, Dorothy, would invite us to her home for Christmas, where my father's loving eyes devoured me. Irish blood connected us with stories and laughter that camouflaged the family rupture. I felt awkward there, knowing my father slept alone in the basement on a urine-stained mattress.

At 39, my marriage dissolved, leaving me dead broke. But I'd acquired ironclad spunk and independence from childhood, enough to embark on a risk-taking lifestyle. After five years as a single mother, and to improve my four children's and my future, I asked my ex-husband to return to the family home in Providence's Elmhurst neighborhood. I moved to Spain with four suitcases and then settled in New York City. My career began as a temp secretary. Eventually, I owned a profitable Manhattan bed-and-breakfast agency, my apartment and rental property.

As for men, I adored them. If unavailable, it was familiar territory. One lover compared me to a courtesan (minus the money exchange). I noticed with most men not business related, I'd primp, become subservient and look for their approval. My father's snub made me prone to dead-end choices.

Now recently retired, I'm reflective and forgiving of my father. I feel deep compassion for his life ravaged by alcohol. Today, I recognize his absence had empowered me to lead a fulfilled life, one I love, minus his harmful, hands-on presence. And it's a life he made possible.

But finding his grave to show respect and absolve him seemed unattainable until I found a musty envelope in my basement, saved after his sister's death. Inside was my father's birth certificate, resplendent with the elaborate penmanship of yesteryear, and his three-inch, yellowed Providence Journal obituary clip. He died at 61, younger than I was now, yet no date of death was listed.

He was survived by his sister and a daughter, Mrs. Benedict Albanese Jr., my married name, and two grandchildren. There had been no Irish wake, only a service at the Monahan Funeral Home, followed by a solemn requiem Mass in St. Sebastian Church, both on the East Side.

"I found your father," said the funeral home director after I inquired about old burial records. "He and his brother George are in a two-person grave at St. Ann's Cemetery in Cranston."

"I'll look for the tombstone when I visit," I said.

"I doubt there's a tombstone. That section isn't well marked," he said, as his voice softened.

"There will be one," I said.

TURKISH DELIGHT INSPIRES A SITCOM IN MANHATTAN

By Asla Aydintasbas, New York Times, June 3, 2001

Surrounded by tacky furniture and lots of marble in a suburban mansion close to New York City sits a frustrated, balding, middle-aged man. He makes a good living, but the daily stress keeps him on edge. He has recurrent nightmares about the past, which he confides to a sensible-looking female therapist.

We are not talking about Tony Soprano, but about Askin Karahanoglu, the lead character in a new Turkish television series that is being filmed largely in New York. "Newyorkgiller" ("The New York Family") is a sitcom about a group of Turkish immigrants who have come to New York in search of luck, love, money, fame or, in the case of one character, jazz.

In Turkey there is tremendous interest in New York City and its way of life. "Sex and the City" has wide viewership on Turkish television, and Istanbul is dotted with restaurants and clubs with names—Paper Moon, Downtown—inspired by Manhattan. The TriBeCa Bakery sells bagels.

"I wanted to demystify the city by showcasing the tragicomic events, real stories, psychological problems and even the culture shock Turks experience here," said Ismail Gunes, the Turkish director, who has directed three television series and six award-winning feature films.

About 150,000 Turkish-Americans and Turks, mostly first-generation immigrants, live in and around the city, according to Egemen Bagis, the president of the Federation of Turkish American Associations. "It's a scattered and eclectic group, ranging from high-society types to college students, plumbers, you name it," he said.

The characters in the series, most played by actors who live here, are similarly diverse. Askin is a self-made millionaire who like many Turks entered the United States illegally years ago by jumping from a ship off New York. Talip is a wheeler-dealer who arranges legal and illegal documents for new immigrants. Soner arrives in New York with hopes of making it as an actor, but instead becomes involved in an organized-crime kidnapping.

The 10-part series will be broadcast in Turkey in September. "But if it catches on, we expect a greater budget for more episodes," said Kadir Ali Secer, the production coordinator.

LESSONS LEARNED

By Lorraine Duffy Merkl, New York Family Magazine, November 30, 2001

Never was I so fortunate to have a calm, rational husband beside me, than when my son Luke's Upper East Side school told us they would not be admitting his younger sister.

I had always assumed my daughter, Meg, would be just like my boy, who was smart and funny, athletic and popular. He fit in wherever he went. I was realistic enough to figure they'd have their own interests, but assumed they would fundamentally live the same life.

"She would not do well here," said the principal, explaining that Meg, in their big classes, would not get the one-to-one attention she needed, pointing out how their traditional learning style would not do right by a child who "learns differently."

Intellectually, I understood, but emotionally I couldn't accept that my family was being divided. I looked to my husband, Neil, to pick up my slack and fight for our daughter's rightful place. To my horror he sat listening intently, nodding.

Seeing our opportunity to persuade the principal slipping away, I began begging—offering to hire tutors, even announcing that I would foot the bill to put an assistant teacher in the classroom. Where I would get the money I wasn't sure, but my mouth just kept running.

As I made my pleas, I felt the warmth of a familiar hand on mine. Neil's touch however, was not one that said, "I've got your back," but, "Sit back and be quiet."

The next thing I knew, we had said our good-byes, I had my coat on, and we were standing out in front of the building. We walked the half a block to the corner, in which time I ranted so loudly my voice echoed on the otherwise quiet block, I mentally enrolled both my children in a different school, and the word "sue" left my lips several times.

A cab pulled up and before getting in to go to work, Neil broke his silence to tell me that Luke should stay put and that Meg should attend a school where she is wanted. Then he kissed me and went on his way.

That night, Neil asked if I had investigated possible alternatives for Meg. I told him how I'd spent the day trying to get through to a contact high up on the educational food chain who would surely be able to change the principal's mind.

With a chest-heaving sigh, he slipped his hands into the pockets of his navy blue, Brooks Brothers trousers and like a stately Abraham Lincoln, this man, who is the oldest of seven, began his lecture: "People are different, even if they grow up in the same house," he said. "Everyone has to get where they're going in their own way and time."

I am an only child and was not exposed to the daily anthropological study on human behavior that was his household. I didn't want Meg to be different. I wanted her swathed in a blue blazer with a crest on the pocket. Plus, I couldn't help but think that word would spread along the gossipy mommy grapevine about my failure to procure a place for my child.

"Who cares what people think?" asked my husband.

In the end, it took less time than I thought to find a beautiful school that welcomed my girl. You'd think I would have been grateful, yet after dropping her off the first day, the way I carried on rivaled Meryl Streep's performance in "Sophie's Choice" when she handed her daughter over to the Nazis.

That year, I harassed my son's principal with meeting after meeting to share the progress my child was making at "that other place," hoping to turn the educator's "no" into a "yes."

After a while, my relentlessness lost its charm. Neil put a moratorium on even discussing my ideas. He instead encouraged Meg to do her best and enjoy where she was.

She took her father's advice, and not long after, stopped asking when she'd be able to join her brother.

I was finally able to put to rest the saga of the school that might have been, when last June my son graduated. Only then could I appreciate that, while I was looking over my shoulder at what I couldn't have, Meg had found her groove where she was enrolled. As my husband had predicted, she was getting where she needed to be. A bit more slowly, so is her mother.

THERE WAS NOTHING FUNNY ABOUT THIS COMEDIAN'S APPROACH TO LOVE

By Danielle Sepulveres,
Los Angeles Times LA Affairs
column, November 14, 2015

"Sending direct messages on Twitter is the easiest way to confirm that someone is not to be trusted," my friend declared over brunch, causing me to choke on my $18 Bloody Mary with a mini-cheeseburger garnish. Nonetheless, I remained silent instead of sheepishly announcing that a Twitter DM did, in fact, spark my fairly serious relationship with a comedian.

He had written: "Do you have any plans to come to L.A. any time? Because if so, I would love to take you to dinner. I think you are pretty darn adorable."

Another comedian had warned me about him. "He's a road comic. I've traveled with him and he doesn't know how to be a loyal boyfriend. One night he'll call you from Middle-of-Nowhere, South Dakota, and tell you he's so sorry but he kissed some girl after a show. That's just what happens. And then I'll say, 'I told you so.'"

But I happened to be headed to Los Angeles (my work necessitates lengthy trips from New York to L.A. every few months) and I was feeling pretty adorable. I knew, at least, that we had one friend in common; he, on the other hand, was unaware of any connection. I was just a girl on the Internet whom he happened to find intriguing.

THE BYLINE BIBLE

"I hate how L.A. gets a bad rap," he said when we finally met in person. "I grew up in Los Angeles, so I'm not like those people who moved here from Ohio. I'm so grounded.

"I gotta run, though," he continued. "There's this private screening I was invited to and then a cool after-party."

He told me later that dating a performer, especially in the digital age, requires a strong sense of self—you have to understand that you come second to his work, and you must be secure enough in the relationship to not get jealous about eager audience members or overzealous fans.

He admonished me that I should know the difference between a flirty front-row fan and the faithful woman (me) waiting for him backstage who knows his secrets—such as the fact that he talks in his sleep. I should know the difference between a girl with stars in her eyes and the woman who talks him off a ledge (me) on the days when he's feeling wildly insecure.

"You understand, right, babe?" he said distractedly as he cropped me out of a photo he was posting on Instagram. "I just need to keep my personal life private, so don't tag me if you post it on yours."

When I protested the existence of these two versions of life, he replied: "If we know each other's hearts, that's all that matters."

He'd found me on social media, displaying his public image. I fell for it. But the Internet became the instrument he utilized to halt our progression as a couple in the name of pursuing his career. He needed to appear single and available, insisting that he didn't need to publicly acknowledge me in order for me to understand what I meant to him.

I silently watched him embark on the road to carpal tunnel with his incessant posting about every single person who crossed his path besides me. Still clinging to the thrill manufactured by his initial 140-character promise of something more, I ignored all the red flags.

"If you were a performer," he'd say, "you'd probably understand. This is what's good for my brand."

I understand that "always respect the light" is one of the most basic and important principles for comedians. Even if the audience members are tweeting out your every word, hashtagging your name with "hilarious," and tears are pouring down their faces, when that light comes on, a comedian understands that there's a minute left to wrap up. When the light starts flashing at the 30-second mark, he'd better be ready to smoothly make his exit.

I learned this from many nights watching in clubs, ranging from seedy to opulent. The red light beckoned and the seasoned professionals wrapped up without the slightest hint that they were racing to annihilate that last minute. The less experienced tended to tense up, stilting the delivery of that final joke. Or worse, they blew right through the light, rambling into an incoherent finish.

By ignoring what was right in front of me and blindly putting my faith in him, I was blowing the light. I was overstaying my welcome and breaking my cardinal dating rule. Because loving someone who kept me a secret? Not good for my brand. Babe.

Different Regional Pieces I Published

- "Westside Profile: The New Yorker's Helen Stark is an Institution Within an Institution" (*Westside Press*). Interview with my boss, the head librarian at *The New Yorker*
- "Hidden Upper West Side Galleries Thrive In Clever Spots" (*Westside Press*). A round-up piece of hidden galleries in unusual spots in this Manhattan neighborhood
- "Standing Firm Against the E-Tide" (*The Wall Street Journal*). A third-person reported piece about how the independent Strand bookstore is thriving
- "Adult Education: Teaching at Holy Apostles Soup Kitchen" (*Flatiron News*). An essay about the soup kitchen writer's workshop where I taught
- "Where Creativity Is Cooking: Soup Kitchen Writers Tell Stories of Their Struggles" (*New York Times* Metro section). A roundup of pieces by members of the soup kitchen writer's group where I taught
- "Downtown Feuding Writers Get Nasty" (*The Village Voice*). A round-up piece on all the biggest famous writers' feuds
- "Hey Truman Is My Story: New York Playwright Says Mega-Hit Movie is Based on his Script" (*New York Post*). An investigation into whether a big movie producer stole the theme from a small Off-Off Broadway show
- " A Leg Up For NYU's Aspiring Authors" (*The Wall Street Journal*). A third-person reported piece on a new "book machine" offered at NYU Bookstore
- "Regrets, Even Critics Have a Few" (*The Wall Street Journal*). A third-person reported piece on an unusual event where book critics confessed to mistakes they'd made in the past
- "Another Susie's Story: I Dated a Dylan Biographer" (*The Villager*). A first-person account of how I dated a Bob Dylan lookalike who was writing a biography of the singer/songwriter in the West Village, near where Dylan and his ex-girlfriend once lived

Great Regional Reads by My Students

- "Inside One of Tinder's Controversial Hamptons Parties" by Dale Markowitz (*The Cut*) www.thecut.com/2017/08/tinder-select-hamptons-party-fine-montauk.html
- "While I Adore My Adopted City, I Miss Philly's Strong Tech Community" by Kathleen Garvin (*Technical.ly Philly*) technical.ly/philly/2017/02/10/kathleen-garvin-penny-hoarder
- "No More Summers: The End of the Coney Island Mom-and-Pops" by Valerie Georgoulakos (*New York* magazine) www.grubstreet.com/2011/09/no_more_summers_the_end_of_one.html
- "Profiling for a Seat" by Dvora Meyers (*The New York Times*' Metro section) www.nytimes.com/2010/10/24/nyregion/24nystory.html
- "The Joy of Sax: I Busked Without Getting Busted" by David Sobel (*The Villager*) thevillager.com/2015/07/23/the-joy-of-sax-i-busked-without-getting-busted/
- "A Bronx Boy's Life With Cerebral Palsy, Revealed in Tumblr 'Aaronverse'" by Justin Matis (*The New York Times*' City Room blog) cityroom.blogs.nytimes.com/2013/10/28/a-boys-life-with-cerebral-palsy-revealed-in-tumblr-aaronverse
- "Flunking Out at the Food Co-op" by Alana Joblin Ain (*The New York Times*' Metro section) www.nytimes.com/2009/10/25/nyregion/25coop.html
- "Need Hits Home: When Her Mother's Health Took a Downturn, She Called the Bayonne Visiting Nurse Association" by Petra Michelle (*New York Post*)
- "The Fire, and the Mystery" by Laura Silver (*The New York Times*' "The City" column) www.nytimes.com/2008/04/20/nyregion/thecity/20fire.html
- "A Sidetracked Ivy Leaguer Remembers Rye's Chaotic Playland Summer" by Patricia Crowley (Hudson Valley *Journal News*)
- "A Bush In My Yard: Greenwich Democrat Endures a Fundraising Visit by the Presidents" by Robin Horton (*Fairfield County Weekly*)
- "BackTalk, A Tennis Love Feast" by Janet Lee (*The New York Times*' Sports section) www.nytimes.com/2003/08/24/sports/backtalk-a-tennis-love-feast.html
- "Wonderland" by Nicole Ferraro (Mr. Beller's Neighborhood) mrbellersneighborhood.com/2010/03/wonderland

- "The Wise Plumbers" by Merrill Black (*The New York Times'* "The City" column) www.nytimes.com/2008/12/21/nyregion/thecity/21plum.html
- "Revenge of the Mouse Coffins" by Sari Botton (*The Village Voice*) www.villagevoice.com/2007/03/27/revenge-of-the-mouse-coffins
- "A Prodigy, Poised to Sell" by Megan M. Garwood (*The Wall Street Journal*) www.wsj.com/articles/SB10001424052748703992704576305974142659938
- "Fedora Bar Closes" by Mark de Solla Price (*WestView Newspaper*) markdesollaprice.com/wp-content/uploads/2012/09/Fedora_Closes_WestView_2010_August.pdf
- "Tenant Dispute Becomes Battle of Bedsheets" by Seth Kugel (*The New York Times'* New York City section)
- "After Hastening Gentrification, a Brooklyn Super Has Regrets" by Tyler Kelley (*Gothamist*) gothamist.com/2014/05/12/gentrification_brooklyn.php
- "Jersey Teacher Trades PATH for Kayak Paddle" by Alyssa Pinkser (*New York Post*) nypost.com/2008/12/01/sea-train
- "The McNabb Conundrum" by Kelli Gail (*The New York Times'* Sports section) www.nytimes.com/2010/12/05/sports/football/05cheer.html
- "Gossip Swirls" by Paula Roth (*New York Post*) www.pressreader.com/usa/new-york-post/20071205/281844344293330
- "Cars as Closet: Solving the Storage Problem in NYC: A Car Parked On a Chelsea Side Street, Packed to the Gills" by Joe DeBlasio (*Chelsea Now*)
- "Why Going Around with the Top Down is a Breast Bet for Some: Topless Sunbathers in NY Parks" by Christopher McVey (*New York Post*)
- "A Place for a Fan and the Giants to Start Fresh" by Sara Murphy (*New York Times* Sports section) www.nytimes.com/2010/08/15/sports/football/15cheer.html
- "Fung Wah Buses: The Lines are Long, but the Price is Right" by Daniel Derouchie (*GoNomad*) www.gonomad.com/1605-fung-wah-buses-the-lines-are-long-but-the-price-is-right
- "Clothes lines: A Reading Series at Laundromats Adds More than Just Detergent to the Laundry" by Marin Resnick (*Time Out New York*)

CHAPTER 7

It's My Opinion

If you have a volatile personality with a list of pet peeves you keep adding to daily, this is the assignment for you. An op-ed, a brief first-person argument on a timely topic, can also be the fastest and most furious piece to get into print. It's especially good for new writers with strong beliefs and day jobs in other fields, since editors want quick commentary about the ever-changing news cycle from experts who can illuminate different angles of stories as they unfold. You don't need clips or any publishing experience on your résumé to appear on—and get paid by—a top op-ed page. You mainly need an engaging or unusual point of view on a current public conundrum, usually about 600 words. If you're thinking 6,000 words, you're in the wrong section.

The name *op-ed* originated as an abbreviation for "opposite of the editorial page," where short, pithy commentaries by freelancers ran regularly in daily newspapers. Yet "opinion/editorial" is a better way to think of these topical rants that appear around the clock these days. To decide what to write about, scan the daily newspaper or watch this evening's CNN or Fox News. For a prompt, think: *It really pisses me off that ...*

To have success with this format, it's helpful to utilize a relevant "platform" you might not even know you have. Depending on your topic, that could be being a student, teacher, parent, athlete, voter, veteran, immigrant, child of immigrants, businessman, lawyer, doctor, clergy, disabled person, divorcée, pet owner, coin or stamp collector. You also need quick thinking and an understanding of this type of article. Paying attention to news cycles and geography can also work to your benefit.

I once sent a hastily written rant sharing my displeasure over the huge Kmart that landed in my Greenwich Village neighborhood to *The New York Times* at noon, had an acceptance by 2:00 P.M., was sent a copy by midnight, and received a check within a week. Here are the essential elements of a successful and sellable op-ed.

1. **BE TIMELY OR EARLY.** I submitted my Kmart kvetch in the fall of 1996, a month after the local branch opened two blocks from my home. Luckily, that coincided with a front-page debate about whether Manhattan should allow superstores—like Costco and Walmart—to infiltrate the already overcrowded city. (www.nytimes .com/1996/12/12/opinion/learning-to-love-superstores.html) Timeliness is essential in this genre, especially now that online news sites update around the clock. The 2016 presidential election was hot for op-ed writers until November. Then, regular columnists took over the topic so outsiders had to be more idiosyncratic. (My colleague Kate Walter published a piece titled "Hillary Clinton's Loss Made Me Closer to My Mom" in *Newsday* in November, and I used the voter recount in my home state of Michigan as a topical lede that December.) Be sure to factor in lead times and how long it can take an editor to reply, especially if he doesn't know you. If the Fourth of July is next week, your patriotic piece might already be too late. Consider retooling it for Labor Day. Holidays are reliable hooks because they happen every year, so you can plan ahead (or try again next time).

2. **BE A HOTHEAD.** Now's the one time it's good to be an outspoken loudmouth. When my Northwest Airlines flight was cancelled, I penned a scrawl mentioning "Northworst" in the *New York Post*. You should actually avoid coming off too mild-mannered, tactful, or diplomatic. Do not offer all angles of the story. Fight for your side. In this genre, an argument is much better than a discussion.

3. **CONVEY A STRONG LINK TO YOUR SUBJECT.** When you're an expert on a topic, emphasize your authority with the first-person voice, especially if your story resonates in a universal way. Just make sure you do have authority. Unless you have fought in the Iraq war, have lost a family member there, or are from Iraq, your chances of sell-

ing a piece about it are slim. On the other hand, several veterans from my classes have sold pieces on their military experiences. My former student Sharisse Tracey published widely about being an Army wife and mother of four, trying to get work and healthcare for her autistic son while her husband was deployed. (www.dame magazine.com/2015/11/10/marrying-military-can-kill-your-career)

4. **ADD FACTS.** When crafting your piece, keep asking yourself what's new, fresh, or unusual. Include specific or obscure factual information, up-to-date statistics, and direct quotes from top scholarly publications and university studies to support your argument. In an op-ed I wrote for the *Los Angeles Times* and *Newsday* timed to marijuana legalization, I chronicled my past addiction to the drug. I carefully weaved in statistics about pot use from the *New England Journal of Medicine*, the *Diagnostic and Statistical Manual of Mental Disorders*, a Columbia University research study, and the National Survey on Drug Use and Health, which estimated that half of daily marijuana smokers become addicted—approximately 2.7 million people in the United States. The piece caused a stir and was picked up by twenty other newspapers. (No, I didn't get any more money for it, but it got great exposure.) A reporter from the *Atlanta Journal-Constitution* even did a separate article fact-checking my information—which she found to be correct. (www.latimes.com/nation/la-oe-shapiro-marijuana-danger-20150104-story.html)

5. **DON'T ADD THESE FACTS.** Please don't Google and add lines verbatim from blogs, Wikipedia, or a source you've never heard of. Beware of the fake news that's out there. When in doubt, use established, accredited publications like *The New York Times, The Wall Street Journal, The Washington Post,* or *The Economist*—with correct attribution to one person. ("According to a recent *Wall Street Journal* column by Peggy Noonan ...") Also feel free to cite the president or dean of such famous organizations as Planned Parenthood, Alcoholics Anonymous, Harvard Law School, the U.S. Bureau of Labor Statistics, or the *Journal of the American Medical Association*. Someone could still make a mistake or repeat

misinformation. So double—or triple—check your accuracy. Try to get a direct quote by e-mail whenever possible since, if there's any later dispute, that quote could exonerate you.

6. **DON'T RESTATE THE OBVIOUS.** Even if you can pen a smart argument on a topical subject, nobody wants to print what everyone already knows: War is bad, public schools have no money, healthcare is expensive. Instead, play devil's advocate, be counterintuitive, find an offbeat solution, argue a more original point, or elucidate as only you uniquely can. Instead of saying "Medical insurance is too expensive," my student Justin Matis's *Slate* piece about finding cheaper doctors out of the country was titled "How to Solve the Health Care Crisis—With a little help from some Indians."

7. **BE A CONTRARIAN.** While many minorities were decrying the unfairness of standardized testing in New York schools, my student Miral Sattar wrote a piece titled "Foes of Standardized Tests for Students Have It All Wrong." She told the story of moving from Pakistan to a Queens classroom, where the school's administration mistook her quiet disposition for an inability to speak English. They put her in English as a Second Language courses and the lowest level groups for reading and math. In fourth grade, her entire school took required tests and she shocked everyone—including her teacher—by scoring the highest in her grade. The exam saved her education—and later won her a clip in the New York *Daily News*. (www.nydailynews.com/opinion/foes-standardized-tests-students-wrong-article-1.968369)

8. **KEEP IT SHORT AND SOUR.** Most of my successful cranky op-ed pieces and those of my students are between 300 and 900 words—in such national publications as *The Wall Street Journal* and *The Washington Post* and as local as *amNewYork* and New Jersey's *The Star-Ledger*. Longer pieces tend to be penned by well-known scribes, senators, and regular columnists. Many editors post guidelines on their websites about exactly what they are looking for. Stick to their word lengths. If you send a 2,000-word screed to an editor looking for 500 words, you might be deleted without any response.

9. **TARGET YOUR AUDIENCE.** Here's a sneaky way to learn about a publication's politics, geographical preferences, and tone—read it first! *The Wall Street Journal, The Washington Times, New York Post*, and *Commentary* magazine are slanted to the right politically and probably won't run many left-wing screeds by unknowns. The left-leaning *The Nation, Newsday,* and *Slate* aren't likely to print a newcomer's anti-blue-state rant. Beware of citing New York or Los Angeles landmarks in a piece aimed for *The Boston Globe*, the *Miami Herald*, or a website with national or international readers. Similarly, financial references should depend on demographics. Mentioning private schooling, Ivy League college, and Neiman Marcus will probably go over better in *New York* magazine or the *Palm Beach Post* than in *The Nation* or *The Detroit News*.

10. **MINE YOUR MULTIPLE PERSONALITIES.** To publish lots of op-eds, divide and conquer, like the heroine played by Toni Collette in the 2009–2011 Emmy Award-winning Showtime series *United States of Tara*. I don't mean lie, fake it, or get a psychological disorder. Just focus on your different interests to take on varied subjects. If you trash the verdict of a public trial and you're a lawyer, identify yourself as such. Commenting on parenting issues, mention if you have two children or three grandkids. To write for *Ebony, The Irish Times, The Christian Science Monitor, The Forward,* or *Asian Fusion*, state your religion or ethnicity in the cover letter, the piece, and your bio. I've explored many identities in various voices. To share my side of an education debate, my byline was "Susan Shapiro is a journalism professor at The New School and New York University." Arguing in a women's magazine that a human matchmaker is better than an algorithm, I bolstered my street cred with "Susan Shapiro has fixed up thirty marriages and was set up with both her husband, and his runner up." Aiming for *The Fix*, a website about substance abuse, I called myself "a former addict." Pitching *The Jerusalem Post*, I'm a "nice Jewish girl who often visits her thirty-two beloved cousins in Tel Aviv."

11. **LAST MINUTE USUALLY LOSES.** While sometimes you have to rush a very newsworthy piece before somebody beats you to the paper,

many timely pieces can be well planned. I wouldn't recommend submitting a Thanksgiving op-ed on November 22, since most editors pick their Turkey Day kvetches weeks earlier, or a Christmas-themed saga on December 24, when many staffers are on vacation. My students often point to essays that run on the eve of a big day. I often point to the byline of the full-time columnist who probably filed his story a week earlier. Frantically sending your screed to editors you don't know over a holiday weekend is more likely to lead to a headache than a happy ending.

12. **DON'T SIMULTANEOUSLY SUBMIT.** Aim your piece for one specific publication, write a great cover letter, and send it in. Then wait—at least a few days. The system does work and many top opinion editors will read (or at least skim) hundreds—if not thousands—of pieces from strangers they are sent 24/7. It is not considered fair to submit the same op-ed to many places at the same time. Often an editor who likes your submission must shore up support from higher-ups at a meeting. Imagine the dismay when the editor comes back to give you good news and you have to say, "Oops, already sold it elsewhere." You may end up on that editor's blacklist.

13. **DON'T COMMENT ON ANOTHER COMMENTARY.** Although it seems like an editor might want to print your contrary opinion to the essay she ran yesterday, she doesn't. (Unless you want to publish a comment or letter to the editor, which you won't be paid for and doesn't count as a clip.) Editors are also reluctant to run pieces trashing another specific article. I remember trying to publish a piece on *Newsweek*'s sexist cover story saying a woman would be more likely to get killed by a terrorist than find a husband if she's over forty. Several editors told me they didn't want a freelancer trashing another publication and suggested I try a broader piece on the proliferation of sexist attitudes about middle-aged females in the press. Furthermore, a rant wrapped solely around one movie, book, play, or TV show can feel more like a review than an op-ed. You're better off depicting trends or commenting on a bunch of current movies, books, plays, or TV shows in an overview or cultural commentary, which can still work as an opinion piece.

14. **BE TRENDY.** If it happens three times it's a trend, and editors love arguments and diatribes about what's hot and happening in the world. My former student Erica Kennedy launched her career with a piece in the New York *Daily News* decrying how Gwyneth Paltrow, Reese Witherspoon, and Scarlett Johansson-type blondes were not a good standard of beauty for New Yorkers of color. Finding a triplet of new first-person books by women that were a little too graphic for her taste, another student bemoaned the trend of female memoirs filled with bodily fluids in an article for *Salon*.

15. **FOLLOW UP.** Some editors say if they don't get back to you within 48 hours, the answer is no. But maybe they never received your submission because of a fluke. A *Village Voice* editor I thought was ignoring me turned out to be on maternity leave (and wound up taking my piece). I was hurt that another editor I knew from *The Wall Street Journal* wasn't returning my e-mail, only to find that he'd left the publication. Another time I had the wrong e-mail address. To make sure your op-ed landed where you intended, make sure you're following up politely within a few days. Attach and paste your piece again. And if anything happened that makes it timelier, make sure to mention that you have a newer lede.

16. **ASK FOR DETAILS BEFORE IT RUNS.** Some places, like *HuffPost*, don't offer remuneration for op-ed pieces. Even publications that pay run many pieces in their op-ed section by elected officials and charity heads who don't expect payment. So several newspaper editors I know won't mention their usual fifty- to four-hundred-dollar fee for op-eds unless the writer asks and sends an invoice. Don't wait until it's too late. The minute an editor e-mails or calls to say she is interested in taking your piece, speak up. Inquire if the publication pays, how much, if she'll need a revision, when, and how to properly send an invoice. The squeaky writer gets the clip—and the check.

17. **PREPARE FOR TROLLS.** Because op-eds spout controversial, risky takes on hot-button issues (like abortion funding, legalizing drugs, and euthanasia), those who disagree relish weighing in, often rudely or insanely. My mentors advised me not to read the comments, or at least not to respond to the crazies. After my anti-marijuana

piece ran, readers who seemed threatened that I could take away their stash wrote vociferous commentary. A few critics found my phone number and called me screaming I was wrong. (Though I also had a sad grandmother who called to lament that her sixteen-year-old granddaughter was dating a dealer and had dropped out of school to be with him.) A student who published an op-ed about noise pollution in her new neighborhood felt freaked out by the vehement response. (She was white and mentioned loud rap music blasting at a local club until 3:00 A.M., prompting some to call her racist.) She took the piece off her website and Facebook page and decided to pursue less explosive subjects for a while. Anything can set people off. If you can't stand the storm, don't submit a screed to this intentionally provocative section.

18. **BE SOCIAL MEDIA SAVVY.** Some people love courting controversy and use it to further their success and stardom. The cranky Ann Coulter, Maureen Dowd, Camille Paglia, and Howard Stern come to mind, as well as Al Franken, who launched his writing career with the books *Rush Limbaugh Is a Big Fat Idiot*[1] and *Lies: And the Lying Liars Who Tell Them*[2] (before winning—and then losing—his senatorial seat). If you want to throw gasoline on the flames and watch it explode, don't be afraid to be out there in your title, piece, and bio, offering clickbait. The minute your op-ed comes out, share, tweet, and post it and ask your friends and colleagues to join in. This is what the Internet is great for. Often the more hits, shares, and comments you get, the more an editor might pay attention to your voice and even solicit you for another piece. After someone reads my newspaper op-eds, I've been asked to do a column, TV spots, and several radio interviews. If it's just in print, I take a picture of the page with my iPhone and share my byline that way on Instagram, Facebook, and Twitter. Also check to see if and when the publication posts it and boost their audience with your own. An opinion page can be the perfect place to share your witty, wise,

---

1. Delacorte Press, 1996
2. Dutton, 2003

or warped perspective with a huge audience and initiate your own career launch or relaunch.

POINTED OP-EDS BY MY STUDENTS

NEW YORK'S COLUMBUS ESCAPES A TOPPLING

By Jakki Kerubo, Wall Street Journal, January 16, 2018

New York mayor Bill de Blasio last week announced the city will retain monuments to disputed figures like Columbus and Theodore Roosevelt but "focus on adding nuance and details." As an immigrant from Kenya, where all colonial symbols were removed at independence, I kept my head down as the Robert E. Lee monument debate raged on last year. I didn't fully fathom why it took nearly a century for Americans to confront the problem with Confederate fountains.

But my thoughts about the debate bubbled to the surface on a recent trip to London. While chasing the elusive sun, I felt the dull throb of my intricate past with England. On previous visits, I hardly noticed the memorials of war heroes in Westminster. This time, I did—and they made me angry. I was reminded of the torture and killings of tens of thousands of my home country's freedom fighters under the orders of these British generals. I now understood why many Americans were wounded by bronze casts.

At the height of anticolonialism, writer and activist Ngugi wa Thiong'o wrote "Decolonising the Mind," which offered a radical solution for Africans: Abandon the language the possessors used to transmit their culture, and speak and write only in the mother tongue. A noble idea, for as Tom Wolfe has written: "Speech, and only speech, gives the human beast the power of accurate memory and the means to preserve it." For me that meant, impossibly, renouncing the English language and all it's come with: Jane Austen, George Orwell, Netflix's *The Crown*, my Christian faith, and a thousand other things.

There was no escaping history's jagged edge and its long reach. Despite the rage I felt toward the British Empire, and the occasional pang of self-loathing for not possessing a purely African sensibility, I recognized that much of what I enjoy in life is the result of the cultural influence of imperialists. From boarding school to afternoon tea rituals to romanticized safaris, my native traditions were very much intertwined with those of the colonialists. King George V's statue may have been removed in Nairobi, but his legacy lived on through the churches, tea farms, and the powdered horsehair wigs Kenya's Supreme Court justices wear.

I am now an American, and fast accumulating new histories. Although I may not connect deeply to America's past, I share its future with fellow citizens. Mr. de Blasio's moderate resolution after months of deliberation and public debates across the city reflects the personal and complicated nature of our collective history. Obliterating offensive sculptures won't miraculously convert supremacists who idolize the darker side of history. Nor will it ameliorate our racial strife.

Centuries ago, great figures in U.S. history were also responsible for great evil. Statues were erected in their honor to reflect the values of their time. Our ethics have evolved, but today our cultural maturity should allow us to view these sculptures as part of a record. It's not an honor. It's a lesson.

YOGA TEACHERS NEED A CODE OF ETHICS

By Sarah Herrington,
New York Times, June 7, 2017

I was relieved when Bikram Choudhury, the 73-year-old founder of Bikram yoga, was finally served a warrant for his arrest late last month, after failing to pay nearly $7 million in legal fees he owes for a sexual harassment lawsuit. Many in the yoga world had been waiting for that moment, after years of rape and assault claims against Mr. Choudhury, the millionaire creator of a 26-posture "hot yoga" sequence and studio system. But the news brought only a grim satisfaction; many of us wish he'd been arrested for the assault claims themselves.

Unfortunately, the case of Mr. Choudhury is not unique. In 2016, a beloved teacher in the New York City-based Jivamukti Yoga center, known for its celebrity clientele, was sued, along with the center and its leaders, for sexual abuse by her mentee. John Friend's Anusara community was rocked and dissolved in 2012 after he was discovered having affairs with married students and performing Wiccan-like sex rituals. Kripalu's Amrit Desai was accused of sexual misconduct and abuse of authority in 1994 and a $2.5 million settlement was paid (the Kripalu Center in Massachusetts divorced itself from Desai and reorganized). And there are, of course, countless under-the-radar stories of yoga teachers coming on to students or touching them inappropriately in class.

This must stop. As a practitioner of yoga for 20 years who has been teaching for a decade, I know that people often approach spiritual practices like yoga and meditation when they are vulnerable. They come recovering from broken bones and hearts, and usually at some greater personal crossroads. They come with trauma, addictions or eating disorders. They come after divorce. They come with hope.

In this state of vulnerability, it is absolutely critical that students feel safe. Teachers, like therapists or educators in other fields, have an inherent power, which can be used to either heal or exploit. But because it is also easy to conflate the goodness of yoga with the teachers themselves, instructors can benefit from an aura of ethical conduct, or even holiness—what some call a spiritual blanket that protects those who abuse their power. While it is up to students to discern between teacher and teachings, those in authority have a responsibility to protect.

According to the 2016 Yoga in America survey co-sponsored by Yoga Journal and Yoga Alliance—the largest nonprofit in the United States representing the yoga community and providing teacher-training requirements—there are 36.7 million yoga practitioners nationwide, 72 percent of them women. Though Yoga Alliance has published a bullet-point code of conduct, few know it exists until they are explicitly looking, and by then it may be too late.

I have personally seen things go wrong. Early in my practice I became involved with a meditation teacher and learned, after the breakup, that he had dated students serially. I lost my community. I've received inappropriate sexual Facebook messages from well-respected teachers and have had my bottom slapped (*not* an adjustment) in a balancing pose. Though these actions are not as serious as the egregious behavior Mr. Choudhury and others have been accused of, they provided a personal window into the hurt and confusion crossed boundaries can create.

Yoga transformed my life: healing a back injury, giving me tools to work with my anxiety and providing a spiritual home. Had it not, I would have quit. Some victims have quit, and face years of trauma from what should have been a refuge from the hurt of life: spiritual practice. This sort of violation denotes rape on many levels: spiritually, mentally, emotionally and, yes, sometimes physically.

When I began teaching yoga at an all-girls charter school in Lower Manhattan, we took the first class to create a "yoga contract." Girls from 5 to 12 years old brainstormed and signed lists of rules to "keep everyone safe and happy" during practice. Rules they themselves invented included "respect others' space" and "use active listening." As the teacher, I signed, too. We ended each class with a Sanskrit chant that translates to, "The one true teacher lives in the center of your heart." I wanted these young girls to know, though teachers are helpful guides, the one true authority is inside of them. I wanted them to carry this lesson forward into their adult yoga world as women. Mr. Choudhury and others like him could learn plenty from these girls.

I'm hopeful the arrest warrant for Mr. Choudhury will ignite this conversation in spiritual communities. I believe all organized yoga teacher training should include training in ethics and, if affiliated with Yoga Alliance, point students toward that resource. Each community center, meditation group and yoga studio should post a code of ethics, as Jack Kornfield's Spirit Rock community recently did. Every center should have a formalized, safe place to report abuse seriously and anonymously. Even secular yoga studios should provide this service, alongside mats and towels. We cannot rely on karma alone.

THIS SELFIE WILL BE FOR THE AGES

By Ralph Ortiz, AMNY, February 8, 2017

My 21-year-old daughter, Mimi, loves Bernie Sanders and sharing her life through social media. I was with Hillary Clinton, and I'm sick of social media. Yet we share this in common: We're graduating college in May.

Mimi is a senior at St. John's University, while I'm at The New School. We've shared study sessions, and she's even asked for my help.

She went to college at 18. My wife and I worked hard for that. I didn't want her to be like me; it took me 24 years to get here. I dropped out of high school at 16. I tried to earn a degree in that time, but school was interrupted by marriage, parenthood and homelessness.

Last fall, Mimi and I met at Washington Square Park and walked toward NYU's Elmer Holmes Bobst Library. We sat on a bench and I turned to her: "When I was at New York University, I was homeless and slept on this very bench."

"What happened?' Mimi asked in shock.

I was a clerk at an insurance company that took a financial hit paying policyholders impacted by a hurricane. When the dust settled, I got $1,000 in severance pay. I had fallen behind on my rent, by two months. I had the money but paid my tuition at NYU.

My landlord was a friend so I thought he wouldn't mind. He did. After I was laid off, I went to see my then-girlfriend who had invited me to lunch.

I was happy to see her. But before I could tell her what happened, she said, "We need to break up." She was starting to get busy with classes and hospital rotations and didn't have time for me.

Two days later, after looking for work, I came home. Agustin, the landlord, stood by my door. "You gotta leave," he said. A month later, I was still sleeping on the streets. I hated the stigma of being poor. I didn't say anything to family or friends.

At 4:45 one morning a police officer woke me up and said that sleeping in the park wasn't allowed. I walked out, reaching a garbage can on the corner of Waverly and Washington. I was hungry, so I went digging. The first time I ate from the garbage, I had a bologna sandwich with mayo. Disgusting.

I still had my NYU ID card, so I sneaked into the recreation center for a shower. Homeless and 22, I didn't have the skills or degree to get a job. I wanted to go to the public assistance office. But pride would not let me.

During my time at NYU, I met Gene Redondo, a 50-year-old NYU employee. He hired me for a temp job and allowed me to stay in the empty rooms of the dormitories I had to work in. To get me started, he gave me clothes, money and a job as a janitor and painter at NYU.

After I told Mimi the story, there was a long pause. "So my dad slept on a park bench and ate from the garbage?" she asked.

"I knew things were gonna get better," I said.

Later, Mimi and I were in the library. We read, took notes, and shared highlighters. On graduation day, the one selfie I want is of Mimi and I in our caps and gowns. That picture I'll post on Facebook, Snapchat, and Instagram.

WHAT TRUMP TAUGHT ME ABOUT BEING ASIAN AMERICAN

By Stephanie Siu, New York Times, January 20, 2017

Tonight, my Chinese family and I will be at a restaurant in Brooklyn's Chinatown eating fried tofu and Peking duck while Donald J. Trump attends Inaugural Balls. If you told me a year ago that we would be commiserating banquet-style while an internet troll was sworn in as president, I would have snorted derisively into my illegal shark fin soup.

Growing up in Manhattan, the American-born child of immigrants from Hong Kong, I was embarrassed by my family's strange holidays. I never learned to speak the language, or even use chopsticks. Disney's "Mulan" felt like a caricature of every stereotype I was teased about in school. When "Fresh Off the Boat" aired on television, it seemed that people like me were the butt of a nationally understood joke—especially when Chinese people were portrayed by Korean actors.

I dreaded answering "Where are you from?" When I told an elementary schoolteacher "New York," she shook her head and asked, "But where are you really from?" As an adult, I cringed when a classmate asked, "What kind of Asian are you?"—or worse, presumed to guess. On a date two years ago, the blond lacrosse player I met from OkCupid said between bites of sushi: "You're Korean, right? I'm really good at telling Orientals apart." I was horrified at being fetishized for my race—especially one I didn't identify with. I just wanted to be American.

It took a trip to Asia—and Donald Trump—to help me embrace my identity.

After resigning from my Wall Street analyst job because of a chronic wrist injury, I took a solo trip to Asia and went everywhere but China. I didn't want to be around people who looked like me. And indeed, people often treated me like an outsider. In Penang, Malaysia, a smiling woman brought me a bowl of hokkien mee with hot sauce on the side instead of mixed in—a practice reserved for Caucasians. While surfing in Indonesia, a dark-skinned aboriginal laughed at my thin "city people" arms. "You paddle like chicken," he said, before showing me a better way to propel.

In America, I was viewed as Asian. In Asia, I was viewed as American. I had feared being boxed in by what others thought I was. But belonging is personal, fluid and multicultural. I had clung to being an American as my one immutable identity, not realizing that who I was could not be diluted. Being Asian did not make me less American.

Which brings me to Mr. Trump. Sitting on a stool at my mother's house in Brooklyn during one of the presidential debates, I watched him accuse China of using the United States as a piggy bank and of inventing climate change. Though I had spent my life distancing myself from Asia, his xenophobia made me feel personally rejected.

Before I knew it, my brother and I were both shouting at the television. I knew who I was. I am Chinese-American, and he was talking about me.

MOM, DAD, I'VE BEEN FIRED

By Steve Doppelt, Chicago Tribune, June 17, 2012

When my company let me go last month, I never imagined the hardest part would be breaking the news to my mother and father.

As the son of Depression-era Jewish parents growing up in the Chicago suburbs, I had been conditioned to measure success by my salary and job security. My dad ran a scrap metal business, and his career advice had always been a combination of cautious practicality mixed with lessons from Arthur Miller's "Death of a Salesman."

"How's the superstar advertising executive doing?" my dad often asked on the phone, echoing the current Tony-winning Broadway revival. "Are the clients happy with your work?"

"Sometimes you just have to give them what they want," my mom chimed in.

Unfortunately, I wasn't giving them what they wanted. I'd won awards as a copywriter in the early years of my career. Yet as a creative director, I lacked the Don Draper charm needed to make my clients feel like they were the center of my universe.

"Shouldn't you be on a beach somewhere?" I joked at the end of one prolonged Memorial Day email exchange with a demanding chief marketing officer. The following day I was asked off the account.

When I was fired from my latest job, I wasn't terribly surprised. In fact, I was relieved. I was tired of endless meetings, sick of heated arguments over things I was pretending to care about and ready for a change. I reached out to my contacts and made "to-do" lists every morning. But one task eluded me.

"Have you told Mom and Dad?" my brother Rick asked after I broke the news.

"No," I said. "And I'm not going to."

"Smart move."

Like me, he had spurned the family business to pursue a more corporate career.

"You're eventually going to tell them, right?" my girlfriend, Kristin, asked.

"No," I said. "No point."

I explained that at age 83, they didn't need additional worries. I feared that if

I told them, and then either had a heart attack or stroke soon after, I would spend the rest of my life feeling responsible.

But it wasn't just guilt driving my decision. It was shame. I had never been fired before. None of my three older siblings had, either. Unemployment was something that happened to other people's children.

Confronting my parents with failure was uncharted territory. Throughout my straitlaced adolescence, my greatest rebellion was going through a brief period of overquoting Thoreau. The few times I was disciplined in middle school and given a "pink slip," I told my parents it was my friend Sam who'd gotten in trouble. Then I'd strategically wait until they confirmed it was a silly infraction before admitting that it had really been me.

As a grown man of 45, I was now terrified to tell them I'd gotten a much more significant pink slip.

"You have to tell them eventually," Kristin urged.

I knew she was right. My cryptic answers to their questions about work would eventually give me away, and if they somehow found out from another family member, the repercussions would be worse. So I decided to reveal my dark secret during my next visit, so they could see my face as I spoke openly and honestly.

"Well, there's been one big change in my life," I said at their dinner table, feeling like a 16-year-old who'd just totaled the family car.

"You left your job," my dad guessed.

"Yeah, I did," I said. "How'd you know?"

"Well, you've been so unhappy," my mom said. "And lately you've seemed happier."

"Where are you going to be working?" my dad asked. "What did your boss say when you told him?"

I still wasn't off the hook.

"I didn't exactly tell him." I said. "He told me. He let me go."

"They had layoffs?" he asked.

"No, just me."

My dad looked confused.

"Maybe it's for the best," my mom said. "I would cry every night I got off the phone with you. You sounded so miserable."

Kristin jumped in to assure them I'd already been offered several project-based assignments and that I'd have no trouble finding more work.

I explained that as a freelancer I could avoid office politics, choose my own clients and have greater control of my schedule. My dad lit up.

"Ah, so you're going to be a consultant," he said.

Looking at him, I could see how important that word distinction was. A freelancer is out there desperately hustling for work, whereas a consultant is sought out for his expertise. Willy Loman would be a freelancer. My father's son would be a consultant.

"So how's the superstar consultant doing?" my dad now asks every phone call.

"The consultant's doing just great," I always say.

Sometimes you just have to give them what they want.

CALLING THE KARDASHIANS "AMERICA'S FIRST FAMILY" IS AN INSULT TO THE OBAMAS

By Tiffanie Drayton,
thefrisky.com, October 15, 2015

Cosmopolitan just released its 50th Anniversary cover, which features the Kardashian women whom the magazine proudly declares as "America's First Family." Somehow, the magazine must have forgotten that America already has a first family: the Obamas. The presidential family whose mere presence at the forefront of American politics was meant to represent "progress," a legacy that stood as proof that the country could, indeed, overcome its racist past. Sadly, *Cosmo*'s trivialization of the title "first family" shows a blatant disregard for that legacy and for people of color to whom it represents generations of dreams and aspirations realized.

This is not the magazine's first racially insensitive transgression this year. Only a few months ago, the fashion magazine published an article titled "21 Beauty Trends That Need to Die in 2015" which featured photos of women of color in styles *Cosmo* claimed needed to "RIP" beside photos of white women representing the trends the mag approves of, their images captioned "Hello, Gorgeous!" In response to the outcry on social media, which deemed the article racist, the editor responded with this note:

This article focuses on beauty trends with images that represent those trends. Some images have been taken out of context, and we apologize for any offense. Celebrating all women is our mission, and we will continue to work hard to do that.

For a magazine that supposedly aims to "celebrate all women," the visibility of mostly white women versus WOC in that article told quite a different story. And now, calling a family of white women "America's First Family," despite the fact that the country already has a first family (who happens to be Black) shows the magazine continues to fall short of its goal. *Cosmopolitan* does not seem to be genuinely interested in celebrating "all women." White women are still apparently the most important.

Which bring us back to the conversation about the six white women who have somehow supplanted Barack, Michelle, Sasha and Malia Obama as "America's First Family." Yes, designating the Kardashians—who are most famous for a sex tape, reality television, hair extensions, modeling and plastic surgery—the "first family" is unremarkably absurd and obtuse. But more importantly, it trivializes the hardships endured by America's first family throughout Obama's presidency. From the resurgence of White supremacist hate groups when Obama was elected, to cartoon drawings depicting the president as a monkey, constant references to Michelle as a man and the untenable constant scrutinization of Malia and Sasha by the media, there is no shortage of examples that highlight the struggles of America's real first family. What, precisely, have the Kardashians done to earn this title? Let's review.

I suppose, among the aforementioned accomplishments, marrying and/or dating rappers should be listed. Or perhaps parading a big, round derriere on the cover of a magazine while imitating racist Black Jezebel stereotypes is also noteworthy? If not that, then maybe the continued commodification and appropriation of other cultures without remorse? Such are the criterion for a family of white women who aspire to being called "America's First Family"?

The criteria for a Black family, on the other hand, must have at least two Ivy League college graduates, a mother who spearheads various social movements, two teenage daughters who are among the 25 Most Influential Teens of their time, and, you know, a two-term President. Oh yeah, and they must also continue to battle the racist demons birthed by centuries of inequality—gracefully, no less.

Cosmopolitan evidently does not understand why these two families should not share a title. Anyone with a modicum of respect for the legacy of America's (first!) Black first family, however, most certainly should.

RAGE OF THE ASHES

By Richard Dodd, Newsday, May 29, 2015

My memory returned with jagged edges, raw nerve endings, and a panic attack as I filled out the 2015 World Trade Center Health Registry survey this week.

I revisited the apocalyptic sights, sounds and smells rising from Ground Zero that rivaled—not surpassed—the graphic movie trailers for the release of "Mad Max Fury Road."

The registry, the largest post-disaster public health registry in U.S. history, tracks the health of more than 71,000 people directly exposed to the World Trade Center disaster. I enrolled in the program in 2004 and completed the last health questionnaire in 2011. This year's update recorded disturbing changes to my quality of life.

May 30, 2015, also marks the 13th anniversary of the end of the recovery and cleanup operations at the World Trade Center site. For many of the workers and volunteers, this date has life-altering significance. It connects their lives like an umbilical cord to the 9/11 toxic womb that gave birth to respiratory disorders, mental health issues, cancer and other ailments.

In 2001, I was a middle-age business executive living and working near Wall Street. With a faltering marriage and a start-up venture teetering on the brink of collapse as our development team was forced to cease operations and vacate Battery Park City, I volunteered in the rescue and recovery efforts.

On Sept. 28, 2001, I was selected with a team of five other volunteers at the Salvation Army headquarters in Greenwich Village to man a food-and-supply depot called Canteen 1. We were issued security badges and bright-red Salvation Army Disaster Services T-shirts and dispatched to the disaster site in mid-afternoon.

As we navigated through security checkpoints, an opaque dust cloud swallowed our van. Then things went terribly wrong.

I volunteered to find help and stepped outside. Immediately my eyes began to burn. The smells were awful and reminded me of brake pad dust mixed with melted plastic. The air was so thick and grainy—I could chew it.

I approached a tent where a medical professional was meticulously tagging items. He screamed, "This is a restricted area. Get the hell out of here." I realized the items were body parts. In shock, I walked until I found a National guardsman. He guided me back to the van and directed us to our destination where we relieved the previous night's crew.

The canteen reminded me of the food trucks that pull up to work and school locations. We took our positions. I served hot food in the form of Dinty Moore Stew while others handed out candy bars, salty snacks, water and respirators.

Throughout the night we breathed in the smoldering air and wiped hot embers from our eyes. We witnessed bravery. We witnessed heroism.

In the weeks that followed, I coughed the World Trade Center cough until my lungs screamed. I was diagnosed with asthma the following year. Then my health deteriorated severely in 2013.

I remember the meeting with my urologist to diagnose the cause of my urinary tract bleeding.

"Sir, how many packs of cigarettes do you smoke a day?"

"Doctor, I don't smoke."

"Do you work with chemicals?"

"No, I'm a white-collar computer executive. The only time that I recall ingesting large amounts of smoke was when I lived and worked in Lower Manhattan at the time of the 9/11 attack."

"Maybe that's your link," the doctor replied.

I had surgery to remove a cancerous bladder tumor in June of 2013 and underwent six months of chemotherapy. I did some research and discovered that bladder cancer is one of more than 50 types of cancer listed in the James L. Zadroga 9/11 Health and Compensation Act that was signed into law by President Barack Obama in 2011. In February of 2014 the World Trade Center Health Program certified my cancer along with asthma and post-traumatic stress disorder as being linked to my exposure to the toxic air in Lower Manhattan. Ongoing studies funded by the federal government and the New York Fire Department indicate 9/11 responders and volunteers have a 20 percent higher chance of contracting cancer than the general population.

I'm proud of my decision to join the real heroes and the accidental heroes who came together to make a difference. While I signed up as a volunteer, I didn't expect to have my health compromised. Fortunately, my health issues are treatable and there has been no reoccurrence of cancer. I am entitled to receive state-of-the art medical evaluations and treatment for my conditions through the World Trade Center Health Program.

I just completed the registry questionnaire. I wonder how many of the other 71,000 survey responders have experienced significant changes in their health since the last survey.

OK, time to hit the send button ...

I'M HOMESCHOOLED—HOLD THE PITY, PLEASE

By Veronica Andreades, Wall Street Journal, September 8, 2013

"You're home-schooled? That's bad, right?" Another teenager started off a conversation with me that way recently. We're both actresses, and we were waiting for a theater rehearsal to begin.

"Bad? Where did you get that idea?" I replied.

"Well, you don't have any friends, right?"

"I have lots of friends," I said, laughing to hide my annoyance.

Welcome to the life of a Manhattan home-schooler surrounded by supposedly open-minded liberals. This was hardly the first time I've confronted unsolicited comments about going to school at home. Not long ago, after a ballet class (yes, home-schoolers sometimes sign up to study elsewhere), I mentioned in the locker room that I was being educated by my mother. One of the other dancers said: "No offense, but don't your parents care about you being socialized?"

When I asked my mom why she chose to teach me, she said: "I did not want to be at the mercy of my ZIP Code." When you're from a middle-class family supported by a father who is a minister, chances are you aren't going to live in a wealthy area and therefore in a good school district.

I've gotten used to seeing pained or perplexed reactions when I talk about going to school in my apartment, as if I'm this nerdy, introverted alien. The truth is that my parents wanted to give me the freedom to pursue my passions so I'd be better prepared for college and career.

Considering how often people mourn the failure of the U.S. school system, it's remarkable that so many still recoil from the thought of learning at home. They might be surprised to learn that children receiving an education from their parents generally score higher than students in regular school. A 2009 study by the National Home Education Research Institute tracked nearly 12,000 home-schoolers and found that they score an average of 34 to 39 points higher than the average public-school student on standardized tests.

As for home-schoolers' supposed deficit in socialization, research also shows that teenagers studying at the kitchen table can be more socially adept than their peers in the classroom. In a 2012 report on the social development of home-schoolers, Lisa Bergstrom of the University of Wisconsin found: "Many of these home-schooled children surpass their public school counterparts in all areas of development and are successful in college and in careers." Contrary to the stereotype, I am regularly in social situations—like that locker room at the dance academy or the karate studio I go to in the East Village.

Although I enjoy figuring out chemistry problems while lying in bed, I do wish I could go to prom or attend a school basketball game. For years, I've also secretly desired to do my work on one of those chairs with the little desk attached.

Sure, I don't know what a home room is. But I do know what goes into organizing a church retreat for 50 people.

I can balance a budget and navigate an acting audition in New York on my own. The flexibility afforded by home-schooling allowed me to get a focused education while pursuing real-world skills and jobs.

So while others are convinced that home-schooling will stunt me, I take my inspiration from icons like Agatha Christie, Thomas Edison, Venus and Serena Williams, Whoopi Goldberg, Sandra Day O'Connor and Charlie Chaplin—all of whom were taught in their own residences.

THE REDDIT CONNECTION THAT GOT ME INTO COLLEGE

By Eli Reiter, New York Times On Campus, December 25, 2017

I met him online. He texted me on Christmas. Two weeks later, we met in person at a Barnes & Noble.

This is the story of an internet connection that has nothing to do with romance. At 22, I was lost and living at home. I wasn't looking for a date. I was trying to ace the SATs.

It was 2011 and I had recently dropped out of a Maryland rabbinical seminary and moved back into my parents' house in Brooklyn. Although I was back in the community I grew up in, I felt different from everyone I knew. I was depressed and friendless. The internet provided solace and distraction, a community of fellow lonely people. I was particularly drawn to Reddit, which is essentially a mix of popular, crowdsourced links and conversations. The

site has everything, from photos of the cutest kittens to long posts by NASA engineers about designing vehicles for the International Space Station.

One day I came across a post that caught my eye: "IAmA SAT/ACT tutor at the top end of the market in Manhattan. AMA." AMA, in Reddit-speak, means "Ask Me Anything." This generous citizen was answering questions in real-time about how he tutored the best and brightest of the Manhattan prep crowd. He framed the SAT not as a test of knowledge but of "college readiness," and wrote about his strategies for, say, making "Beowulf" relatable to a high schooler. He charged almost 300 dollars an hour, but he got results: Some students added over 700 points to their exams. I was fascinated. Here was someone who held the logical keys to a foreign world I aspired to succeed in: college.

I grew up in an Orthodox Jewish community going to a Yeshiva high school where we got three hours of secular studies each day. Most of our teachers were never formally trained and some were community members who were between jobs. After grade school, I went to seminary both for self-edification and because it was what was expected of me. It's not that college was ever off-limits. I just had no idea how to get there.

But peering into the world of this competent stranger on Reddit, I was overwhelmed by a mix of desperation and hope. I sent him a private message and asked for an hour of his time, but I was upfront about the fact that I couldn't pay. I knew it was a really long shot—his time was clearly very valuable—and I didn't expect him to respond.

But on Reddit, sometimes magical things happen. Although the community is a disparate group of millions of users all around the world and there are plenty of trolls, the website fosters real human connections between strangers. I once received a hand knit scarf and a random assortment of local beer from a Secret Santa whom I never met. Another time, when I expressed interest in astronomy on another conversation thread, someone sent me science textbooks.

So, hoping for the best, I reached out to the SAT tutor, and a few days later he texted me back, introduced himself as James, and we made an appointment to meet.

On a clammy and cloudy Tuesday, I found James in the stacks of Barnes & Noble, wearing fancy boots, jeans and a plaid shirt. He was tall, confident and extremely articulate.

"So, why did you drop out of rabbinical school? Crisis of faith?" he joked.

I told James that I was completely lost about how to get to college. My younger sister, a first-year student at the University of Chicago at the time, was an inspiration, but I had seen how hard she worked to get there, studying for her SATs since the seventh grade, diligently reading daily emails from the College Board with prep questions.

At 22, one glance at the college essay prompts would plunge me immediately into self-doubt. But I passionately wanted to go to school, to foster a curiosity that could not be sated with Talmud. I imagined being mentored by men in tweed jackets sitting in oversize armchairs, our faces illuminated by a crackling fire.

And James was supportive of that (although possibly amused by my vision of college). He spent hours with me that day demystifying the test-taking and application process and sharing study tools that I still find useful. He taught me the tricks to multiple-choice, and how to strategically answer math questions that I didn't recognize. He walked me through my difficulties with subject-verb agreements and showed me how to "hack" large passages of text in order to answer reading comprehension questions.

At one point, we moved our study session to a nearby diner and James talked while I furiously scribbled notes in the back of an old SAT book with yellowing pages. He told me a little bit about himself: He had gone to the fancy prep school where "Dead Poets Society" was filmed and had taken four years of Latin there.

At one point, through bites of bacon and eggs, he started speaking in a strange dialect.

"What are you saying?" I asked when he stopped for breath and another slice of bacon. I was never that close to bacon, and it was distracting: It smelled like pastrami but was a little off, like being on a blind date with someone who is charming and likable but there's no romantic spark.

"That's Chaucer. 'Canterbury Tales,'" he said. "We had to memorize it in high school."

Through our conversation, I felt James's confidence rub off on me and my fear of failure dissipate. I sat higher in my chair. When I went to pay for the breakfast, however, my credit card was declined and I was mortified. A perfect stranger had given me hours of his professional time—free—and I couldn't even pay for breakfast. But he brushed it off, as if it was a nonissue.

For the next two months, I studied incredibly hard. I'd spend long afternoons and evenings at Starbucks, doing practice tests in a zombielike state. The night before the SAT, James sent me a good luck text and reminded me to eat a light breakfast, and bring snacks, a clock and extra pencils. I don't remember much

of that day. I hit the ground running and didn't think. Eight weeks later, I received my score. I had jumped 400 points from my original test, and my writing section was in the 95th percentile.

I thanked him profusely, but didn't see James again for another four years or so. By that point, I was a senior at Hunter College, pursuing a degree in history and minors in linguistics and English. My research on Yeshivish, a dialectical English spoken among sections of Orthodox Jews, had won an award at a conference and I wanted to tell James about the wild success story that had come from his act of charity, and buy that breakfast I owed him.

At a restaurant in Jersey City—this time, kosher and bacon-free—we talked about his life and mine. I was working on applications to fellowships abroad. He was engaged to a doctor and they were moving out West for her job. We were both closing chapters in our lives and starting new ones.

Now I'm an English teacher in a Yeshiva similar to the one I attended, hoping to be the James that I wish I had when I was the students' age. I've been to college and back, prepared to counsel the next generation of students who decide to venture to worlds unknown.

MY ASIAN PUSSYCAT PARENTS

By Kate Chia, New York Times
On Campus, October 17, 2016

The day I received my letter of acceptance to New York University, I was ecstatic. It was my dream university,

and my parents were pleased for me. But they also hadn't pushed me to get into such a competitive school. In fact, the best thing they ever did for me was to discourage my perfectionist tendencies—indeed, when I was in elementary

THE BYLINE BIBLE

school, my dad offered to buy me a present if I got a C.

It happened when I was in third grade. An only child in an Asian family, I had just moved with my family from Taiwan to Los Angeles. Months into third grade, I developed a consuming worry about getting subpar grades. Seeing my anxiety, Dad said, "Kate, tell you what. If you get a C or lower, I'll buy you a present. If you score higher than that, I won't buy you anything, because you won't need it."

"You don't have to break your neck to make a living," my dad said via Skype.

Eventually, I did switch out of the pre-med track, not at my parents' persuasion, but because I realized I didn't enjoy the subjects. I switched to psychology, after falling in love with the Intro to Psych class I took my sophomore year, and graduated with an honors in psychology.

I think it was my parents' lack of emphasis on grades that gave me room to foster my own desire for achievements. I developed a strong work ethic of my own accord, instead of doing it to placate my family. Intrinsic motivation, as it's known in psychology, is doing something because that activity is inherently rewarding. Extrinsic motivation is doing something for outside rewards—praise from parents, money or recognition, for instance. Goal pursuit directed by intrinsic motivation is not only more powerful, but exponentially more fulfilling. I believe that when parents oppressively push their children toward academic success, it prevents them from forming intrinsic motivation for scholarly accomplishments.

That's not to say the harsh tiger parenting tactic isn't effective. Statistics show that Asian-Americans tend to excel academically. They make up just 5 percent of the United States population, but constitute about 20 percent of the student body at Ivy League colleges.

This academic edge, however, comes at a hefty cost. Asian-American students have higher rates of suicidal ideation than white college students, and these pernicious thoughts translate into behavior. At Cornell University, there were 21 on-campus suicides from 1999 to 2006, 13 of which were Asian students. At the Massachusetts Institute of Technology, Asians accounted for 42 percent of student suicides in the last 15 years.

I now realize I was mistaken when I thought I didn't receive a present from my dad that day. He gave me two invaluable gifts: the space to cultivate my own desire for excellence, and the healthy psyche to pursue it.

IN NEED IN NEW YORK

By Alex Miller, New York Times, June 21, 2012

A native of Chicago's South Side, I was raised in poverty. Several times my mother and I had to take refuge in other people's homes, and sometimes in shelters. I thought that by joining the Navy at 18, I would get the training and education I needed to improve my life and help my family.

Yet once I was honorably discharged in 2008, with good conduct medals and, from a service-related injury, seven screws in my foot and ankle, I found the recession had left few available jobs. I worked as a server at a pizza joint and as a salesman at a retail store. Finally I did maintenance at the veterans hospital in the Bronx. I should have taken a full-time job there when it was available, but felt sure I could find something that paid higher. I was proud, and I was wrong. For a long time, I got by on the G.I. bill benefits and scholarship grants I received from going to community college and, more recently, the New School. But eventually I couldn't get by anymore; I couldn't even pay rent.

One in seven homeless people have previously served in the military. This year, at 25, I became one of those homeless veterans. One of my most vivid memories of New York City shelters is of watching a fellow black veteran having a heated argument with himself. The oddest thing was that no words were said—the man spit and sputtered and pounded his fist on his chest, all while only moving his lips. It was as if a mime was violently illustrating anger to a person who had never experienced it.

It reminded me of a conversation I'd once had in the middle of the Indian Ocean. Bored of waiting to hit land, which could take two months or more, my shipmates and I made up games. One such game, which we called "Wish List," was simple. We had to envision the most extravagant thing we'd do in order to get an early discharge from the Navy. One guy said he'd pretend he was crazy—eat foreign objects and pull his

pants down while pledging allegiance to Harvey the pooka instead of the United States of America. That got laughs.

It was hard to laugh at that veteran in the shelter, though. And others were worse off than he. The mistake that the shelter system makes is to clump everyone together. Those unstable vets lay in cots directly next to stable soldiers who lay next to ex-cons with any number of offenses. It was hard sleeping at night not knowing how innocent or guilty the former prisoner in the bed next to me was. Just about every shelter had gang members or former gang members and stories of violence and theft. Sadly, there was always someone who had taken, or at least claimed to have taken, the life of another. There was speculation that sex offenders were being quietly shuffled through the system, too.

I experienced firsthand the frustrations veterans feel in shelters each day. We were told how little we mattered by social workers with limited patience and even less training in working with recently deployed soldiers, and pushed into applying for public assistance. I wanted a job, not welfare, but I was told that no New York City shelter would house me if I didn't apply for food stamps and warned I would fail to find work.

Despite the setbacks, I am grateful for some of the acquaintances I made. I met a former service member who worked for NASA before a crack addiction led to theft, a prison sentence and homelessness. I got to know an Army doctor who served in Vietnam. Doc, as we called him, lost it during combat and even admitted to enjoying killing people, but his charm and patience made that hard to believe. Another former-Navy man was an astronomy geek, just like me, so we hit it off instantly.

In the beginning, I blamed the government for our fate, for training us for sophisticated equipment that is found only in the military, thus limiting our job opportunities in the civilian world, and for failing to put better safeguards in place to keep veterans off the streets. I pointed fingers at my college for only granting me a small sum for food and transportation while my world was crumbling. I even found fault with my mother, for dying and leaving me and my siblings to pay for her funeral and burial costs.

But ultimately, my experience has made me realize that I'm more responsible for my situation than I'd like to admit. Drinking to excess and my uncanny ability to withstand hardship when help should be requested are two of the main culprits. Today I'm focusing on my education; I moved out of the shelter last month and am now living in a beautiful duplex in New Jersey. I have been able to find purpose in all of this: a persistent determination to do better for myself, ironically the very lesson the Navy instilled in me when I joined eight years ago.

DATING WHILE ILL IS ILL-ADVISED

BY LIZ MONTGOMERY, AMNY, JULY 5, 2017

One thing Netflix's show "Girlfriends' Guide to Divorce" doesn't cover is how to date when you are a 46-year-old woman, twice divorced, and recovering from abdominal cancer with a feeding tube in your arm. This was not the first time in the past seven years that I needed the 12-hour feedings, but it was the first time I decided to date in that condition.

My 78-year-old mother, Theresa, who cared for me, called me "foolish" for being on Tinder. She wanted me to focus on recovering—not love. I rolled my eyes and decided to meet Alan, a dermatologist from Manhattan. My mom was concerned, and looking back I can see why: I weighed 85 pounds at 5-foot-7. But I wanted to feel normal again, if only for a night.

The sweater dress I wore camouflaged the catheters. We met at a hotel near my Manhattan apartment. My mom watched me walk to the hotel, worried I might collapse. Alan, a rotund, 42-year-old, was at the bar, having just ordered appetizers to share. I explained I had eaten dinner and ordered a pinot noir. He asked me questions about my life as the room began to spin.

When I said something funny, he hit my arm, right where the catheter was. Then he did it again, and a third time. Finally, I said, "Ouch, I hurt myself working out yesterday. Be careful." He questioned, "You aren't one of those skinny girls addicted to working out, are you?"

I told him I was naturally thin.

He attempted to feed me the zucchini and ricotta salata appetizer, saying, "We need to put some meat on those bones."

Laughing, I excused myself and went to the bathroom. In the mirror I saw my face, eyes sunken, lips cracked. I wondered what he must have been thinking.

Seeming oblivious to the fact that I was on the verge of passing out, he spoke about his dermatology practice and beach house on Long Island. About two hours in, I felt my body giving out. He walked me home. At my door, he hugged me and said, "Please take care of yourself." I never saw Alan again, but I was grateful for his affection.

I walked into my apartment crying, but also feeling a sense of normalcy. Two hours in the company of a man was something I hadn't had in several months. I hooked myself up to my feeding tube as I lay down in my bed with my mom beside me. We talked like two schoolgirls about boys until I fell asleep, happy for the first time in a long time. I proved to myself that it didn't matter what I looked like, I was still me on the inside.

I no longer need intravenous feedings, but I'm still looking for love. With my mom's blessing.

WAYWARD TEENAGERS IN YOUR BACKYARD: LET FACILITIES TAKE ROOM IN NEW YORK CITY NEIGHBORHOODS

By Gigi Blanchard, New York Daily News, June 22, 2015

At age 15, I was arrested for stealing a car and was sentenced to juvenile prison until my 21st birthday. In mid-90s Illinois, the sole female juvenile prison was located in a Chicago suburb, five hours north of my rural town. Visitations were held weekly, but without public transit options, my single mother—who bicycled to work—was unable to come.

In the two decades since, several states have shifted from warehousing delinquents in remote prisons to localizing them in treatment centers that address their psychological needs. In 2012, Gov. Cuomo approved the Close To Home initiative, which relocates young offenders nearer to their communities, where they can restoratively transition back home.

The idea is sound and progressive: Being within MetroCard proximity to their families allows kids to stay in touch with their support networks while receiving transferable school credits, reducing both dropout and re-entry rates. Close to Home facilities offer enhanced counseling services, too.

But not everyone believes in the project—especially not when it's in their backyard. On Tuesday, residents of South Ozone Park celebrated the city controller's decision to reject a contract to operate a facility putting up to 18 teenagers in their neighborhood. This comes after months of heated protests and a civil suit filed against the children's service agency, which locals claim was trying to turn their neighborhood into a dumping ground.

After hearing plans to build a treatment center in Queens Village, neighbors there erupted into their own revolt, vowing to follow South Ozone's example.

Opponents say they have safety concerns. It can appear they are more motivated by fear of diminished property values. Neither reason justifies blocking the program.

Kids eligible for it are either non-violent offenders like me or do not pose a clear or present danger. They're just young people in need of a second chance.

If, that is, they're anything like me. My delinquency started when I was 13, after my parents divorced and my siblings fanned out among friends. I went from a crowded bedroom to an empty trailer and was left confused and angry. I didn't understand my mother's need to work 16-hour shifts and sleep during her time off.

I began running away, committing petty crimes and using various substances to numb my sense of loss. By the time I was arrested, I knew that being taken off the streets probably saved my life.

During the first year, letters home were frequent. I sent, "Miss you," crayoned with blue bubble letters, followed by, "Please send a photo, I'm afraid I'll forget your face." Correspondence rapidly dwindled, and in a final note, I wrote, "Sorry for the pain I caused, wish I could have gotten it together sooner."

I got used to the locking of steel doors, barbed-wire fences and caged windows. Stifled cries echoing down the hall as I tossed in my sleep became home.

After two years, I was paroled for good behavior to a group home in a small town, still out of my mother's reach. My progression into independent living was hinged upon finding a job—but the revelation of my facility's address sabotaged employment opportunities. The resentment among the locals in Illinois mirrored the current climate in Queens. My existence had pockmarked their town.

New laws bumped my release date to age 19, but I couldn't celebrate; I wasn't really ready to be freed. Landing in a battered women's shelter and acquiring a mentor was my turning point. Through her nurturing, I was able to find something positive within myself and walk a different path.

I'm now a 33-year-old college grad who lives near South Ozone with my husband. I've been in the city for almost a decade, and as I witness these protests, I'm reminded of how it felt to be loathed by people who didn't understand my predicament.

If they keep juvenile facilities out of their neighborhood, NIMBY opponents may win a small victory. But it will pose a larger, lasting threat to the city's future.

More Sharp Op-Eds by Students

- "How to Solve the American Health Care Crisis" by Justin Matis (*Slate*) www.slate.com/articles/health_and_science/medical_examiner/2013/08/a_solution_to_the_health_care_crisis_indian_doctors_on_indian_reservations.html
- "Inside Prince's Paisley Park" by Jeff Vasishta (Rollingstone.com) www.rollingstone.com/music/news/inside-princes-paisley-park-my-amazing-day-with-the-purple-one-20160422
- "A Kenyan Story of Forgiveness" by Jakki Kerubo (*The Wall Street Journal*) www.wsj.com/articles/a-kenyan-story-of-forgiveness-1502144216
- "How I Went From Dropout to Ivy League Graduate" by Julie Charnet (New York *Daily News*) www.nydailynews.com/opinion/dropout-ivy-league-grad-article-1.3176236
- "My Time to Stand Against Sexual Abuse" by Tiffanie Drayton (*Newsday*) www.newsday.com/opinion/my-time-to-stand-against-sexual-abuse-1.12457415
- "Two Muslim Brothers Who Took the Assimilation Path" by Kenan Trebincevic (*The Wall Street Journal*) www.wsj.com/articles/SB10001424127887323789704578443473812237556
- "An Independent Comes out of the Closet" by Zollie Maynard (New York *Daily News*) www.nydailynews.com/opinion/independent-closet-article-1.337659
- "1,000 More Cops—The Last Thing We Need" by Josmar Trujillo (New York *Daily News*) www.nydailynews.com/opinion/josmar-trujillo-1-000-cops-article-1.2121970
- "Globalism and Barbie's Behind" by Jennifer Tang (Los Angeles Times) www.latimes.com/opinion/la-oe-tang5sep05-story.html
- "Pampered Dogs, Miserable Humans" by Ryan Stewart (Daily News) www.nydailynews.com/opinion/pampered-dogs-miserable-humans-article-1.3684284
- "Info Overload: How The Intern is ruining food and music" by Tara Cox (New York Post) nypost.com/2016/05/02/the-internet-is-ruining-food-and-music-for-me/
- "The Lives We Live-On Line and Off" by Nick Lioudis (AMNY) www.amny.com/opinion/the-lives-we-live-online-and-off-1.18501010
- "Remembering Langston Hughes's Anger Alongside His Joy" by Renee Watson (*The New York Times*) www.nytimes.com/2018/02/01/opinion/langston-hughes-birthday.html

CHAPTER 8

Selling Short Humor

ASSIGNMENT #4

Around the time I wed, I wanted to exploit my marriage to plug my hopefully humorous book *The Male-to-Female Dictionary*.[1] My husband had just left his Los Angeles sitcom job, and we were going broke buying a Manhattan apartment. So when a colleague offered to pay us to co-create a weekend comedy seminar in my hometown of Southfield, Michigan, we agreed to make money in lieu of spending money on our honeymoon. Here's what I learned from that jest-fest: Many people think they're side-splittingly uproarious. Yet day-to-day laugh riots can't necessarily transform their funny bones into funny prose on their own. However, with the right instruction and revision, most witty writing can be made wittier and publishable.

Later I taught humor classes at New York University and The New School and had editors in the field come speak. Turns out, there's a market for humor on the web, in magazines, and in newspapers. Those willing to learn the rules and formats, listen to criticism, and rewrite can get clever clips while laughing all the way to the ATM. Here's how:

1. **DON'T PITCH OR PROPOSE HUMOR.** While investigative news stories, profiles, and reviews can be "pitched" (as we discussed earlier), humorous prose usually doesn't fall into the category of ideas that will get you a contract from just a query. Unless you're Issa Rae, Ian Frazier, Lena Dunham, Aziz Ansari, or Andy Borowitz, don't tell an editor you don't know, "I want to write a really hilarious piece on my relationship with my mother" and expect to hear "Great! I'll

---

1. Berkely Trade, 1996

send you a contract." Instead, complete the piece first, aiming for 400–900 words (depending on the publication). A finished product is better than proposing just an idea. The funniness factor can be idiosyncratic, so you usually need to show what you've got up front.

2. **FIGURE OUT THE SUBGENRE.** You can take in-person or online courses or seminars with experts in sketch comedy, sitcom writing, TV pilots, animation, videography, cartoons, screenplays, stand-up comedy, or sit-down humor writing that's fictional or first-person nonfiction. Each has a different look, format, style, length, and raison d'être. It's much easier to get paid if you know which form to market to whom. Make sure to check the credits, bylines, and work of any professors or professionals you study with. If you have zero money or time for classes or research and decide to post your knee-slappingly silly videos on YouTube or try your hand at a short humor piece, at least study the successful ones first.

3. **DETERMINE YOUR SPECIFIC TARGET.** A literary parody for *The Rumpus* or *McSweeney's* is a different animal than a ridiculous *MAD* magazine, *Cracked*, or *National Lampoon* TV satire (they all have online incarnations). And those are not the same as a manic political cartoon in *Funny Times*, a sophomoric tirade for sophomores in Collegehumor.com, a *New York Times'* "Loose Ends" column, or the famously droll fictional *New Yorker* "Shouts & Murmurs" column.

My mentor Ian Frazier explained to me the history of "Shouts & Murmurs." It seemed Harold Ross, the *New Yorker* founding editor from 1925–1952, used to run humor pieces that he called "casuals" that were supposed to seem effortless, tossed-off, and ideally funny and brilliant at the same time. He hoped to create a different type of column from the hokey, corny, jokey humor of his era and the dumbness he believed pervaded *The Saturday Evening Post.* Casuals could be long and take up as much as two or three pages in the front of the magazine, though they were mostly written by old white male staff members. James Thurber's 1939 "The Secret Life of Walter Mitty" was a classic casual, as was Frazier's 1978 classic "Dating Your Mom," bought by William Shawn (the editor from 1952–1987), which turned into a humor collection. When Tina Brown took over the helm of the magazine from 1992–1998, she changed the title to "Shouts & Murmurs" and put it in the back of the magazine. The current editor David Remnick came in 1998 and returned "Shouts & Murmurs" to the front pages of the magazine, where it remains. While Remnick added more women writers and editors to the mix, it's still very hard to break into. Happily, a shorter "Daily Shouts" version was launched online in 2012 by editor Emma Allen—who also edits comedy videos and the cartoons—and is open to new, younger, weirder, more diverse voices.

4. **READ MANY PIECES THEY'VE RUN.** Each market necessitates a different type of spec material. The aforementioned "Shouts & Murmurs" tends to be kooky, timely fictional send-ups that zigzag and build up to a surprising conclusion. While a great title, subtitle, or epigram helps, you can't just riff or repeat the same jokes—they need a twist. Read multiple issues of the publication and column you want to break into, which will help you get its distinct style, length, view, and voice. I've included examples of published pieces after each assignment that you should scan before starting your own.

5. **GET REALLY PERSONAL.** There's a reason why Jerry Seinfeld does kvetchy guy from Long Island bits and Larry David wrote and played versions of his annoying Jewish personality. Mindy Kaling covers a non-skinny non-white single woman trying to find a mate. David Sedaris chronicles being a gay guy of Greek heritage who grew up in a big crazy family in North Carolina. Chris Rock and Dave Chappelle brilliantly riff on being black in America. Amy Schumer, Julia Louis-Dreyfus, and other females make sharp jokes about women who aren't twenty-year-old size-two starlets trying to make it in Hollywood (check out their hilarious Comedy Central skit "The Last Fxxkable Day.") Similarly you should, by all means, poke fun at yourself—or your type—with self-deprecation, trying to emulate the sublime Tina Fey and Jerry Seinfeld (versus the sometimes more callous Kathy Griffin or Andrew Dice Clay).

6. **REMEMBER THAT HILARITY IS HIGHLY SUBJECTIVE.** Although your brother, college roommate, or water cooler co-workers find your one-liners amusing, that might not translate to clips, stand-up club ovations, or big sitcom deals. At my Midwestern comedy seminar, a lawyer acquaintance known to ambush strangers with a barrage of yuck-yuck jokes tried it on my husband, who'd worked as a writer for *Seinfeld, Saturday Night Live, In Living Color,* and *The Jon Stewart Show*. My mate whispered his mean but spot-on verdict later: "He's funny—for Southfield." Tread humbly around editors and comedy professionals.

7. **CURB YOUR OFFENSIVENESS.** Yes, Sarah Silverman, Amy Schumer, and Ari Shaffir get away with dry "dyke," rape, genitalia, and race relation quips, while Bill Maher, Stephen Colbert, Jon Stewart, and Samantha Bee eviscerate the president daily. Still, for newspapers, magazines, and the web, there's hard competition for political screeds, scatological silliness, rage, and profanity. Although much of what cracks us up isn't politically correct, dirty jokes and nasty jabs that go too far can land wrong. In most of the publications I've written for, you can't swear. And remember Kathy Griffin's photo of Trump's severed head that almost guillotined her career? Trash talk can be dicey and offend editors, agents, producers, readers, and bloggers, who could soon be trashing you. Read a publication carefully to determine its politics, audience, and language limitations.

8. **IF YOU MUST BE NASTY, AT LEAST PUNCH UP.** Making fun of wealthy white celebrities, pretentious socialites, authority figures, and powerful politicians is widely permissible and encouraged. That's because 1) Many deserve it. 2) They choose to be in the public eye. 3) Your words usually won't hurt them. 4) Jealousy and bitterness "play in Peoria." On the other hand, fat shaming and trashing poverty-stricken minorities, disabled people, sick defenseless children, or victims of catastrophes—not so much. Punching down can make you look like a despicable elitist or racist bully. Consider your targets carefully.

9. **UNDERRATE, DON'T OVERRATE.** Even in a cover letter, the more hilarity you promise an editor, agent, or producer, the larger likeli-

hood you'll disappoint. So don't ask if she wants to see your "hysterically funny" take on millennial job interviews. Instead use the words "parody," "satire," "spoof," or "sketch" without adjectives to indicate you hope she'll laugh. Notice at the beginning of this chapter I mentioned my "hopefully humorous" book. Not a bad way to introduce your project. Though don't go the other route and undermine yourself with a warning that your material sucks.

10. **SUBMIT SCRUPULOUSLY.** Find the name of the right section and editor to e-mail and visit the publication's website for submission guidelines you should try to follow. Magazine, newspaper, and web zine work is almost always sent directly by the writer to the editor. Yet if you are trying to sell book-length humor, a TV pilot, or romcom script for decent money, you'll probably need an agent or manager to help you. Getting a job on *Saturday Night Live* or a similar show requires crafting a packet of the kind of sketches they air. My brilliant friend Guy Nicolucci, who was on staff at Conan O'Brien's show for a decade, got his break by writing fantastic, topical monologue jokes that convinced both an agent to handle him and an executive producer to offer him the job.

11. **FIT THE KNOWN FORM.** It's fun to invent your own half-science-fiction, half-slapstick, thirty-two-page rhyming verse and, as they say, "you can do anything as long as it works." But if you plan to get paid this decade, I'd begin by following existing formats. My students have sold many types of humor pieces. The first is the short parody (check out *The Onion*, which is filled with parodic pages, albeit infamously hard for freelancers to break into). That type of take-off requires the title to reveal what's being spoofed. For example, my college lampoon of T.S. Eliot's "The Love Song of J. Alfred Prufrock" was called "The Love Song of A. Suzy Co-ed." Then there are whimsical first person 500–900 word newspaper op-ed essay kvetches that are often timely (think Dave Barry and Joyce Wadler). Another format is 1–10 humor, in which you use a topical conceit in the title and intro and—often nonsensically—prove it in ten bullet points. That's longer and fleshier than a BuzzFeed

listicle like "29 Tweets That'll Make You Laugh Louder Than They Should." My oft-reprinted 1–10, which ran in *The New York Times Magazine* and *The Barbie Chronicles* anthology[2] was a 900-word "10 Ways Barbie Was a Modern Girl's Dream Mentor" timed to the doll's thirty-fifth birthday. It was such a hit I retooled it for her fortieth, and then her fiftieth, too.

12. **PUT IT TO THE TEST.** Read your humor pieces aloud to a class or workshop where you can hear whether the instructor, classmates, or critics are groaning or guffawing. Your mother, spouse, or kids saying "You killed it!" doesn't count. Brave souls have tried out new material publicly at readings, storytelling events at The Moth, improvisation schools like Chicago's The Second City, and stand-up comedy clubs. What works in late-night open mics may not work on the page by daylight. Reactions from these (possibly inebriated) audiences might not translate to those of producers, agents, and editors who'll pay you.

13. **USE HUMOR IN ALL YOUR WRITING.** Don't limit levity to categories labeled *comedy* or *humor*. I attempt to work wit into everything, whether it's wedding toasts, service pieces, seminar introductions, or book subtitles, like my memoir *Lighting Up: How I Stopped Smoking, Drinking, and Everything Else I Loved in Life Except Sex*.[3] Some fear humor will keep you from being taken seriously or your work might get marginalized as light or commercial. Not me! By eliciting laughter, I've increased my pages, publications, and payments— as well as warm reactions from my readers. Regina Barreca's great book on female comedy, *They Used To Call Me Snow White ... But I Drifted*[4] points out that the one making people laugh is often the most powerful person in the room.

EXERCISES TO WRITE FUNNIER FAST

When I asked my husband how to become a successful humor writer, he said, "Be born funny." While some feel you can't teach anyone to

2. Touchstone, 1999
3. Delacorte Press, 2005
4. Viking, 1991

be amusing if they're not, I argue that all writing can be improved on every level with work, good feedback, editing, and revision. Here are ways to quickly make your work more comical.

1. Try to replicate the exact humor page you want to emulate, but in your own words. You can download or order film, TV pilots, and sketch comedy shows from the web. When you do, underline the lines that make you laugh. Sometimes I even count words and syllables to copy the exact length and sound.

2. Experiment with a variety of forms: a 600-word online "Shouts & Murmur" column, timely late night comedy monologue jokes, a *MAD* magazine parody of a new TV show, a 400-word *Onion* news story satire. See which best suits your voice and your topic.

3. Watch repetitions. The third time you do something, it has the opposite meaning. If a character cries or screams once or twice you may fear or feel bad for them. Three times, it stops being sad or scary and becomes maudlin. My comedy writer pal Guy Nicolucci gives this example from the classic film comedy *Airplane*: Whenever Robert Hays's character talks about his broken heart, the person in the seat next to him kills themselves. A woman hangs herself, a Japanese soldier commits seppuku. The third time, the Hindu man doses himself with gasoline, then lights a match ... but Robert Hays is called away, interrupting the story. Relieved, the Hindu man blows out his match. Beat. Then he explodes.

4. Laughing is said to be a reaction to being surprised. So remember that lists are funnier when the last item you end on is surprising. In my piece on my nicotine withdrawal, I listed reasons why I should quit smoking: "Look younger, get healthier, have fewer wrinkles, spite enemies."

5. Visit comedy clubs and see what works and what doesn't work with comedians there. Try out material before an audience, class, or friends and see if—and where—anyone laughs.

6. While I wouldn't send fart or oral sex jokes to an editor at *The New York Times*, if you're going to be offensive, you're better off joking around with good friends or testing out material at comedy clubs.

Sometimes the best humor is edgy, outrageous, or creepy. Think Sarah Silverman's incest riffs or Amy Schumer's masturbation routines. Though it's said, "comedy equals tragedy plus time," don't be afraid to inappropriately poke jokes at current tragedies. *The Onion* reacts ironically to mass shootings and after their darkly hilarious 9/11 issue two weeks after the World Trade Center attacks, they were inundated with positive comments from readers.

7. Don't tell the reader something is funny, using the verb "he joked" or "chuckled" or saying "and they all laughed." Show a scene and let your audience decide.

8. Self-deprecation is comedy gold. Start by writing a list of all the horrible things you hate about yourself. (Though if you trash your weight, race, or age, you have to be careful not to cross the line into also shaming others these days.)

9. Be unexpected by twisting clichés. A white grandma who talks like a gangsta rapper is funnier than a gangsta rapper speaking like you'd expect him to talk. Betty White's off-color sexual jokes seem funnier because she's a 96-year-old lady with beauty parlor hair.

10. Tell the truth about dark emotions nobody admits, like feelings of failure, jealousy, and loneliness and stories of bad breakups. "My college boyfriend didn't sleep with one of my roommates. He slept with two of them" often gets a laugh, since everyone can relate to lousy love stories. The topic led to my first book.

11. Try a funny unusual word you don't hear often. The Dilbert Blog lists words that are funny within themselves: Mongolian, herdsman, vagina, trouser, shish kabob, storm drain, Johnson, slap, canoe, pulverize. These are especially good to weave into your work out of context. Use a thesaurus to find better verbs, nouns, and adjectives. "I hit him," isn't funny. "I pulverized him" might be. Dissecting his jokes, Jerry Seinfeld recently told *The New York Times*, "You want things that are just fun to say. It's fun to say Cocoa Crisp and Fruity Pebbles. It's not fun to say Oat Bran."

12. Use odd juxtapositions. I saw @Cheeseboy22's Tweet "Homemaking tip: In a pinch, the end slices of bread can be used as toilet paper." Gross, but I admit I laughed.

13. Try observational humor. I know it feels old-fashioned, but trashing everyday things that seem odd offers a good humor structure. Think of the questions, "Did you ever notice?" and "What's the deal with …" à la Seinfeld and Larry David. To be updated, poke fun at mistakes you've made with the latest technology.

14. Specifics make everything funnier. "I ate too much junk food," isn't as good as "I ate seven bags of Chips Ahoy chocolate chip cookies," just as "I haven't had sex in years" doesn't sound as original as "I haven't been laid since the Reagan administration."

15. Exaggerate a lot. I often interject "Then $400,000 worth of therapy kicked in," though I haven't spent that much on shrinks over the years. And I always get a chuckle in my classes talking about my difficult childhood when I explain, "I was the weirdest, drunkest, angriest, most drunk and stoned person in Michigan who flunked the entire state."

16. Nutty metaphors and similes add color, like Dennis Miller's lines "America may be the best country in the world, but that's kind of like being the valedictorian of summer school," and "I'm one of the more pessimistic cats on the planet. I make van Gogh look like a rodeo clown."

17. Cut extra words, unintentional repetitions, and clichés. The end of a sentence, paragraph, or piece should land the weirdest or funniest. Often great humor pieces, like poems, are tight and succinct.

18. Half of what's out there now is topical humor. Take a page from Stephen Colbert, Trevor Noah, Samantha Bee, and Seth Meyers, who upped their comedy games the minute Trump became president, along with *Saturday Night Live*, now reinvigorated by political mimics. Minutes after the picture was posted of Melania Trump going to the Houston hurricane in five-inch stilettos, a comedian colleague posted "Melania Heels the Nation." Remember to keep a pen and pad handy when you watch the news.

My Top Five Humor Pieces

- "It's Over, Isn't It?" (Barnesandnoble.com) www.barnesandnoble.com/review/its-over-isnt-it
- "My Mentor, Barbie" (*The New York Times Magazine*) www.nytimes.com/1994/11/06/magazine/endpaper-my-mentor-barbie.html
- "Marrying in Midlife is Better" (*Funny Times*)
- "Barbies for the Modern Age" (*New York Post*)
- "10 Reasons Why Sex is Better Over 40" (*More* magazine)

WINNING HUMOR BY MY STUDENTS

HACKS FOR DEALING WITH YOUR CLOSETFUL OF APPLE BOXES

By Keysha Whitaker, New Yorker Daily Shouts, August 17, 2016

We know you love them as much as we do—Apple-product boxes are the mother of all boxes. Just feel how tight those corners are.

But we get it: you accumulated way too many, and now you can't bring yourself to throw the magnificent containers out. If you're anything like us, for years you just stacked them in the closet and checked in on them every few months. Then, suddenly, your closet was overflowing with Apple packaging and you had no room to store your coats or hundreds of outdated chargers or cat.

But don't dump them! We scoured the Net and found the best hacks for dealing with your Apple boxes. Follow our suggestions below and, soon enough, those boxes will be worth as much as the product that came inside them.

Regive Them

Apple boxes can serve as great gift boxes. Imagine the joy on your loved one's face and her squeals of delight when she opens up that pristine Apple box and finds a gift card to Rite Aid lovingly stowed inside.

Repair a Bridge with Them

Unlike metal or cement, Apple boxes do not corrode or rust. They can withstand twelve tons of force per square inch. Crowd-source America's closets and collect enough boxes to repair some of the country's sixty thousand crumbling bridges!

Renovate Your Home with Them

Forget Sheetrock—increase the value of your property with a perfectly proportioned Apple room. Apple boxes are made of a NASA-designed material that will keep you warm in temperatures as low as ninety degrees below zero (Celsius!). In fact, Apple boxes have replaced ice blocks in forty per cent of igloos. (The other sixty per cent have melted.)

Build a Boat with Them

This D.I.Y. watercraft is Silicon Valley's update to that old milk-carton boat you made in elementary school. Use your marine-grade Apple boxes to create a vessel without having to get your Sperry Topsiders dirty during chores like sanding, fibreglassing, or painting. Simply place the desired number of MacBook boxes side by side and tell Siri to "make a boat." The edges of the boxes will then merge, creating a waterproof seal that'll keep you safe and dry from here to Cupertino!

Bake a Cake with Them

Apple boxes can be used in place of cake and muffin pans and are actually edible when baked at three hundred and fifty degrees. Move over, Betty Crocker—nothing says lovin' like an Apple-box cake. Stack your Apple boxes for an inexpensive multilayered wedding cake: iMac, MacBook, iPad, iPhone 6, iPhone 4, and iPod Nano as the topper!

Construct Your Own Coffin with Them

Funerals are expensive. Why not take your boxes and build a custom casket? The box material doesn't decompose and will keep your body perfectly preserved well past the second-thousandth coming of iOS. If you prefer cremation, three MacBook Pro boxes will hold a standard-size adult.

"THE HANDMAID'S TALE": THE LOST PENCE PREQUEL

By Fiona Taylor, New Yorker Daily Shouts, March 31, 2017

June 9, 2029

Dear Diary,

I can't lie to you—in part because you're my only confidante, but also because I fear being struck by lightning. I must admit that I don't think my sanity and my marriage can endure another baby. But ever since birth control was declared illegal by our Exalted Leader Pence, my options have seemed limited. And I fear that I have been living on the edge, tempting my husband, Greg, by flaunting myself in my neck-to-floor calico dress. He's only human, after all, and when I wear it you can almost see the outline of my form. Yes, it's my own fault that I ended up with ten kids in just eight years!

After the fourth set of twins, I was quite overwhelmed, and then—surprise! I found that I hadn't known what desperate really meant until baby

Malachi followed only ten months later. I must have been a tad hormonal, because late one night, after our wet nurse/indentured servant escaped, I followed her lead and sneaked out, with the plan of leaving little Malachi on the firehouse steps. I knew he'd be safe there, but, to my surprise, the steps were just filled with babies. There was no room! I guess a lot of other women were feeling desperate, too, even though they all wear fixed, bright smiles when I see them out and about.

Luckily, I discovered how to prevent an eleventh baby. I went to the government-sponsored clinic, It's God's Plan If You Get Knocked Up™, where the nurses introduced me to two new scientific breakthroughs: an abstinence sack and chastity board. They weren't cheap, but, then, new medical technology never is! I tried to trade baby Malachi for a sack, but the nurses wouldn't go for it. Instead, I paid them with a barrel of salted cod, my three best donkeys, and a hundred and forty gold coins commemorating our dearly departed Exalted Leader Trump. (I still get teary-eyed thinking about the tragic spray-tan accident.)

All the way home, I fondled the rough burlap of the abstinence sack. It has two openings and drawstrings at the top and bottom—perfect for a couple that likes to stay close, but not too close. Apparently, the sack is normally sufficient birth control for people nearing thirty, but I confided to the nurses that Greg is a randy devil.

The first year of our marriage, he kept his distance from me—so much so that I asked the minister at my church for advice. But after Greg was sentenced to the Official Government Conversion Camp™ for three months, he came back raring to go! The electroshock therapy may have even worked *too* well. Now he often wants to have relations more than the one night each month officially allocated for procreation—especially after he checks out Ann Coulter's Twitter feed. He often insists that our bedroom be totally dark, and, for some reason, he calls me Andy, but, then, we all have our quirks.

When the nurses heard about my concerns, they exchanged knowing looks and recommended that I keep a candle lit when Greg makes non-condoned overtures. If that fails, they said that I should try the chastity board. It's a long wooden plank that fits down the middle of the bed so Greg can't accidentally touch me or catch a glimpse of my enticing sack. I've learned from experience (ten kids!) that you just can't play it too safe.

Since Greg sometimes gets amorous even by candlelight if he has indulged in a home-brewed ale, the nurses also gave me a Bible. If he tries to breach the chastity board, my first line of defense will be to read scripture to him. (No Song of Solomon!) If that fails, then, apparently, God will forgive me for knocking him unconscious with the Bible. This is a form of birth control that consistently demonstrates a ninety-five-per-cent effectiveness rate. Hooray!

I feel much more confident now, armed with my new knowledge and this heavy Bible. The best news of all? I only have to fend him off for twenty years until I hit menopause!

A LIBERAL LEARNS TO ACCEPT THE FAMILY TRUMPSTER

By Sybil Sage, Boston Globe, June 9, 2016

With enough political buttons strewn about for our apartment to pass as Democratic headquarters, I assumed my 35-year-old nephew was teasing at a recent Sunday brunch when he volunteered, "Donald Trump is the best candidate."

"What makes you say that?" I asked, expecting he'd snicker.

"Because he'll surround himself with good people" was his answer.

"Like Chris Christie?" I scoffed. "Or David Duke?" How could I be hearing this from the adorable, dimpled nephew whose every birthday, graduation, and marathon I'd taped? I realized I'd just served hand-sliced smoked salmon at $29.98 a pound to a Trump fan.

Sign Up

The rest of us banded into a unit of nova-noshing Navy Seals charged with saving our country from a threat. I'd been the first to deploy, but my son, a 32-year-old attorney, parachuted in to ask, "Have you considered what he could do to the Supreme Court?" The nephew shrugged as if that were not an issue. My son continued, "Look, even if you have problems with Hillary, you have to admit she's the most qualified." The nephew remained quiet, which prompted my son to point out, "If you don't care about women's rights, you should." His reward was approving smiles from his wife and me.

Politics have always been important to me. When I met my future husband, Jimmy Carter was in office. Before we did anything that might transmit germs, I made sure he was a liberal. I wasn't about to share a bed, or the TV remote, let alone raise a child, with a Republican. My husband's entire family, like mine, was solidly Democratic, but my nephew's stance was evidence that genetics guarantees nothing.

Desperate to understand how my nephew had been seduced, I messaged a relative in Florida who'd "liked" the Donald J. Trump page on Facebook: "You have no problem voting for a man who was praised by Louis Farrakhan for not accepting money from the Jews?" Maybe she'd be more explicit and articulate.

"OK," she replied, "here goes. Hillary, she was in the White House for four years. What did she do?"

So much for that plan. I restrained myself from pointing out that Hillary was there for eight years and her role was as the first plus-one. All politics is local, so I decided to question people I encountered as I roamed around. I took my listening tour to different parts of the city, bringing up the election at every opportunity. A man sitting next to me on a bus said, "He's the only one who gives me hope."

A tourist asking for directions insisted that the billionaire is unafraid, perceiving Trump as an alpha leader capable of reinvigorating the country. I imagined there were many who confused brashness and bragging with strength.

In my dentist's waiting room, a woman getting an implant was convinced the man whose Chicago hotel minibar includes a $25 bottle of water will make America great again. My teeth clenched, making it almost impossible for the dental hygienist to clean them; she repeatedly pleaded, "Can you open any wider?"

Someone working in a bakery who'd moved here from Guatemala admitted she hoped Trump would win because he tells it like it is. "You don't care that he's anti immigrants?" I asked. "Not Guatemalans," was her response. "It's Mexicans he hates."

The survey didn't help me come to terms with my nephew's position, but other family events were coming up and I was eager to get back the warm relationship I've always had with him. (In fact, I'm still hoping he'll agree not to vote for a Republican in return for the anonymity I'm giving him here.)

Though I'd failed to figure out what he saw in Trump, maybe I could at least understand why he'd made that announcement to us. He had to know it would be provocative.

Psychologists attribute many personality traits to birth order. From what I read, it was conceivable my nephew had "middle child syndrome." Sandwiched between an older and a younger sibling, he may have felt invisible or neglected. (Maybe I was even partly responsible. Had I played enough games with him as a child?) His brunch declaration may have given him a moment as speaker of the house ... even if it was only his aunt and uncle's house.

These realizations (rationalizations?) allowed me to stop conflating the candidate and his follower. I could loathe one and love the other. Respectful, sensitive, and kind, my nephew is nothing like the Donald. And I'm sure he'd happily show me his tax returns. I wonder how Paul Ryan's aunt is handling her nephew's endorsement.

11 THINGS NOT TO SAY TO GAY PARENTS

By Haig Chahinian, Cosmopolitan.com, October 15, 2015

Even though my partner and I had met in a Chelsea bar, we'd confided that we'd happily trade in martinis and margaritas for play clothes and playgrounds. Eight years later, we fretted over how to start a family: use a surrogate, ask a favor of someone we know, or adopt. When we chose domestic adoption, I imagined being let down by people's naïve comments, since we'd be the only nontraditional clan in our New York City apartment building. As expected, they didn't disappoint.

Over the last decade—our daughter just turned 10—my now-husband and I have endured a Tonka truckload of bumpy interactions. Rarely have they been funny like Mitch, Cam, and Lily's antics on Modern Family. At dinner parties, strangers have approached us in the same way they might prod a foreign object with a stick. Unless we're on Facebook, I don't like to be poked.

But I get it. Gay parenting's relatively new to the scene. To keep my sanity, I've learned when to sidestep queries, when to give direct answers, and when to educate well-meaning folks. To help other same-sex parents avoid that dance, here are 11 things you should stop uttering.

1. Where's her mother? I live in a rainbow metropolis, and yet this is the most frequently offensive sentence I hear. Simply put, my tween has two dads. And if there's concern about my daughter's safety, simply ask, "Where's her grownup?"

2. Whose sperm did you use? Who carried the baby? Naturally, acquaintances are curious about the origins of a couple's baby-making. Consider flipping the tables. Are you willing to tell a stranger that you and your girlfriend conceived while she straddled you in reverse cowgirl position? It's called TMI.

3. Aren't you afraid your toddler will play with your sex toys? Because I had to reject the shame surrounding sexuality when I came out, like so many queer people, I did emerge from the experience more sex-positive. That doesn't mean all homosexual mums and pops leave dildos, nipple clamps, and vibrating rings lying around the living room. That's what closets are for.

4. Who's the mother: You or your significant other? I appreciate the desire to fit people into preset categories, but don't box me in. Not all gay couples subscribe to traditional gender norms or roles. As fathers, my husband and I both do plenty of parenting.

5. Does your baby have HIV? Stemming from the 1990s fear that men who are intimate with men must have AIDS, and ignorance about how the virus is transmitted, this inquiry earns a blank stare.

6. Is she in touch with her mother? I've been driven batty by people's preoccupation with assigning a mom to every child. "Her BIRTH mother," I've retorted, or, "Her biological mother." My reply depends on my mood and how close I feel to the asker.

7. Are you concerned your kid might be like you? When I sought out young women's camouflage shirts at a department store, the clerk cautioned, "Your child could be lesbian." I chuckled so much I forgot to feel insulted by her tone.

8. But what will you do for Mother's Day? Our household celebrates the more inclusive Parents' Day, the last Sunday in July. It was signed into law by President Clinton, and brunch reservations are much easier to make for the mid-summer holiday.

9. Doesn't your princess need a role model? She's not a Disney character, but yes, she does need strong, successful women to emulate. And she has plenty. My spouse and I have found "aunties" among our siblings, our circle of friends, and at school. As the teen years approach, we're fully supported.

10. Is your tot adopted? We say our little one "was adopted," referring to

that wonderful day when she joined our family. Never would we say "is adopted" or "is an adopted child," because the process rests in the past.

11. I bet your child gets confused about what to call you. No, and most have this figured out. My daughter calls me the Armenian word for Daddy, and my hubby is "Dad." I know two men who let their tykes call one "Dad" and one "Mom," like they hear their schoolmates do. To each their own. More welcomed and less judgmental is, "How does your kid refer to you?"

FOR NYC, A FEW RULES OF THE SIDEWALK

By Rob Williams, New York Daily News, April 7, 2014

New York City has the nation's highest rate of commuters who walk or use public transit. A whopping 56% of households in the five boroughs don't own a car, tops in the country.

In the East Village, where I live, it's tempting to envision the city as a symphony, with millions of people weaving around each other in choreographed harmony. But then some guy with a yoga mat cuts in front of me, stopping me short and sending coffee down the front of my coat.

In this city, where battle lines have increasingly been drawn between walkers, bicyclists and cars, we take it for granted that cars don't respect pedestrians. Should we also take it for granted that pedestrians don't respect each other? I grew up driving my grandfather's Ford LTD upstate and, ironically, I've noticed a few big things we pedestrians can learn from car culture.

Stay on the right. The most basic rule of the road applies to sidewalks as well. Whenever I see someone strolling down the left side of a sidewalk, I can't help thinking, "I hope to God that ma-

niac is British."

Don't drift out of your lane. Walking diagonally is inconsiderate. Straight lines and 90-degree turns mean fewer hassles for you and everyone else. Definitely don't veer to one side, then overcorrect and veer to the other. Your unpredictability makes you difficult to maneuver around.

Don't pop out into the middle of a busy street. It's amazing how often people coming out of stores walk straight into the middle of the sidewalk, as if they take precedence over everyone else on the street. Would you exit a parking lot that way—zooming into the middle of the road without regard for oncoming traffic?

Don't turn a corner into the "oncoming" lane. If you've ever walked around a corner and nearly bumped into someone coming the other direction, one of you was doing it wrong. When rounding a corner to the right, stay inside, close to the corner. When turning left, stick to the outside and give the people turning right the inside track.

DEALING WITH TRAIN LITTERBUGS: 5 RULES

By Brian Pennington,
Metro NY, June 7, 2006

One morning, while riding the A train to work, I confronted a litterbug. The culprit, a well-dressed professional woman, had crumpled her half-eaten cream cheese bagel and tossed it—paper, napkins and all—coolly under her seat, adding a slight heel kick for good measure. Stupefied, I reached under the seat and offered to pitch her trash. She gazed fiercely and bellowed that I was a nitwit, even suggesting where I should shove her partly finished breakfast. I retorted clumsily, something about how this is my city and it should be cleaner and free from trash. I hadn't expected such vitriol. I thought the issue about littering and the scurrying rats it brings was settled. I thought all reasonable New Yorkers were on board with making our city cleaner. Apparently this is not the case. Since that uncomfortable moment on the train, I have arrived at a few trusted guidelines to soften my (or anyone's) dealing with subway trash-lobbers. Here are some tips that could guard you from getting an earful—or worse, a punch in the chops.

RULE 1. DON'T SWEAT THE SMALL STUFF: Avoid confronting the guy who let lint fly loose out of his pocket. Do not grab a newspaper left unwittingly behind and chase its unsuspecting owner. Littering is the deliberate chucking of one's rubbish (a Coke bottle, a coffee cup, a half-eaten sandwich). A straw wrapper bears little impact compared to a greasy french fry carton. If it's large and can attract pesky rodents, then it's probably trash. Use discretion.

RULE 2. ABOVE ALL, SMILE: When you witness a garbage-hurling miscreant, you are to approach, pick up the item and say, in a helpful voice, "I got this." Then smile, turn and walk away. Avoid derision or sarcasm or you may trigger a regression to some raw, painful childhood moment of parental chastisement. Grab the dumped trash and walk in a purposeful manner to the opposite end of the train or toward the closest trash receptacle. Note: This distance could serve as a head start if a chase ensues.

RULE 3: IT IS THANKLESS WORK: Don't expect a pat on the back. The rewards are not of this Earth.

RULE 4: MY BODY MASS TO THEIR BODY MASS QUOTIENT: Before I approach, I calculate the likelihood the person could turn on me and inflict bloodshed. I target mostly women and men my height or shorter. Being only five-foot-six, a sizeable number of men escape my vigilantism. Since I wear plastic frame glasses and it's apparent my wife cuts my hair, I give off little menace.

RULE 5: WEEKDAYS ONLY: The workweek is the most acceptable and safest time to confront a litterlout. Steer clear of very late evenings, especially on weekends, when the sour odor of alcohol breath hangs in the stale air of the train. Riding home one late evening to Brooklyn, I spotted a hefty, inebriated, dodgy-looking man with large, tattooed knuckles. He opened a piece of candy and, whoa, let the wrapper fall onto the train floor. I stepped forward, staggered from the effects of several drinks imbibed at an earlier event, and reassessed. My hazy mind and the tightly crammed L train worked to my disfavor; I would be unable to abscond safely (see rule 2). So I let it go this time. Not to mention that I didn't want him to smudge his tattoo on my carefully placed nose.

CANDY COMPANIES' PREWRITTEN STATEMENTS ANTICIPATING THE TRUMP CAMPAIGN'S NEXT CANDY-RELATED GAFFE

By Jennifer Byrne, New Yorker
Daily Shouts, October 12, 2016

Here we are, less than a month before the election, and two candy makers have disavowed the Republican Presidential candidate. Tic Tac made its remarks after a video first published by *The Washington Post* showed Donald Trump having a lewd conversation about women with then-host of "Access Hollywood" Billy Bush ... This came only three weeks after Donald Trump Jr.'s tweet comparing Syrian refugees to poisoned Skittles.

Reese's Pieces:

"Like Skittles and Tic Tacs before us, we unequivocally condemn recent remarks made by Donald Trump that make reference to our candy. We have nothing but respect for the fine work of the Academy Award-winning actress Reese Witherspoon, and Mr. Trump's comments regarding her 'pieces' were lewd, vulgar, and entirely unacceptable. Our candy's name was never meant to be used in the service of such crass wordplay. We hope that, this Halloween season, our entire line of candies will continue to represent what they have represented since 1928—wholesome and sweet American treats that in no way promote the reduction of powerful women to their anatomical parts."

Bazooka:

"We deeply regret that Mr. Trump felt the need to encourage America's Second Amendment enthusiasts to 'give a Democrat a Bazooka to chew on,' referring to the recoilless anti-tank rocket launcher with which we unfortunately share a name. In light of the highly inappropriate nature of Mr. Trump's remarks, we have decided to relaunch our classic chewing gum under the name Finger-Gun Gum, a playful, nonviolent allusion that we hope will convey the totally harmless spirit of our popular chewing gum. Parents should rest assured that their children can enjoy Finger-Gun Gum without the threat of military-grade destruction."

Oh Henry!:

"We are honestly baffled that Mr. Trump would choose to invoke the Oh Henry!

name in his tasteless implication that Hillary Clinton flirted with former Secretary of State Henry Kissinger in an effort to gain his endorsement. Mr. Trump is actually correct in his winking assertion that Oh Henry! is 'more than just Hillary's favorite fun-size candy bar.' It is, in fact, the product of familial entrepreneurship that has delighted the nation with quality confections for nearly a century. But we cannot distance ourselves more emphatically from Mr. Trump, whose apparent preoccupation with 'fun size' clearly seems rooted in his insecurity about the size of his own hands."

Marshmallow Peeps (Halloween Marshmallow Monsters):

"The Halloween edition of our cherished Easter marshmallow snack was simply meant to be a holiday-themed variation on the classic. In no way were the Marshmallow Monsters intended to be used to fat-shame women including Rosie O'Donnell, Alicia Machado, or Mr. Trump's own wife, Melania, during her 'majorly hormonal and scary-huge pregnancy.' It is our wish that Marshmallow Monsters, which, incidentally, contain only twenty-eight calories per piece, should be enjoyed by humans of all shapes and sizes."

Joint Statement by the Makers of Runts, Nerds, and Dots:

"On our own behalf and on behalf of hardworking Americans across the political spectrum, we deeply resent Donald Trump's recommendation that consumers package our products together in Halloween 'loser bags.' This is clearly a weak rejoinder to the 'basket of deplorables' and is a thoroughly reductive portrayal of Hillary Clinton's supporters. We strongly disavow Trump's bigoted bundling strategy and intend to combat it by selling our own pre-made 'diversity pouches' containing these same products."

Mike and Ike:

"For Mr. Trump to even joke that Mike and Ike are engaged in an 'unholy union' is altogether reprehensible and potentially dangerous, given the polarized social climate to which he has so gleefully contributed. This is a candidate who has stated that he would 'strongly consider' overturning same-sex marriage. Even when said with 'sarcasm,' his remarks should be viewed by voters and candy lovers alike as a threat to social progress and equality. We hope the makers of Jolly Ranchers will follow our lead and condemn him as well."

QUIZ: DID YOU WIN THE INTERNET TODAY?

By Caren Lissner, McSweeney's, March 27, 2018

Instead of regretting the time you spend on social media, why not score it so that you can base even more of your self-esteem on it? You probably accomplished something during those hours.

1. You got insulted by a troll on Twitter this morning. You:

A) Spent the whole day arguing and came away frustrated

B) Put up a bold defense and felt satisfied

C) Got the troll to admit that no, Jesus would not have wanted him to call you a "leftie snowtard"

2. While snooping through your ex's vacation photos on Instagram, you:

A) Accidentally faved one, then unfaved it, then locked yourself in a room

B) Shrugged and decided it was time to move on

C) Realized the photos are from rehab and enjoyed a satisfying cackle

3. You made one of your best political quips ever on Twitter. As a result:

A) It got liked and retweeted by dozens of your progressive friends

B) It got liked and retweeted by an A-list celebrity

C) It got you blocked by Donald Trump

4. Your boss caught you looking at Snapchat. You:

A) Said you were only drawing whiskers on yourself to enhance your design skills and become a more versatile employee

B) Pointed out that at least you weren't vaping in the stairwell like Mike from Accounting

C) Said that clearly, you're bringing a millennial sensibility to a company that has long needed one—and asked for a raise

5. Drawing upon all of your recent internet experiences, you wrote an insightful Facebook post that went viral, eliciting hundreds of likes, comments, and shares—and landing you as a guest on three prominent podcasts. As a result:

A) Nothing in your life has changed in any way

B) Nothing in your life has changed in any way

C) Nothing in your life has changed in any way

SCORING

Two or more A's: You wasted time on the internet. Tomorrow is another day.

Two or more B's: You're becoming a more productive loafer. Good job.

Two or more C's: Congratulations! You have won the internet! And … nothing in your life has changed in any way.

ONLINE SHOPPING FOR DUMMIES

By Seth Kugel, New York Times, December 19,1998

More Americans than ever are avoiding taxes and crowds by ordering Christmas presents over the Internet. But does the Web really offer anything that the local mall doesn't?

It didn't take much cyber-surfing for me to find a sleighful of novel gifts that would disappoint even the easy-to-please. And no, I'm not making any of this up.

MANMADE BROWN ONION STRING, $158.98. The vegetable lovers in your family will be speechless when they see this ready-to-hang "food replica" onion display from the Fax Foods company website. Why buy the real things for 59 cents a pound when you can have a fake bundle of them for so much more? And while you're at it, why not get a few leaves of RepliKale to garnish the Christmas roast. (Yes, this is real, too.)

DENTIST SPEECHES, $45. With three speeches to a set, this gift from a speechwriters' website may seem like a deal, if one of limited use. Each speech is meant for use at a dinner or function for dentists and ends with "a toast to the profession." Accounting and Australia Day speeches are also available.

LEATHER TRUNK WITH MOTORIZED TELEVISION PLATFORM, $6,200. The Frontgate catalogue website pitches this 240-pound, 41-inch wide treasure chest at those who find a television obtrusive. Click the remote control and a 27-inch television set (not included) rises into view. Perfect for living rooms with a pirate motif.

KOMATSU D65PX-12 BULLDOZER, $164,900 (USED) A company called Con-Equip is offering a 1996 model, and Dad will approve of the 190 horsepower and straight blade with tilt. The only problem is trying to fit a living-room-size dozer under the Christmas tree.

THE COMPLETE PROFESSIONAL BASIC-THROUGH-ADVANCED HYNOTHERAPY VIDEO COURSE PACKAGE, $2000. The Omni Hypnosis website should fulfill your hypnotherapy shopping needs. This set of 43 videotapes includes more than 100 hours of instruction from the dapper hypnotism guru Gerald F. Kein. And completion of the course makes you automatically eligible for certification by the National Board for Hypnotherapy Anaesthesiology.

TWENTY-FIVE POUNDS OF GROUND OSTRICH MEAT, $99.75 PLUS $31 SHIPPING. The Ostriches OnLine Website, the self-proclaimed World's Largest Ostrich Shop, advertises its meat as low in fat and cholesterol and hormone-free. Soon after you receive this bulk order, your friends and family wil trip over one another to avoid ostrich stroganoff leftovers.

Note: the order must be picked up in person at a major airport.

TWO THOUSAND POUNDS OF CAYENNE PEPPER, $2,700. The Trading Company offers the highest quality spices, delivered straight to you from New Iberia, La. If your relatives think a net ton of the stuff is a bit much, tell them to browse the website for Cajun recipes, then multiply the ingredients by 700.

More Humor by Students

- "Yuca Chips With Your Back Rub?" by Seth Kugel (*The New York Times*) www.nytimes.com/1999/02/14/nyregion/soapbox-yuca-chips-with-your-back-rub.html?sec=&spon=
- "Dating Don'ts: 9 Tinder Profiles That Made Me Swipe Left" by Gina Fitch (*The Frisky*) www.thefrisky.com/2014-02-11/dating-donts-9-tinder-profiles-that-made-me-swipe-left/
- "8 Photos You Don't See on Instagram (But Probably Should)" by Jessica Siskin (*Thought Catalog*) thoughtcatalog.com/jessica-siskin/2013/05/8-photos-you-dont-see-on-instagram-but-probably-should/
- "Father's Day Advice for Freeloaders" by Zach Valenti (*The Wall Street Journal*) www.wsj.com/articles/zach-valenti-fathers-day-advice-for-freeloaders-1402700161
- "How Not to Burn Your Toast: Urgent Advice for Prince Harry as He Prepares to Roast Prince William" by Victoria Wellman (New York *Daily News*)
- "10 Reasons to Date a Guy Who Lives At Home" by Rainbow Kirby (*Newsday*)
- "10 Things I Learned About Men Through Online Dating" by Tiffanie Drayton (*The Frisky*)
- "Give Me My Nobel" by Carli Entin (New York *Daily News*)
- "Short Imagined Monologues: Ted Nugent Reviews A Christmas Story" by Jennifer Byrne (*McSweeney's Internet Tendency*) www.mcsweeneys.net/articles/ted-nugent-reviews-a-christmas-story
- "College Poverty Can Be a Blessing" by Kristian Costello honeysucklemag.com/college-poverty-blessing/
- "Your Russian Connection: Is There Any There, There?" by Keysha Whitaker (*The New Yorker*) www.newyorker.com/humor/daily-shouts/your-russian-connection-is-there-any-there-there
- "Classic Holiday Dishes You'll Now Have to Make Yourself Because They Were Previously Made by Trump Voters You Disinvited" by Jennifer Byrne (*The New Yorker*) www.newyorker.com/humor/daily-shouts/classic-holiday-dishes-youll-now-have-to-make-yourself-because-they-were-previously-made-by-trump-voters-you-disinvited

CHAPTER 9

Secret Service

....

ASSIGNMENT #5

To craft, sell, and get good service clips, ask yourself: What do I do well? What unique wisdom can I impart quickly? Can I teach readers something interesting in a succinct page or two? Luckily, you don't need a Ph.D. in a subject to provide a service to readers in a service piece that's broken down into easy steps. You *do* need to be creative and have talents, knowledge, or experience in areas others might care about. A healthy cook can share ten secrets to making lower-calorie recipes. A parent might offer seven ways to help a toddler sleep better. A TV addict who knows what's worth watching can share summaries of twelve new Hulu or Netflix series worth binging on this month. A physical trainer may offer eight reasons why being a "Weekend Warrior" could sideline you for the entire season. Yes, these pieces are big on numbers and lists.

Many young people think *BuzzFeed* invented illustrated "listicles" like "32 Cool and Colorful Tattoos That Will Inspire You to Get Inked." These short-form, roundup pieces—like *The New York Times'* Smarter Living section—also proliferate on such sites as *Bustle*, *HelloGiggles*, and *Mic*. While these latest web incarnations entertain, they also offer advice, opinion, or help and seem derived from the more old-fashioned print model. Some credit modern "service journalism" to Clay Felker, who founded *New York* magazine in 1968 and filled it with pages of film, book, and restaurant reviews. He included tips for better urban living and eventually devoted entire issues to such subjects as "The Best Doctors in New York." But I'd argue that articles providing specific, pragmatic advice to readers became prominent in the late 1800s with the inception of *McCall's*, *Cosmopolitan*, and *Ladies' Home Journal* magazines—filled with recipes and helpful hints for women to improve their health, home, and love life in five or ten easy steps. Then Dale Carnegie's 1936 bestseller *How to Win Friends and Influence People* jump-started the self-help genre. Having thirty million copies in print proved there's money in teaching people how to improve their lives fast.

While two of the well-known women's magazines nicknamed "The Seven Sisters" have gone out of business (*McCall's* and *Ladies' Home Journal*), five are still alive and kicking your homes and marriages into shape: *Better Homes and Gardens, Family Circle, Good Housekeeping, Redbook,* and *Woman's Day.* They continue to be stuffed with recipes and hints for women to spruce up their health, home, and love life in five or ten easy steps. *Vogue, Elle, Glamour, Cosmopolitan,* and *In Style* feature all kinds of advice as well as cutting-edge fashion for every season. And these how-to articles are not just for women. *Esquire, GQ, Maxim,* and *Playboy* offer males tips on how to invest soundly and buy a great tux, wet suit, and work wardrobe. *Men's Health, Men's Journal,* and *Men's Fitness* provide information on fitness and adventure travel while *Out, Gay City News, The Advocate, Washington Blade,* and *GO Magazine* offer lifestyle, social, and political advice to gays and lesbians.

After an early mentor told me, "Sex sells," and "Write about your obsessions," I wound up selling many relationship service pieces to women's and men's magazines. Yes, I admit in public that I, an ardent feminist, published the advice feature "How to Score Your Own Rock N' Roll Romeo." In my defense, it wasn't my idea or title, women's and men's magazine pieces were fun and easy to write, it took only a few hours, and they paid between one hundred dollars (for website work) and five thousand dollars (from top print magazines). They also led me to publishing self-help books on topics I was better suited for: *Secrets of a Fix-Up Fanatic: How to Meet & Marry Your Match,*[1] *Only As Good as Your Word: Writing Lessons From My Favorite Literary Gurus,*[2] and the co-authored *Unhooked: How to Quit Anything,*[3] which was a *New York Times* bestseller. Although highbrow literati love to trash self-help

1. Bantam Dell, 2007
2. Seal Press, 2007
3. Skyhorse Publishing, 2012

THE BYLINE BIBLE

articles and books, I find them addictive. You're not allowed to knock the genre until you've tried making a living as a freelance writer.

Meanwhile, this type of consumer reporting and ranking is still popular and lucrative. NY1 TV station lists Best Theatre in town, NPR promotes Best Books of the Year, *U.S. News & World Report* is known for influential Best Colleges and Best Hospital rankings, and *Brides* offers everything you want to know about planning a wedding. Almost all newspapers, magazines, websites, radio, and TV news shows these days recommend food, travel, and budget guides packed with tidbits promising instant deals, steals, and improvements. Service journalism might actually be the most recession-proof publishing market out there. Here are ways to come up with unique, sellable, helpful how-to articles.

1. **LIST YOUR SKILLS, TALENT, AND WISDOM.** This doesn't just mean the particulars of your job or your best subjects in high school or college. Perhaps you can share tips about knitting, shopping, or running, or finding good lawyers, doctors, business consultants, or editors. A student who volunteered with the New York City Board of Elections used her experience for a piece on ways to make your vote count more. I've mined my past neuroses and pathologies, selling service pieces about quitting addictions, leaving bad relationships, getting into therapy, fixing a faltering marriage, and recovering from getting fired. I once joked to my students that failure was my favorite expertise. My recent piece in *Writer's Digest* magazine was titled "Lemonade: Beyoncé Isn't the Only One Who Can Turn Pain Into Art. Here Are 13 Sweet Lessons We Can Learn From One Writer's Sour Moments."

2. **DETERMINE WHO YOUR AUDIENCE IS.** Who would benefit from the items on your list of what you know? If you're a mother or father, think: *Parenting, FamilyFun, Babble, Brain Child, Aeon,* or *The New York Times'* Well Family section. A wine connoisseur can aim for *Food & Wine, Wine Spectator, Decanter,* or *Wine & Spirits.* There are separate subcategories for health, cars, sports, and fashion. Google to find out where you should aim your work. Of course—as

with any kind of piece—read issues of the publication so you get its style before submitting.

3. **WRITE YOUR TITLE AND SUBTITLE.** While editors often change your "head," "subhead," and "dek," as they call it at newspapers, if you come up with something fun or creative, they'll sometimes keep it. When I wrote the five words "How to Forget Him Fast," I could see it in a woman's magazine. Luckily, so could the editor who bought it. Make your headline frank, funny, or self-explanatory. Mix numbers, promises, and spilled secrets.

4. **FINISH THE WHOLE HOW-TO PIECE FIRST.** As in personal essays and op-eds, if you don't have many clips or connections to editors, I recommend crafting the entire short how-to. I have found it easier to sell an already written short service piece, usually between 300 and 900 words. After your title and subtitle, you'll need an engaging one- or two-paragraph introduction, explaining your point. After your lead-in, add your list of recommendations. These are not just 20-word David Letterman top-ten lists—think at least 200 words.

5. **LEAD WITH YOUR PERSONAL EXPERIENCE.** Service pieces don't have to be as intimately revealing as first-person essays. Yet it can be valuable to begin by sharing distinctive material from your own experience. My *New York Post* "A New Yorker's Guide to Quitting Smoking" started, "Now that cigarettes in the city are more expensive, I'm extra happy I quit my twenty-five-year addiction sixty-five days ago through a creative combination of popcorn, nicotine patches, and the treadmill." My *Cosmopolitan* piece "How Therapy Changed My Life" began, "When I was twenty years old, I moved to Manhattan against my parents' wishes. I was wracked with guilt and confusion. My exciting big-city career was a bust. My relationships with men were a mess. I was miserable, depressed, and suicidal. My friend Claire gave me the number of a therapist ..." After it ran across a three-page spread, my parents called me to complain, "Why don't you just tell the whole world you're in therapy?"—until I mentioned that I'd received a $3,500 check for that many words. After I finally quit drinking and smoking cigarettes, I crafted how-to stories on ways I'd learned to stop my

addictions for *Time Out New York, New York Post, Psychology Today,* and a recovery website called *The Fix* that led to my addiction books. The money I made allowed me to claim a tax write-off for nicotine patches and part of my addiction therapy as business expenses.

6. **STUDY DIFFERENT TYPES OF SERVICE.** The most common how-to articles I see in newspapers, magazines, and webzines fall into these categories: Health and Fitness ("How to Lose 10 Pounds Doing Yoga Before Memorial Day"), Food and Drink ("The Best French Wines That Will Get You Drunk For Under $7"), Romantic Relationships ("Ways to Heat Things Up Under the Covers"), Entertainment Recommendations ("Best New On-Demand Movies to Binge-Watch This Summer"), Travel ("Japan on $100 a Day"), and Business/Money Advice ("Safest Investments for a Beginner"). *The Byline Bible,* for instance, could be considered a Business/Money how-to book for creative people interested in careers in writing and journalism.

7. **SHOW ORIGINALITY, CREATIVITY, OR ATTITUDE.** Most editors say what they really want is to read something they haven't seen before, though it may feel like everything's been done. "Tiny Town" was a roundup of which restaurants and movie theaters offered children's discounts (and checked ID) written by my petite baby-faced twenty-eight-year-old student who did research dressed in overalls, pigtails, and glitter. Another student had luck with "Valentine's Day Movies to Make You Happy You're Single," listing love-gone-wrong films, like *The War of the Roses* and *Fatal Attraction.* (I notice this take has been picked up in different ways in many webzines every year since.)

8. **FIND A TOPICAL, FRESH, OR LOCAL ANGLE.** To sharpen the appeal of my quit-smoking piece, I added every single timely mention I could find. I updated smoking statistics from the Centers for Disease Control and Prevention and included the latest anti-smoking laws in the state. Plus I added local luminaries—like *Rolling Stone*'s Jann Wenner and Knopf exec Sonny Mehta—who'd recently attempted to kick their smoking habits, while former New York City Mayor Michael Bloomberg kept raising the cost of cigarettes.

9. **PURSUE EXPERTS.** Supplement your own knowledge by citing leaders in the field. I find authors are often happy to be quoted if I men-

tion their book on my topic, as are professors known in their fields. For an Atlantic.com story, I once posted a query for recent graduates of M.F.A. programs in the United States on a writer's Facebook group, and within minutes I had one hundred private messages. When I wrote the aforementioned quit-smoking piece, I interviewed an addiction specialist, hypnotherapist, acupuncturist, psycho-pharmacologist, Stop Smoking Medical Center group leader, director from the American Cancer Society, holistic healer, yoga teacher, and aerobics instructor—all with unusual methods for helping clients quit. Had I just wanted to share the opinions of the addiction specialist, that would look more like a profile of one individual. Depending on the length and publication, many service pieces share a roundup of different opinions and expertise. Yet unless you have an editor officially committed to your piece, while you gather quotes, be humble and ambiguous about where you'll be submitting it. You're better off being understated and saying, "I'm a freelancer doing research, and I hoped you'd have time to answer a few questions," or "I'm a student," or mention your previous clips. But don't promise a source he will be included in or say, "I'm aiming this at *The Washington Post*." (What if the piece is rejected or the editor cuts their lines out?)

10. **CONSIDER YOUR READERS' BANK ACCOUNTS.** The writer Patricia Marx's engaging "On and Off the Avenue" shopping column for *The New Yorker* listed a $2,495 Armani silk blazer, appropriate for that affluent audience. The New York *Daily News'* readership isn't as wealthy. Thus my student Alyssa Pinsker sold the paper a piece on how to travel the world for free. *New York Post* readers also differ from the Armani blazer crowd, so my lede for my quit-smoking article began, "Now that cigarettes are so expensive ..." In fact, under the headline "A New Yorker's Guide to Quitting Smoking," the subtitle mentioned the rising cost of a pack and said, "Fuggedaboutit! With sky-high cigarette prices, now's the time to kick the habit."

Stressing the importance of the demographics of different readerships to my journalism classes, I shared the legendary rumor about *New York Post* owner Rupert Murdoch bumping into Alfred Bloomingdale, owner of the famed luxury department store, at a party. Murdoch asked, "Why doesn't your store advertise in the *New York Post*?" Bloomingdale supposedly answered, "Because your readers are our shoplifters."

11. **PUT YOUR PERSONALITY ON DISPLAY.** You can be snarky, revealing, or funny. (But the main purpose has to be helpful advice to readers, not just to make them laugh.) My former student Marci Alboher shared an engaging story for her *Time Out New York* travel piece on reasons to vacation in Wildwood, New Jersey, where she grew up: "For years I shuddered at the mention of my hometown. When college friends asked me where I was from, I mumbled, 'Jersey Shore.' These days, I'm glad that I grew up in such a kitschy place."

12. **DON'T REPEAT THE OBVIOUS.** If you're going to pen a service article, cough up secrets that your audience might not be familiar with. I don't need to be told how to apply lip gloss, that I'll "catch more flies with honey than vinegar," or why using frequent-flier miles might get me a cheaper plane ticket. However, my former globetrotting student Seth Kugel's *New York Times* Frugal Traveler piece "8 Things You Can Do Now to Save Money on Travel" shared insider info I'd never heard before about how switching airlines, times, days, schedules, and even my cell phone plan could get me cheaper seats. In my favorite tip, he suggested applying for a special Citi Advantage credit card that would give me fifty thousand miles if I spent three thousand dollars in the first three months. I needed to buy a computer, so I put it on the new credit card and wound up upgrading two American Airline seats to Los Angeles from coach to business class. It worked so well I told my husband to apply for that credit card, too.

13. **BE COUNTERINTUITIVE.** As someone who has written a lot of addiction advice pieces, I never want to state what people already know or can find in minutes by Googling, like "many people quit drinking by going to AA meetings." For my *Salon* service piece aimed at New Year's resolutions, I went against the grain by calling it "New Year's

Is Actually a Bad Day to Quit." The editor liked that unusual take so much he expanded the title to "New Year's Is a Bad Day to Quit Sniffing Glue—Or Anything Else: Make Those Resolutions, Sure, But Don't Dream of Starting Today." Underneath was a picture of an actor dressed as a pilot from the film comedy *Airplane*, sniffing glue. (Did I mention that the writer doesn't get to pick his own headline or illustration?)

14. **PROVIDE READERS WITH CONTACT INFO.** Whether it's phone numbers, e-mail addresses, or websites, be sure to include a fast way for readers to find the services you discuss. I admit to having a gung-ho reaction to a service piece promising all-you-can-eat sushi. Clipped article in hand, I checked out several of the restaurants mentioned in my neighborhood that same day. In retrospect, the author could do a follow-up on foods that should never be all-you-can-eat.

What Not to Do

1. Don't share obvious, completely dumbed-down advice without a new spin, for example "Lose Weight by Eating Less and Exercising More." (A more recent, idiosyncratic piece I read was "Lose 10 Pounds in a Month Micro-Fasting" that suggested cutting back to 750 calories two days a week.)
2. Don't make it a stale and general "evergreen," as if your piece could have been written generations ago, like "How to Find a Job, Happiness, and a Husband."
3. Don't include quotes or facts from a study without triple-checking its veracity and date.
4. Don't pick a topic you're not interested in or know zero about, thinking you can wing it.
5. Don't ever pitch an editor by asking, "I'm going to Japan, you need anything?" Do the work and come up with a much better, more specific pitch.

Service Pieces I've Sold

Here are some links to self-help ideas that editors paid me for over the years.

- "The 8 Biggest Money Questions Asked by Live-In Lovers & What Not to Share" (*Glamour*)
- "Ways to Loosen Up With a New Lover" (*Cosmopolitan*)
- "Understanding Your Girlfriend: The Male-to-Female Dictionary Guide" (*Penthouse*)
- "What Not to Do After You've Been Dumped" (*Woman's Own*)
- "Get Rid of Him Fast: How to Forget the Man You're Obsessing About" (*Hamptons* Magazine)
- "No Strings Attached: 10 Benefits of Keeping a Man at Arm's Length" (*Woman's Own*)
- "Why Marrying in Midlife Is Better" (*The Forward*)
- "Stop Smoking: There's No Magic Trick, But These 10 Methods Can Take the Sting Out" (*Time Out New York*)
- "Ways New Yorkers Quit Smoking" (*New York Post*)
- "Therapy Changed My Life" (*Cosmopolitan*)
- "The Dangers of Over-Exercising" (*Swing* magazine)
- "Jewish Women Gamble Too: Where to Get Help" (*Lilith* magazine)
- "How to Tell If It's a Habit—or an Addiction" (*Psychology Today/ HuffPost*)
- "13 Ways to Quit Anything" (*Psychology Today/HuffPost*)
- "Don't Quit Addictions on New Year's and Other Advice for Addicts" (*Salon*)
- "Make Me Worry You're Not Okay: How to Use Humiliation in Memoir" (*The New York Times*)
- "City's Getting Verse: Where to Hear Performance Poetry" (*New York Post*)
- "They Only Come Out at Night Downtown: Late Night Performance Art Shows" (*New York Post*)
- "Ways to Fake Art Expertise" (*Smock* magazine)
- "Best Books by Male Authors of the Season" (*Penthouse*)
- "Why Not Be Footloose and Freelance: Dreaming About Self-Employment? Put Some Foundation Under the Fantasy With This Get-Set Guide to Working on Your Own" (*Cosmopolitan*)

- "8 Secrets of Persuasion: Strategies for Selling Your Ideas, Yourself, Anything Related to Work—Over the Phone or in Person" (*Bottom Line* magazine)
- "How to Make It Through Adversity: Quitters, Campers, and Climbers" (*Bottom Line* magazine)
- "How to Find a Writing Mentor" (*The Writer*)
- "How to Sell Your First Book" (*The Writer* cover story)

SERVICE PIECES BY MY STUDENTS

5 WAYS TO UNDERSTAND TODDLERS

By Jessica Milliken, Washington Post Parenting, May 26, 2015

"A key test is resisting the temptation to control everything," said Tovah Klein, also known as "The Toddler Whisperer." She would know, with three kids and more than two decades of research as the Director of Columbia University's Barnard Center for Toddler Development. She's an expert from the land of tiny people.

At a recent interview in New York, the 50-year-old mom to a trio of boys looked like she never skipped a night's sleep. Impressive, because in addition to being a Psychology professor at Columbia, Klein is also on tour promoting her book "How Toddlers Thrive," just released in paperback. According to her research, the early years are critical for predicting self-regulation later in life.

In her new book, Klein demystifies what's happening in the brains of children ages 2 to 5 that makes their behavior so turbulent. She reveals tools caregivers can use to plant seeds of lifelong success in children during this "lab for later." Klein notes the needs of kids haven't changed, but with ample information on the Web and obsessive comparisons with other parents via social media, parents are more self-doubting than ever.

"Family life can feel like a competitive arena rather than the very personal process that it is," she said.

Klein believes that well-intentioned parents can get in the way of their toddlers' development by overcorrecting, criticizing and trying to tame erratic behavior. She explained that, when children feel securely loved and adults step back a little, a child who is resilient, empathetic, and curious will authentically emerge on his own.

As a mother to two-year-old son, I wanted to know her secret to raising such grounded and well-behaved angels.

"Try to see the world through their eyes," Klein suggests, encouraging moms and dads to get to know their offspring. She insists life with little ones can be calm, fun and enjoyable, but says it starts with recognizing their shifting cues and adjusting our reactions.

"Stick to routines, be flexible. And humor can go a long way for everyone," she adds.

Klein shared her five principles for parenting from a child's point of view:

1. Stay close even when it's hard. Don't see resistance as defiance. As parents, we are the rocks. Kids need us to stay calm even when they are difficult. When they push us away, we should move toward them. They don't really want to be left alone. They are navigating complicated feelings of independence and attachment.

2. You're in charge. Toddlers need limits and are looking for authority. Some parents are anxious that their children might become more challenging, and they get stuck in emotional battles, thinking they can't give in. Other parents give up completely. But setting firm limits builds trust. By allowing our little boy to be upset with us, we are teaching him to handle his emotions in a safe place, and that love remains even when he misbehaves. Also we need to pick our battles—junior can't cross the street alone, but let him win sometimes, such as when he wants to press the elevator button.

3. Be consistent. Your schedule should frame the day, not overwhelm it. Toddlers lack a sense of time. Having a routine teaches them organization, which they will build on for the rest of their lives. A big part of child be-havior comes from the attitude of the parent. They watch us, how we react to things, and how we treat other people. Birth to age five is an important time to establish a caring relationship. Kids need a supportive environment where they can play, have fun and learn about themselves through problem solving. They don't need dual language classes. They'll be happy just building Legos with you on the floor.

4. Be realistic. In order for little boys and girls to feel self-assured, we need to have reasonable expectations of what they can and can't do. Sometimes we are in a hurry to move on to the next stage—whether it's learning to read, sitting at the table or staying on the toilet. But development is not a straight line. With growth, there will also be tantrums. Sometimes, especially with social media, we look at their milestones as a reflection of us. It's not. Development is slow, and individualized.

5. Accept your child for who she is. We all have hopes and desires for our families. They get in the way when we can't separate our dreams from seeing who our little ones really are. Too many demands can disappoint us, and end up causing them shame—like pushing them into social situations, assuming they want to be popular or outgoing, because we wanted to be. Stop and ask yourself "Who is my child? What does she want and what do I want?" She might be very different from you. If you can accept your child the way she is, she'll thrive.

7 WAYS TO STAY HAPPY (ALL YEAR LONG)

By Joe Antol, Your Tango,
February 15, 2008

Hint: Treat every day as if it's Valentine's Day.

Ah, Valentine's Day, the one annual holiday where couples-only need apply. It's one thing to keep your Valentine happy in the short term. Expensive baubles and dinners will do that. For the long haul, however, more original techniques are required. Having taken the vow, everyone wants a long, loving and happy marriage, yet half of all marriages are destined to fail. As a 42 year old male Manhattanite who's been with the same woman for 17 years, married 12 and had a child for 5 I think I have a few tricks to keep your mate happy. To whit:

1. Sex. Put out or get out. Marriage is, among other things, a convenient means of getting laid on a regular basis. Or it should be. Granted, the pelvic coals may dim a bit with time, but if they're completely dark then Fix The Problem. Do it even if you don't want to; and if you don't want to, figure out why. A shrink, Viagra, porn, whips, chains, shopping, whatever it takes. If you're too busy, put an entry in the calendar. Just tired? Get more sleep.

2. Kissing. Do it early, often and randomly. When you or the Missus leaves for work in the morning, give each other a kiss. Just had a fight over who forgot to make the coffee? Kiss anyway. There's no better martial lubricant than a good smooch. As for the random part, I kiss my wife whenever she sneezes.

3. Flowers. Men, listen to me. Never, never buy flowers for birthdays, anniversaries or, most importantly, Valentine's Day. If she expects floral delights and you fail to satisfy, you're screwed. If you remember these occasions with flowers, she's happy, but you're just doing your job. Instead, give on a whim. Since it's a surprise, there's no possibility for disappointment. For The Big Day, save yourself the 60 bucks you'll sink on a dozen American Beauties and FedEx her a couple of pieces of Stroehmann's finest with a note telling her she's the greatest thing since sliced bread. She'll *love* your originality and fiscal restraint. Women, just buy flowers. Guys do like them. Your man may feign embarrassment, but he'll be warm and happy on the inside.

4. Shave. Women: shave the legs, the pits and anything else you dare. Keep in mind, if he wanted to hear the gentle rustle of armpit hair he'd have married a Wesleyan woman studies major. And he doesn't care what French women do. You're not French and we're not in France. And guys: that weekend growth you're sporting is only tolerated because you're heading off to the Home Depot in the performance of your manly duties (fixing something). You don't look suave and Latin, you look like a slob. And it chafes her skin.

5. Sleeping. If you're sleeping under the same roof, always sleep together. No excuses. Women, don't banish your man to the couch or stomp off to pout in the spare bedroom. If you've had a fight, and they do happen, either make up or suck it up. Lie precariously at the edge of

the mattress and fume if you must, but lie in the same bed.

6. Size. Don't kid yourself: Lust Matters. Women, he may tell you that extra girth means "more of you to love," but he's lying. Guys, my wife says: "Outgrow that wedding ring and I'll outgrow you." You may have convinced yourselves that those 20 extra pounds make you "cuddly," but no matter how many sweaters or layers you pile on, you're still fat. When I've asked my wife if she'll still love me if I get chubby, she replies: "Of course, but I'll miss you."

7. Children. Don't have kids to have a happy marriage. Have a happy marriage, then have kids. Women, if the relationship is circling the bowl, children won't help. They won't bring you closer and give you a common bond. If you already have problems a baby will dial them up to eleven. Children are the most frustrating, annoying creatures in existence, but they're also the most wonderful little beings in the world. A good, strong marriage is made more so by a family. Then there really is "more to love."

SNACK ATTACK

By Cara O'Flynn, New York Post, June 16, 2008

It's 3 p.m. and your stomach's growling—no way you're going to make it to dinnertime. Next stop: the office vending machine.

There you stand, dollar bill in hand, eyeing the selections. Your expectations are low as far as finding anything healthy and/or nonfattening, but some goodies are better than others. So how best to choose?

City chain restaurants are now required by law to post calories on menus so diners can order their Whoppers and Bloomin' Onions with open eyes. But you can't eye the nutritional information on the Snickers bar until it's actually in your hand—and by then it's too late.

So, to guide the hungry worker, we turned to Upper East Side nutritionist

Sophie Pachella, and had her review the offerings in the vending machine here at work world headquarters.

As a rule, says Pachella, "A good snack raises your energy level with a combination of complex carbohydrates, protein and healthy fats." (Examples include dry-roasted nuts, hard-boiled eggs and yogurt—not exactly typical vending machine fare.)

Bad snacks are typically high in carbohydrates or sugar without any healthy fat or protein.

"They cause your blood sugar to rise and then crash about a half-hour later, leaving you rabid with hunger," she says. (Tip: If you must gobble a high-carb snack, pair it with a handful of nuts to maintain level blood sugar.)

With these and other considerations in mind, Pachella picked her five best and worst choices for office grazing. Keep in mind, though: The "good" options are merely less bad than the rest.

Gobbling Guidelines

Nutritionish Sophie Pachella, the founder of EatStrong.com, offered a few general guidelines for packaged snacks that help more than they hurt.

* Don't let fat fool you: Just because something's fat-free doesn't mean a lot of other things aren't wrong with it—and good fats from natural sources aren't something to run from.

"A package of peanuts has 30 grams of fat but is a far healthier choice than jelly beans, which are fat-free but all sugar," Pachella says.

* Avoid products containing hydrogenated oils and high-fructose corn syrup—or try to, anyway (they're in most packaged foods).

* Don't believe everything you read: Some foods marketed as good for you often aren't. Reduced-fat doesn't mean low-fat, just less than the regular version.

 Granola bars may sound wholesome, but they're usually full of sugar and bad, processed fats.

* In general, look for items that have 1) less than 300 calories; 2) less than 2 grams of saturated fat; 3) 7 grams or more of protein; and 4) 3 grams or more of fiber.

Snacks to Skip

Dipsy Doodles. Essentially fried corn, these fatty chips have no redeeming nutritional qualities. (Plus, being seen with a product by this name will do nothing for your workplace credibility.)

 Linden's Chocolate Chip Cookies. This celebration of hydrogenated oil and sugar will spend forever on your hips.

And that moment on your lips is so not worth it.

Twix. It might be fun to get two candy bars in one tidy package, but these have as much saturated fat as a McDonalds double cheeseburger. Enough said.

Skittles. The worst ingredients in food are sugar, corn syrup and hydrogenated palm oil. A bag of these fruity candies hits the trifecta. They're fat-free, but what you eat once the sugar rush ends won't be.

Big Texas Cinnamon Roll. As a rule of thumb, any food with "Texas" in the name is unlikely to shave inches from your waistline. This preservative-filled bun has all the calories of a meal.

Lesser Evils

Baked Doritos. All carbs, but they're relatively low in calories and fat, and that's about all you can hope for in a junk food. If you're hung over these will satisfy your salt craving for a bit, but not much else.

Stacy's pita chips. These are relatively high in fat and low in protein. But they're made with natural ingredients, so you could do worse. Good when you want to indulge in some mindless carbcrunching.

Snyder's Sourdough Nibblers. These boast few ingredients, which is a plus. They're also free of hydrogenated oil and high fructose corn syrup, making them a decent option for a quick boost.

Mr. Nature No-Salt Trail Mix. This mix of nuts, seeds and raisins offers the perfect blend of protein and healthy fat needed to maintain energy and stave off fantasies about your next meal for a few hours.

Reese's Peanut Butter Cups. If you're having a bad day and want to placate yourself with chocolate, go for the Reese's. They have less sugar than other candy bars, and the peanut butter offers some protein.

TALKING TO KIDS ABOUT RACIAL VIOLENCE

By Haig Chahinian, New York Times Well Family, July 16, 2016

My husband is white; as an Armenian man, I am a hue darker, and our 10-year-old daughter is biracial, with brown skin. We've tried to shield her from some of the recent painful news stories related to bias. But after last week's killings of two African-American men by police officers, and then the killings of five Dallas police officers, we need to be ready to talk with her about the terrors of prejudice.

I reached out to some experts who help teenagers and parents make sense of violent racism, and work toward something better. Here is some of the wisdom they offered:

Don't avoid it. "As moms and dads, we can be scared to talk about something so raw, and ugly," said Tamara Buckley, an associate professor of counseling and psychology at Hunter College and the co-author of "The Color Bind: Talking (and Not Talking) About Race at Work." "But not bringing it up doesn't protect your family. It only puts the conversation in others' hands."

All kids—not just minorities—need to talk. "Every youth needs to be nurtured to practice empathy, not judgment," said Renée Watson, who has worked with high school students struggling to process the Black Lives Matter movement and whose work includes the young adult novel "This Side of Home." "It's time for us to get out of our own worlds. To be critical thinkers, young people must be exposed to news about every demographic."

It's O.K. not to have answers. "Don't be afraid to be vulnerable in front of your child," said Ms. Watson. "Even as a teacher I don't know everything. It's not about me trying to get students to think how I do, but to create room for dialogue."

Ask open-ended questions. Buckley suggested asking: "How are you feeling about what you're seeing in the news? What are your friends saying? What bothers you the most?"

Notice changes in behavior. "Your son might answer, 'It's not bothering me,'" Dr. Buckley said. "Some young people may be in such shock they can't take in the news. Keep a close eye on them. Do they seem stressed? Isolated? Watch for changes in demeanor, which can suggest they're upset even if they're telling you otherwise."

Turn to art. "If things get tense, music, painting, and dance are great ways to express yourself," said Ms. Watson, who was a 2013 NAACP Image Award nominee. She said multicultural publishers like Lee & Low "know we need a mix of 'mirror' books—in which we see ourselves reflected—and 'window' books—in which we see others." She offered a checklist to measure the diversity in your home library: Do all the titles featuring black characters focus only on slavery? Do all the ones about Latinos emphasize immigration? Are all your L.G.B.T.Q. books coming out stories? If so, you could consider books that examine broader issues in these communities.

Educate yourself about social justice. "Know the difference between equality and equity," said Shuber Naranjo, a diversity educator at Bank Street School for Children in Manhattan. "It's like in a Broadway theater, there are the same number of stalls in the women's and men's bathrooms. It's equal, but not equitable, because you see a longer line for women."

Don't go it alone. Racism is a tough subject for one person to tackle. "Seek out other dads and moms," Dr. Buckley suggested, "and find ways to support one another. I've noticed all this racial violence has been a real point of connection between black and white parents."

HOW TO GET THE MOST OUT OF YOUR SUMMER OYSTERS

By Branden Janese, Men's Journal, May 14, 2005

Chef Mads Refslund of ACME in Manhattan likes to give oysters the opportunity to shine in and outside of the shell. "I incorporate oysters into unusual dishes such as lamb-and-oyster tartare with green almonds. I also blend oysters with parsley and oil to create a creamy emulsion, almost like a mayonnaise, [that's] great with crudités such as radishes and turnips." You need some serious skills to properly prepare oysters. Luckily, Chef Refslund isn't stingy with his secrets. "Since a lot of cooking is done during the summer with open flames, roasting oysters is easy yet impressive. The heat from the fire opens them (no need to learn how to shuck) and then a dollop of mushroom or herb butter to melt inside them will wow your guests."

As far as a drinking partner is concerned, Refslund mentions, "The juniper notes in a classic gin martini would suit oysters nicely, or a Whiskey Sour." He suggests pairing creamier oysters, such as the East Coast Belon, with big stouts, like Guinness. "Oysters with high salinity will go well with a lager and sour beers, such as pilsners," he says. For diners new to oysters, Refslund adds, "Taste them with different cold white wines to see how a pairing brings out their characteristics."

If you don't love them raw, try oysters grilled or make a stew. To ensure you don't cut yourself shucking, wear a glove or ask your fishmonger to do it for you. I don't know how much truth there is to the aphrodisiac rumor, but there is an unexpected pleasure about the oyster experience. If you're looking to build an oyster plate at home, Refslund has some advice.

"Of course the most important thing is very fresh oysters, and if you are serving them cold, then ice is essential. If you're serving them at home, you can crush ice the old fashioned way: make a sack of ice out of a dishtowel and use a hammer to crush the cubes. At ACME I serve fresh oysters with rose-hip vinegar and grape seed oil, which keep a great balance between the salinity and creaminess of the oysters. We also serve grilled oysters with celery and parsley juice on a bed of pine branches that we light before they leave the kitchen. This gives an aromatic, smoky layer to the enjoyment of the bivalves, which really suits them. Mignonette is traditional but a purist will eat oysters without any accouterments. A few drops of fresh lemon juice are a nice way to enjoy the oysters' flavors with a little extra brightness."

For those of you who aren't fans of raw oysters, there are plenty of other options, including this traditional deep-fried recipe that combines the flavors of the Deep South and the Chesapeake Bay.

Deep-Fried Oysters

Ingredients

1 pint of oysters (usually 20–30, preferably no larger than a half dollar), shucked and stored in their own liquor)

Breading Ingredients

1 pint buttermilk

1 dry pint cornmeal (about 2⅓ cups; I get a crisp crust by using Anson Mills Antebellum fine yellow cornmeal.)

1 dry pint all-purpose flour (about 2⅓ cups)

1 tbsp. Creole seasoning

1 tsp. kosher salt

1 tsp. Old Bay

Directions

Reserve buttermilk in separate container. In a mixing bowl, whisk together the dry ingredients until well-blended. Remove oysters from liquor, draining excess so oysters are still wet but not dripping. Place all of the oysters in buttermilk. One at a time, remove each oyster from the buttermilk, allowing the excess to drip back into the container. Toss to coat all sides in the breading (gently press the breading onto the oyster to help it adhere). Transfer to waxed-paper-lined plate or cookie sheet until oysters are all breaded.

In a heavy stockpot with high sides fitted with a deep-frying (or candy) thermometer, bring at least two inches of peanut oil to 375°F.

Keeping the heat at a steady 375°F and working in batches of six, fry the oysters until they are golden brown and just cooked through, about 90 seconds. (The oysters will curl slightly when they are done.) Using a slotted spoon, remove oysters and drain on brown-paper-bag-lined plate. Sprinkle Old Bay on top.

WILD AT HEART: WILDWOOD, NJ, IS A GLORIOUSLY TACKY BEACH TOWN OF MOTELS, ROLLER COASTERS AND FRIED DOUGH

By Marci Alboher, Time Out
New York, June 22, 2000

For years I shuddered at the mention of my hometown. When college friends asked me where I was from, I mumbled "Jersey shore" and left it at that. If they pressed because they were familiar with the shore, all the worse for me, because then I'd have to admit that it wasn't Margate, Spring Lake or some other affluent area. How I longed to have grown up in a conventional suburb like everyone else. Instead, I came of age in a series of honky-tonk seashore communities, where my parents owned a succession of small motels. From age 16 on, my home was one I could barely say with a straight face—Wildwood, NJ, mother of all cheesy beach towns, with more tattoos per square foot than your local veteran's hall, a nightlife catering to South Philadelphia's prom-age set and an amusement-packed boardwalk.

These days, I'm glad that I grew up in such a kitschy place. When I visit my mother on summer weekends, I revel unabashedly in Wildwood's tackiness. While the rest of America has been taken over by chain stores, Wildwood can boast that the nearest shopping mall is some 30 miles away, and there is nary a Starbucks, Blockbuster Video or Gap in sight. Instead, the town has authentic '50s diners and scores of vintage motels with names like Bali Hi, Astronaut and Ship Ahoy—each with a garish neon

sign and props to accentuate its theme.

The buildings are so distinctive that, in the mid 1990s, Philadelphia architect Steven Izenour launched a project where students from the University of Pennsylvania and Yale come to Wildwood to study its style. Neon signs, cantilevered roofs, kidney-shaped pools, plastic palm trees and exotic themes are the hallmarks of what has come to be called "Doo-Wop Architecture." Now, architecture students from several schools make pilgrimages to Wildwood, and town planners and business owners are racing to capitalize on their newfound cred.

The area known as Wildwood is a five-mile-long island beach community (also known as Five Mile Island) that is actually made up of three separate towns: North Wildwood, Wildwood and Wildwood Crest. Connected to the mainland by several bridges, Wildwood is home to the raucous boardwalk; North Wildwood and the Crest are more sedate, toned-down residential neighborhoods, but they too are packed with restaurants and motels. These towns had their heyday in the 1950s and '60s, when they were a summer getaway for Philadelphia's working class, whose infatuation with automobiles made driving holidays de rigueur. At the time, the motel was just emerging as an American institution, and vacationers chose their lodging from gaudy signs evoking romantic locales that were beyond their pocketbooks but not beyond their imaginations. Inside the motels, efficiencies with kitchenettes, game rooms, free ice and color televisions made for the ideal family holiday.

Wildwood's main attractions today are the same as they were 50 years ago: the motels, the boardwalk and the beach. While many parts of the Jersey Shore lament erosion and engage in expensive dredging to maintain their sandy shores, Wildwood's "too much sand" problem is reminiscent of that annoying friend who just can't gain weight. Since the turn of the century, the town has struggled with an ever-expanding strand (the boardwalk has even been moved east several times to bring it closer to the sea). Along this sprawling shorefront runs a boardwalk that is alive day and night with two and a half miles of games of chance, roller coasters, miniature golf courses, batting cages, go-cart tracks and novelty stores. All three major boardwalk food groups (fried, salty and sugared) are well represented.

Dining

There are two types of eating in Wildwood: on the boardwalk and in a restaurant. Some contend that with Mack's pizza (3218 Boardwalk at Wildwood Ave), Kohr's frozen custard (locations along the boardwalk) and countless purveyors of saltwater taffy and fudge, there is no need for a real restaurant, let alone one with a tablecloth. But if you feel a tablecloth will counter some of the damage done to your diet and complexion by boardwalk grazing, here are a few of the best.

Little Italy (5401 Atlantic Ave, Wildwood Crest, 609-523-0999) is the kind of Italian restaurant you'd never find on a quiet street in Venice. It serves up pasta heavy on the red sauce in a dining room painted with murals of the leaning tower of Pisa and the Colosseum. The food is reliable, portions are huge, and the average entrée, with salad and bread, costs about $15, which is reasonable by Wildwood standards. For a take on a small-town steak house, head to Neil's Steak & Chowder House (222 E Schellenger Ave, Wildwood, 609-522-5226; 12oz. steak costs $15 and comes with salad, veggie and potato), which offers an array of basic steaks, chops and seafood in massive portions (notice a trend?). When you tire of the plastic palm trees, it's time for Sunset Bay (400 W Spruce Ave, North Wildwood, 609-523-0411, www.sunsetbay.net; average entrée $14), a beachfront complex where the real palms and the Jamaican band at the Castaways Beach Grill will transport you to the Caribbean. Castaways offers a casual grill menu; the nearby Sunset Bay restaurant has a wider selection, with an emphasis on seafood and grill choices inspired by the tropics. Make a night of it by staying in the complex for minigolf and ice cream at Shipwrecked Dunes Golf Course.

The latest addition to the dining scene is Restaurant Maureen & Martini Bar (3601 Atlantic Ave, Wildwood, 609-522-7747; average entrée $25), whose imaginative contemporary drink menu, offering 19 types of martinis, could be a sign that Wildwood may soon be catering to more than the beer-and-hot pretzels crowd. The food is sophisticated and eclectic, almost a novelty in these parts, and the sign alone—a 27-foot neon martini glass—is worth a gander.

Accommodations

Choices include inns, bed and breakfasts, and even luxurious townhouses, but it should be illegal to spend a weekend on the island without staying in a motel. The summer season has traditionally lasted from Memorial Day to the end of September, but in recent years many resorts have stayed open longer. Rooms sell out far in advance, so call right away—and be warned, motel rate cards are about as complicated as the periodic table (rates vary depending on room type, number of occupants, date and day of the week). One place I visited had a mind-boggling 14 different room types. All rates quoted are for a standard room for two people in high season (late July) and may be slightly higher on weekend nights.

The original tongue-and-groove paneling in certain rooms and multicolored spotlights at Eden Roc (5201 Atlantic Ave, Wildwood, 609-522-1930, www.edenrocmotel.com; $108 per night, with a three-night minimum) make this motel a classic of the genre. Still, you'll feel more like you're at a bed and breakfast, thanks to owner Linda Goldstein's personal touch. Guests are treated to an itinerary-planning session with Goldstein upon arrival and are given use of her lending library.

The Memory Motel (7601 Atlantic Ave, Wildwood Crest, 609-522-3026, www.memorymotel.com; $70) gives Doo-Wop a modern twist with its oversize guitar sign, wall portraits of rock legends like Jim Morrison, and hot-

pink doors. In 1998, owner Peter Ferriero left his corporate job to follow the Rolling Stones on tour. Once home, he decided to open the motel of his dreams. Targeting baby boomers reliving their past, the Memory sports a Jumping Jack splash pool (whose slide emerges from Jagger's giant plastic lips), nightly movies playing outdoors, and movie- or music-themed rooms.

More proof that Doo-Wop need not mean dated is the Starlux (305 E Rio Grande Ave, Wildwood, 609-522-7412, www.moreyhospitality. com; $139), a newcomer scheduled for a June 30 opening. The latest brainchild of the Morey Organization, the family-operated behemoth that owns most of the boardwalk's piers and enough hotels to qualify for a Wildwood monopoly, this contemporary take on Doo-Wop promises to blend a 1950s sensibility with modern amenities. The Morey family built most of Wildwood's original motels, so all eyes are focused on the unveiling of the Starlux.

From the fabulous lollipop-face sign to the real lollipops at the front desk and the candy-colored room doors, The Lollipop Motel (23rd and Atlantic Aves, Wildwood, 609-729-2800, www.lollipopmotel.com; $99) is a great choice for families with young kids.

At the Royal Hawaiian Beachfront Resort (on the beach at Orchid Rd, Wildwood Crest, 609-522-3414, www.royalhawaiianresort.com; $136 per night), plastic palms sitting on a concrete island in the middle of the pool beg you to think like a 1950s Wildwood vacationer—if you can't go to Hawaii, why not drive to a place that looks like a caricature of it?

For those of you wondering, my mom still owns a place in Wildwood (the Spanish-themed Madrid Ocean Resort in the Crest). Sitting by its pool with the sand at my feet, the boardwalk in the distance, and the smell of fried dough wafting through the air, I realize that, while I'm still a long way from Spain, home really ain't so bad.

Getting there

By car, take the NJ Turnpike South to the Garden State Parkway. Continue on Garden State Parkway until Exit 4B, turn right on Rio Grande Ave (Route 47) to Ocean Ave. The drive takes about three hours. Or take a NJ Transit bus from Port Authority (212-564-8484). For more information, visit www .beachcomber. com (a Cape May County search engine), www.jerseyshore-online. com, www.moreyspiers.com, www .doowopusa.org and www.gwcoc.com.

NEVER LEAVE HOME WITHOUT FIDO—ESPECIALLY NOT CHRISTMAS

By Tracy Charlton, New York Post, December 25, 1998

As the holidays approach, I've begun to make preparations for returning home to California: buying airline tickets, calling old friends and getting the dog carrier out of storage. Many people find it strange that I bring my 80-pound mutt Buddy along with me. Despite the hassles involved in transporting a neurotic animal 3,000 miles across country, I've always found that it's worth it.

Here's why:

1.) Saving Dough. American Airlines charges $100 for a round-trip "dog ticket" to go anywhere in the country. The local kennel is $40 a day. If I stay for two weeks, I save $460, and I get to have Buddy with me.

2.) Inner Peace. Although the plane flight is less fun for your dog than for you, it's only 12 hours of misery. In Buddy's case, the rest of the vacation is spent in my Mother's backyard searching for squirrels and digging holes in her plant beds. In the Manhattan kennel he would be inside 24 hours a day.

3.) Mellow Cab Drivers. Cabbies are always fascinated by the fact that you're taking your dog on a plane trip. This inspires stories of their own dogs from the villages where they grew up. They become so busy talking they rarely break the speed limit.

4.) Never A Dull Moment. A mix between a Doberman and a Husky, Buddy has always been high strung. Traveling does not have a mellowing effect on him. There's nothing like being in an airport full of people trying to control a large, snarling dog. While this is not pleasant, it insures that you're never bored.

5.) "The Child." Since my husband

and I don't have children yet, Buddy has achieved the status of "granddog." Every night my mother makes Buddy a special vegetable plate. He is photographed, groomed and fed gourmet beef sticks. This makes my mother very, very happy.

6.) Burn Calories. After eating all those Christmas cookies and candies I want to wallow in what feels like the early stages of a diabetic coma. Instead, I am invariably pestered into taking Buddy on at least one long walk a day. While I never enjoy this at the time, it does ensure that I can wear something besides my husband's sweatpants for the month of January.

7.) Conversation Piece. When visiting high-school friends you can run out of things to say. If you've just flown with your pet from the opposite coast, this rarely happens. Californians think that anyone who moves from their golden paradise to New York City is crazy. When you start traveling with your dog, they know you're nuts. Somehow this has an energizing effect on conversations.

8.) It Wouldn't Be Christmas ... It's just not the holidays without Buddy lying snoring in front of the fireplace, begging for scraps at the table or being forced to pose for pictures with a fake reindeer hat. We're not quite a family without him.

UNCOVERING SOME OF TRIBECA'S HIDDEN SHOPS

By Victoria Grantham,
Downtown Express,
January 4, 2009

As a longtime resident of Tribeca, I've seen the community's dramatic transformation up close. Once known as an outpost populated by pioneers, it became the epicenter of the 9/11 recovery effort, then it morphed into a haven. Movie stars (Julianne Moore, Edie Falco), families (drawn to P.S. 234, P.S./I.S. 89, and Stuyvesant), and now big business (Bed, Bath & Beyond, Barnes & Noble), have flocked to the neighborhood. Mid-upheaval, mom-and-pop shops have been elbowed out, but distinctive small businesses have also sprouted. Some are so tiny, out of the way, or otherwise camouflaged, however, you could blink and miss them. Here are eight semi-hidden gems—from fitness

to food—worth your time and money in the new year.

Kiva Café, 139 Reade St., 212-587-1198, kivacafe.com. Named after the ancient structures in which Anasazi Indians gathered for ceremonies, this cozy nook pairs a welcoming, meditative atmosphere with organic bites. At 200 square feet (at most), it could be easily missed. Beebe Okoye, an architect and artist from Arizona, opened the café in Tribeca and its sibling space in Soho. In addition to nourishing the neighborhood with vegan morsels at brunch and flatbread pizzas and wine at dinner, Kiva showcases local jewelry, ceramics, paintings and photos.

Tribeca Treats, 94 Reade St., 212-571-0500, tribecatreats.com. Rachel Thebault, a banker turned baker, opened this sumptuous confectionary in early 2007. Thebault sells indulgent, beautifully packaged chocolate, cookies and cupcakes and goes beyond the usual, offering custom flavors of truffles for special events. Gourmet chocolate bars sold by the box contain from 2-25 pieces ($4–$45) and are named after local streets, like Franklin and Leonard. The store, slightly off-the-beaten-path, on Reade between Church and West Broadway, has a simple brown box on its sign. Kids can likely locate the place with their eyes closed.

Soda Shop, 125 Chambers St., 212-571-1100, sodashopnewyork.com. The brainchild of Craig Bero, a serial restaurateur (Grange Hall, Anglers and Writers, etc.), and Linda Donahue, a lawyer, Soda Shop is an ode to old New York. It is filled with lovingly scavenged castoffs—like the century-old white marble fireplace Bero unearthed on a demolition site. The spot features other-era candy including Charleston Chews, as well as frothy egg creams, fluffy cinnamon French toast, and bread-crumbed mac 'n' cheese at student-friendly prices. Wedged between an old school barber and a new nail salon and housed under a nondescript half block-long awning, the eatery is like a Russian nesting doll in that it conceals a secret: It has a hidden back room for parties and high tea. The area, which was excavated by the duo, feels otherworldly since it's separated from the rest of the space by a long passage.

The Hideaway, 185 Duane St. (866) 414-9250, thehideawaynyc.com. True to its name, The Hideaway is a relaxed, sign-less refuge tucked on Duane just off of Greenwich. Chef Alex Oefeli, formerly of Raoul's, turns this mellow bar, which is sophisticated without being stuffy, into a place for a simple bite with friends. With crisp décor, an extensive wine list, dishes like panzanella salad, and flat screen televisions, the space manages to function as a hybrid lounge-pub-restaurant without unduly alienating fans of sports, vino or haute cuisine. The location has been semi-cursed (several bars opened and closed there in the span of just a few years), but judging by the neighborhood's response, it seems The Hideaway, launched in 2005 by two Duke alums, is here to stay.

Cadence, 174 Hudson St., 212-226-4400, cadencecycling.com. Cadence, a new multi-sport training center, is a sleek, high-end facility on the corner of Canal St., practically in the mouth of the Holland Tunnel. This Philadelphia offshoot qualifies as "hidden in plain sight" because when I asked my marathon buddy to meet me there she texted me three times when she was out front, unable to find it. (It's raised above street level and not well-marked.) Staffed by cycling and cross-training experts, Cadence has tapped the triathlon trend. The center sells gear, provides mechanical services and offers cycling classes and coaching in its spa-like 10,200-square-foot space. "Valet bike service," which allows clients to store their bikes on-site, and "cycling concierge service," which includes house calls for bicycle fittings, reinforce the high-touch feel. Intrigued, but not motivated to find the place? Check it out by tuning into "Bobby Flay's Throwdown" on the Food Network in February. Flay went head-to-head against amateur triathletes and professional bakers, Pam Weekes and Connie McDonald, of Levain Bakery, in a taping at the center.

Lotus Salon, 141 Reade St., 212-608-

7788, lotusintribeca.com. Lotus Salon on Reade (right near Kiva Café) is a small, affordable place to pop in for a cut, color, or straightening. Walk-in service, relaxing Asian-influenced minimalist décor and laid-back stylists who provide competent, customized cuts make the experience a pleasure. The salon, which has two sisters, (one in SoHo, one in the East Village), is all about easy.

Daisy Dog Studio, 186 Duane St., 212-431-1616, daisydogstudio.com Sandwiched between galleries and high end furniture shops, Emily McCoy's petite Daisy Dog Studio is like a determined little ray of sunshine. Named after McCoy's beloved pitbull, her shop showcases her lively porcelain pieces. Brightly colored circles dominate Mc-Coy's upbeat plates, pots, jars, bowls and mugs. Described as "porcelain for people," the items, priced from $15 to $100, make a great gift. All the pieces have an image of Daisy at the bottom—(her stamp of approval). McCoy donates 5 percent of sales to PETA. Her hours are limited, so try online.

Tribeca girls, 171 Duane St., 212-925-0049, tribecagirls.com. This is a newcomer to a neighborhood long on kids but short on kids' shops. The store serves girls from two to 14. Free candy is designed to lure young shoppers in and encourage repeat visits. Billed as moderately priced, Tribeca girls carries name-brand fashions from Diesel to DKNY. The staff is helpful, not pushy, but parents beware: Tweens are sure to swoon.

12 TIPS FOR COURTEOUS XMAS SHOPPING

By Kathleen Garvin, Philly.com, December 13, 2012

Like millions of Americans, I work in retail and have for the past eight years.

While I'm grateful to have it, my side gig as a cashier can be filled with full-time annoyances when the holiday shopping season sets in. Here are 12 guidelines on how to be a conscious, gainful consumer and not the subject of a salesperson's exasperated looks.

12. FIGURE SALES PRICES OUT ON YOUR OWN. When stores are crowded and staff is limited, don't harass a worker who's already overwhelmed to figure out the price of discounted items. Use the calculator on your cell phone to determine the cost, or phone a mathematically adept friend.

If all else fails, attempting to figure it out on your own can be a good money-saving effort. After wrestling with 15 percent off of $28 inside my head for a few minutes, I usually come to the conclusion I really don't need the shirt that bad anyway.

11. KNOW YOUR LIMIT. Take all the time you need to shop, but decide what you're buying before you get to the register. It's a simple concept, yet many times my "Hi, how are you today?" is met with "Don't let me go above $40."

Also, forgetting to grab one item and running to get it is forgivable; treating the checkout counter like a deliberation dock to decide what you really need and can afford is not. Step aside before you begin to check out to go over your purchases, and call up that

THE BYLINE BIBLE

same mathematically inclined friend if need be.

10. DON'T COMPLAIN ABOUT THE CHANGE. By the look on some people's faces after I've given them $1 bills, you'd think I had spit in the palm of their hand. When it's busy and people are paying with big money, 5s and 10s run out quickly. Deal with it—it's still currency! I'm building up the courage to hand the next complainer a roll of quarters instead of the cash.

9. PAY IN EXACT CHANGE IF THE SITUATION WARRANTS— AND YOU HAVE IT. Everyone is quick to say "I have the change!" but far fewer actually deliver. Unless you owe 4 cents, don't hold up a line digging through your purse for loose pennies. Or, worse, don't search your pockets for that crumpled dollar bill to give with your $20 so you can get 10 back. You're not going to be happy when my register opens.

8. CHECK FOR PAYMENT. While on the subject of money, make sure you have it on you! It never ceases to amaze me how many people go shopping, rack up a huge bill, then realize their payment of choice is still at home. Also, if you're under the age of 80 and insist on paying with a check, please have it partially filled out and have ID in hand when you get to the register.

7. THE STORE ISN'T YOUR PERSONAL TRASH CAN. I don't know why, but the sight of a checkout counter prompts some customers to empty their pockets of old receipts, used tissues and other unidentifiable, even grosser materials. Worse, they often leave their money in the mix for cashiers to sift through. Until stores accept strange hairs, empty soda bottles and pocket fuzzies as payment, keep it off the counter.

6. FOLLOW COMPANY POLICY. Present coupons up front, ask about a questionable item before it's rung up and hold on to receipts with your merchandise.

One time, a woman I swear I'd never seen before entered the food store where I work and plucked me like a criminal out of a police lineup as the cashier who'd sold her the gallon of milk that she a.) didn't have a receipt for and b.) didn't even have anymore—but wanted to "return."

The holiday shopping season is hectic enough—don't unfairly argue coupons, make someone track down a manager for a void, or be the crazy person trying to send back phantom milk.

5. ARE YOU HAUGHTY ... OR NICE? Whoever coined the phrase "the customer is always right" should be put down.

Too many consumers act like VIPs, and worker cheeriness can only last (or look legitimate) for so long before the countless long, busy shifts take their toll. Remember "please" and "thank you" go further than unpleasant demands. The response to the rude customer who suddenly needs an extra gift bag or box? "Sorry, it's not store policy."

4. EXPLAIN, DON'T EXCLAIM. Seasonal employees or slow machines can result in long lines and frustration. If someone is doing his or her best to help remedy a situation, show a little patience and ask for more assistance if it's needed. Demeaning someone who's already forced to wear a Santa hat is bad for everyone.

3. POSTPONE NOW? DON'T POUT LATER. For three years, I worked in a uniform store where some parents would try to purchase embroidered

sweaters, plaid jumpers and specialty-size clothing the day before school started.

I still remember the shocked-stupid expressions when they found out the items would have to be ordered because tens of thousands of students had bought the same things earlier. No one in retail is making enough money to put up with a customer's bad attitude due to poor planning. If you wait until the last minute, be prepared to be let down. And trust that if the company says something will be in stock and it's not, the lowly salesperson had nothing to do with it.

2. PRACTICE GOOD PAYMENT. If you need to put a hand down your shirt, dig through a boot or look anywhere on your body for funds (there's a story where I work that we refer to as "crotch money"), you need to invest in a wallet. It's not just incredibly crass, it's unsanitary. And no credit cards or writing instruments in your mouth, either.

1. NO, NO, NO "MERRY CHRISTMAS"? Lastly, don't try to correct a salesperson who wishes you a Merry Christmas—it's not necessary to debate religion or non-belief on your way out the door. I'm paler than white in the wintertime, but if someone wished me a "Happy Kwanzaa," I'd graciously accept. The bottom line: Someone is wishing you well! Even if it doesn't apply, thank the person for the sentiment.

More Service Pieces by My Students

- "These Common E-mail Mistakes are Ruining Your Credibility" by Joel Schwartzberg (Fastcompany.com) www.fastcompany.com/40480306/these-common-emails-mistakes-are-ruining-your-credibility
- "7 Steps to a Cheaper Hotel Room" by Seth Kugel (*The New York Times'* "Frugal Traveler" column) www.nytimes.com/2014/08/10/travel/7-steps-to-a-cheaper-hotel-room.html
- "5 Things Not to Say to My Grieving Children on Father's Day" by Barbara Kemp (*Parents*) www.parents.com/parenting/dynamics/single-parenting/things-not-to-say-to-my-grieving-children-on-fathers-day/
- "What's New, Buenos Aires?" by Marci Alboher (*Travel & Leisure*)
- "With a Little Work, You Can Go Far & Travel for Free" by Alyssa Pinsker (New York *Daily News*)
- "How to Keep Kid Athletes Safe" (*The Resident*) by Kenan Trebincevic
- "Crafty When It's Drafty" by Cara O'Flynn (*New York Post*) nypost.com/2008/02/23/crafty-when-its-drafty/
- "Why You Should Never Turn Down a Blind Date: You Could Actually Meet a Darling Man. At the Very Least, You'll Keep Your Friends Howling With Your Fix-up Stories" by Madeline Wolf (*Cosmopolitan*)

CHAPTER 10

Pitch vs. Writing

I've found it's much better to complete an entire personal essay, op-ed, regional article, humor piece, poem, short story, or novel instead of just pitching the idea. Yet there are some kinds of work where an advance pitch letter can be beneficial—or required. That means, before you waste a lot of time writing something that may never sell, query the editor first, to ask if he would be interested in your story. This is especially important if you plan to spend a lot of time and money, travel, do research, or contact elusive sources.

If you're starting out and have no clips, I don't advocate pitching stories you haven't yet written to editors you've never met. It's much easier to finish and publish a completed piece, especially with the five popular assignments I've outlined. Why would a publication give a chance to an unknown when it can use a seasoned pro from their stable? But if you have previous clips, an unusual expertise, or the inside scoop on a good story, pitching first might be the way to go.

A pitch letter is different from a cover letter because you aren't attaching the entire piece with it. You're checking to see if an editor will be interested in your story before you do most of the work.

Coming up with an effective pitch can be more difficult than crafting a cover letter, since you must do more than describe the finished product you've enclosed. With a completed essay, an editor makes a decision only by reading it. Without the benefit of having three brilliant pages you've attached, you have to sell your idea and yourself fast, often in a concise paragraph or two. Try to be enticing, like a sales pitch, selling your story with juicy tidbits that promise more to come. Sum up what research you plan to do, or who you will interview. I do this carefully, without giving away names, e-mails, and phone numbers that could make it easy for the piece to be stolen out from under me. Pitching a piece on ways New Yorkers stop smoking to *Time Out New York*, I said I would interview an addiction specialist, Smokenders founder, Nicotine Anonymous group leader, and psycho-pharmacologist helping smokers quit with Zyban, without giving away anything more specific.

You'll need to find out if the publication covered your topic before, and what they think of your subject. (If they've panned a movie, the editor probably won't want to profile the star, director, or producer.) You can do preinterviews with experts on your topic and sprinkle in dialogue or controversial opinions. Do advance research to ask smart questions. But never say to a source, "I'm pitching this to *Harper's Magazine*" before you have the assignment. Otherwise you may have to go back to tell your source if you are rejected, and you'll lose credibility. Either mention your previous clips ("In the past I've freelanced for the New York *Daily News* and *The Nation*"), say you're a student ("I'm currently working on a piece in my class"), or better yet, just tell them your interest ("I'm a freelance writer fascinated with your latest project. Would you have a few minutes to tell me more about it?").

You may have to prove your expertise or do more legwork to demonstrate you are serious and know something they don't. You have a very short space to convince an editor this is an important or timely subject she should let *you* cover. As my fabulous *Tablet* editor Wayne Hoffman told my students, you always have to answer: **Why you, why me, why now?**

What Should Be Pitched Before Writing

1. Profiles and Q&As where you'll meet and interview the subject
2. Reviews of books, movies, or TV shows that would require getting advance copies or DVDs (but beware: most editors have their own staff critics and assign them months in advance)
3. Travel pieces that might cost a lot (and many publications won't allow free trips or reimburse all your expenses, even if they want your story)

4. News stories and investigative pieces (which can be complicated and you may have to emphasize your platform and provide proof of your facts)
5. Nonfiction books (even a memoir can be sold with a twenty- to one-hundred-page proposal)

Why an Editor May Give You a Shot

1. **You offer a timely, exciting, exclusive story he is interested in.** I broke into *The New York Times Magazine* after I'd learned insider info that Judith Regan, an infamous Simon & Schuster book editor, had been stolen away to HarperCollins by its owner Rupert Murdoch.
2. **You're connected.** When my Michigan junior high pal Brian O'Connor became head of a small Manhattan newspaper, he said yes to my ideas, even though I was green when it came to reporting.
3. **You have expertise she doesn't have.** Since my former student Christine Kenneally had a Ph.D. in biology, she came up with intricate, fascinating science and technology feature ideas. Another former student, Sheelah Kolhatkar, was a former hedge fund analyst, so her business savvy was rare among liberal arts writers. Not that you need an advanced degree or years of experience. In that *Time Out New York* pitch, the fact that I was a former chain-smoker gave me enough of a platform.
4. **The publication is broke/desperate and can't pay much or at all.** A colleague who became editor-in-chief of a regional magazine had a very tight budget. So she allowed several students who were starting out to do travel pieces without pay. She did, however, let them take free press trips and travel junkets—which would be against *Travel + Leisure* and *Condé Nast Traveler* ethics policies, since you could be biased after receiving freebies.
5. **You do your homework and write an endearing, flattering pitch letter** in the voice of the section you're pitching that is so persuasive the editor is won over and decides to give you a try "on spec."

Pitch and Cover Letter Commonalities

1. Find the right editor, section, or column, the same way you do with finished pieces.
2. Start both letters with any connection to the editor you have, for example "My friend David Smith gave me your e-mail" or "As a fellow Wolverine, I thought you might consider ..." Include sincere flattery about the editor's work or what he's previously run.
3. Say exactly what you want to write upfront, as I did for this pithy *New York Post* pitch: "I hoped you'll consider my profile of Bonnie Weisman, a feminist clown who strips on roller skates while playing the saxophone, which I thought might work for your entertainment section. She'll be at the Public Theater October 1–20."
4. End with a line or two about yourself, such as "My work has appeared in *USA Today* and *Variety*." Or, if you have no clips, at least mention your job, hobby, lifestyle, or college major that shows you can tackle the subject you pitched, as in:
   "I'm currently a drama student at the University of Michigan."
   "I've worked in finance for ten years ..."
   "Being an avid stamp collector ..."
   "As the divorced mother of four kids under the age of ten ..."
5. Follow up the same way as essays before moving onto the next editor, but don't submit to multiple publications at the same time.

Make Your Pitches Stand Out

1. Do lots of preliminary homework so you sound like an expert on your topic. Be timely and include anyone famous or important in the field who fits into your piece for a topical/cultural edge and any specific connections you have. A friend used to joke about an idea that would be a no-go "until Madonna peed on it" (meaning until you found a celebrity endorsement).

2. Research the editor and the publication so you can start with something smart and flattering.
3. Pick subjects where you have an idiosyncratic expertise or insider knowledge few others have.
4. Include a sexy title and subtitle of your article in your pitch.
5. Start writing the piece, then steal your best lines for the pitch to show the editor it'll be well written and in the voice of the publication.

Three Pitch Letters That Worked

Note: For examples, I'm using old pitches to real editors over the years who may no longer be at these publications. Make sure to check for an update.

1. My most successful pitch letter for a *New York Times Magazine* profile (to an editor I already knew well)

Dear Harvey,

I love the *Times Magazine*. I'd like to profile Judith Regan, the provocative editrix of mega-selling Howard Stern, Rush Limbaugh, and Beavis and Butt-Head books, who was just lured by Rupert Murdoch's promise of her own TV show to dump her long-time employer Simon & Schuster to work for him at HarperCollins. I have the exclusive. Fingers and toes crossed. Sue

2. My pitch to Brandon Holly at *Time Out New York*

Dear Ms. Holly,

Congratulations on your promotion! I am a fan of yours and a subscriber. I have an idea for a timely TONY feature, "20 Ways New Yorkers Nix Nicotine." I finally quit my long-term two-pack-a-day smoking habit and learned that other Manhattanites—like *Rolling Stone's* Jann Wenner and Knopf's Sonny Mehta—had many crazy ways of giving up tobacco. I'd like to pen a roundup where I'd interview an addiction specialist, a Nicotine Anonymous sponsor, a yogi, an acupuncturist, and a psycho-pharmacologist who prescribes Zyban to help nicotine addicts. My work has appeared in *The New York Times* and other publications.

Thank you for considering! Sincerely, Susan Shapiro

3. My pitch to *Detroit News Magazine*

Dear Kathy Warbelow,

I love *Detroit Magazine*, which I have my West Bloomfield mother send to Manhattan. As a transplanted West Bloomfield girl, my mother also sends me Star Deli tuna in ice packs. My Birmingham-born friend Gayle gets her dad to send her Vernors soda and Sanders hot fudge. I'd love to interview the Michigan grapevine in New York to find out which Midwest delicacies they can't live without for a feature called "Give Their Regards to Broadway, But Their Hearts Belong to Michigan." I've written for *Cosmopolitan*, *Our Town*, and the *Detroit Jewish News*.

Thanks for your time. Susan Shapiro

Two Student Pitch Letters That Worked

1. Subject: Timely Jewish author profile of Alyson Gerber for the *The Forward's* "Sisterhood" section

Dear Phoebe Maltz Bovy,

It was so nice meeting you in Susan Shapiro's class and reading your book *The Perils of "Privilege."* Your event at Book Culture was amazing. I was surprised by your response to "Where is the most absurd place you've seen privilege invoked?" Your anecdote about the young woman gathering money for a $1.50 coffee helped me realize the scale of your argument.

I hope *The Forward* will want my profile of Alyson Gerber, a 31-year-old Jewish author who battled with insecurity having to wear a back brace at her bat mitzvah. She suffered from scoliosis, a medical condition that caused her back to grow in an S-shape. Her debut novel, *Braced*, (out this week from Scholastic) chronicles a high school student's experiences with scoliosis, and the struggles she faces socially and mentally. Interestingly her editor Cheryl Klein also had to wear a brace for scoliosis. And Alyson just sold two more books to editor David Levithan, who wrote his own book about the first gay Jewish presidential candidate (and was mentioned in a 2016 *Forward* piece when another book of his was banned).

Alyson currently works at the Jewish Theological Seminary in New York City. She'll be returning to the Temple Emmanuel in Andover, Massachusetts on April 9th to visit the place where she had her bat mitzvah in the brace. Thank you for your consideration.

Best, Darren Sung

2. Subject: "Lost and Found" *Tin House* submission/Susan Shapiro gave me your e-mail

Dear Mr. Spillman,

I love *Tin House* and it was wonderful to meet you and your wife Elissa, through my professor Sue Shapiro. Elissa's book *Blueprints for Building Better Girls* made me cry.

I hope you'll consider a "Lost and Found" piece about *Travels to Alaska*, the little-read last thing John Muir ever wrote. I found it leaning between a bottle of insecticide and a flat basketball in my parents' garage, brittle and browning, lost there. I was seventeen. I read it in my bed that night. Six months after I found the book I was in Alaska.

Eight months after I was, alone, hiking the 211-mile John Muir Trail through the High Sierra of California. Two years after I was again alone, hiking from Mexico to Canada on the 2,650-mile, devastatingly gorgeous Pacific Crest Trail. On that walk I met rattlesnakes and bears; I forged frigid and remote rivers as deep as I am tall. I felt terror and the gratitude that followed the realization that I had survived. *Travels in Alaska* gave me permission to leave. Thanks for your time.

Aspen Matis

THE BYLINE BIBLE'S TOP-FIVE LISTS

You should read all the pages of this book. But if you're impatient like me, you may want to skim through the CliffsNotes version. Remember publications fold, editors leave daily and resurface elsewhere. While I'll try to keep updating, it's your job to Google, call, or check Facebook and Twitter to make sure they are still there before submitting.

Instant Gratification Takes Too Long Steps

1. Figure out your audience, tone, and topicality by reading many pieces from your target publication and emulate its style and length.
2. Write the three-page piece that editors want (based on my assignments).
3. Get a tough critique of your piece from a professional experienced in the field.
4. Revise accordingly. More than once.
5. Craft a great five-line cover letter with the right editor's name and e-mail.

Mistakes to Make Editors Hate You

1. Don't steal, quote without attribution, or plagiarize—even from yourself. (If you've published it, you usually can't recycle it verbatim.)
2. Don't submit your piece to many editors simultaneously: one at a time.
3. Don't submit your piece Monday, then e-mail the editor Tuesday, asking "Did you read it yet?" Likewise, don't submit a piece, revise it, and then resubmit the newer version.
4. Don't phone an editor you don't know—unless you don't mind the risk of being hung up on.
5. Don't spell the editor's name wrong or include any typos in your pitch.

Five Easiest Short Pieces to Write and Sell

1. The provocative **PERSONAL ESSAY** I have coined "The humiliation essay"
2. An informative **REGIONAL PIECE** about a place where you have a home, job, or platform
3. An argumentative **OP-ED** on a topical subject you're an expert on or connected to
4. **HUMOR OR PARODY** of a timely conflict in politics, dating, technology, or pop culture
5. **A SERVICE ARTICLE** highlighting how-to hints in your area of expertise that others don't know

Advice Stolen From My Mentors

1. Plumbers don't get plumber's block. Don't be self-indulgent, just get to work.
2. A page a day is a book a year.
3. No never means no. (It means revise, make it better, and try another editor.)
4. Three pages can change your life.
5. It's a number's game. Luckily you need only one editor to say yes.

Favorite Rules for Nonfiction

1. Explore your obsessions.
2. Write the story that only you can write and if anyone else can write it, let them.
3. Always question, challenge, and trash yourself in print more than anyone else.
4. The first piece you write that your family hates means you've found your voice.
5. "Lead the least secretive life you can." (stolen from my shrink)

Glossary

Acquisitions Editor: The person at a publisher who can acquire manuscripts and make an offer to buy yours. (They don't all necessarily do the line editing or development.)

Article: This usually refers to a short nonfiction reported piece, which is different than a personal essay, humor, or review.

ASJA: American Society for Journalists and Authors, a group of about one thousand American nonfiction writers I belong to that shares information and presents a fun annual conference in New York.

The Authors Guild: The oldest, largest prestigious organization for writers that provides help with copyright protection and freedom of speech.

Book Doctor: Someone you pay to read an unpublished manuscript who can help you fix it to make it better and more publishable.

Book Proposal: Summary of a nonfiction book manuscript used as a sales technique with the title, subtitle, overview, chapter breakdowns, marketing analysis of similar books, and a bio, usually 20–120 pages.

Byline: A line in a newspaper, magazine, or Web story naming the writer of the piece, often accompanied by the date.

Casual: Old name given to short humorous *New Yorker* magazine pieces before Tina Brown switched the title to "Shouts & Murmurs."

Clip: A copy of a published piece.

Co-author: Someone who co-writes a project who usually gets half of the money and shares a byline.

Copy: Used as a noun, it usually refers to what's written on the page, though more often in advertising.

Copyedit: A thorough editing of writing that corrects grammar, spelling, and punctuation errors, usually by a copyeditor.

Copywriter: Someone who writes advertising copy.

Cover Letter: The short letter or e-mail you write to an editor when you are attaching a finished piece.

Developmental Editor: Someone you hire while producing your manuscript to help you in the early stages.

Editor: Someone at a newspaper, magazine, website, or book publisher who determines the content of writing they publish and fixes the prose.

Essay: A short nonfiction piece of writing that can be first person or third person, but only humor essays can be fictional.

Evergreen: A piece that has nothing timely about it and could run anytime, the way evergreen trees keep their leaves all year.

Feature Writing: Short newspaper and magazine pieces that are not news stories.

Fiction: Writing—usually short stories and novels—that is made up. Don't use the term "fictional novel," which is redundant.

First Person: A writing style using the word *I* from one character's point of view.

Freelance: Working for many different people instead of being employed in one place.

Ghost Editor: Someone behind the scenes you can hire to fix your writing on a freelance basis.

Ghost Writer: Someone who helps authors write and revise their work or writes it entirely, usually for money and without a byline.

Humiliation Essay: A title I coined for my first personal essay assignment, where you write three double-spaced, typed pages on your most humiliating secret that you can put your name on.

Kill Fee: An agreed-upon percentage of a story editors will pay you if they commission the piece, then don't run it. It's often 10 percent, so a killed one thousand dollar piece will get you one hundred dollars.

Killed: When a piece that is commissioned never runs and won't be running in the future. Usually if an editor says it's "killed," you can publish it elsewhere, even if you were paid a kill fee (see above).

Lede: The beginning of a piece.

Line Editor: Someone who goes over each line of your work and marks notes to fix any grammar, spelling, punctuation, or other mistakes.

Listicle: An article, op-ed, or humor piece in the form of a list.

Literary Agent: Someone who will represent your book proposal or manuscript and sell it to book publishers for 10 or 15 percent of your advance and royalties. Most don't handle newspapers or magazines work.

Manuscript Analyst: Someone you hire to go over your pages and give you overall notes on whether they work or not.

Narrative: A written account that can be fiction or nonfiction.

NBCC: The National Book Critics Circle, a brillian group of book critics who give annual book awards (I've been a member for decades).

Nonfiction: Writing that is true and accurate, with nothing made up or fictionalized.

Novel: A book of fiction that is made up and tells one story (versus a collection of short stories or a novella).

Novella: A book of fiction, but usually shorter than your average two hundred- or three hundred-page novel.

Nut Graf: An abbreviated few lines at the beginning of a feature story that telegraph what the story is about.

On Spec: Short for "on speculation," where an editor won't commit to your piece until it's complete. Most essays, humor, poetry, and fiction are published "on spec."

Op-ed: A short, usually timely opinion/editorial piece that runs in a newspaper, magazine, or webzine, average length 600 words.

Peg: The specific timely angle for a story that might help you publish it faster, as in "This is pegged to election day."

PEN American Center: An international literary and political organization that fights for freedom of speech.

Pitch Letter: A letter or e-mail to a newspaper, magazine, or Web editor summing up the idea you want them to publish.

Play in Peoria: An old figure of speech derived from characters in Horatio Alger's novel *Five Hundred Dollars* that has come to mean "Will mainstream middle America like it?"

Profile: An interview with one person that is usually told as a third-person story, not in Q&A format.

Proofreader: Someone who reads through galleys or proofs to correct mistakes and typos.

Q&A: A question-and-answer interview with one or more people where you write out the question then print their answer below. While it reads like it's verbatim, these are often well edited for length and literary cohesion.

Regional Piece: A short nonfiction piece written and published with a specific geographical audience in mind.

Script Editor: Someone working in TV and film who can help script writers develop, write, and correct scripts to make them suitable for production.

Service Piece: A how-to article that gives advice to readers.

Short Story: Usually refers to a short piece of fiction; made-up work that is shorter than a novel or novella.

Special Issues: Many magazines have special issues with annual themes like "Money" or "Love." It's helpful for writers to know in advance what would be a good pitch and when.

Staff Writer: Usually someone who is paid to work full time for one newspaper, magazine, or website.

Third Person: A writing style using *he* or *she* or someone's name, not *I*.

Throat Clearing: An expression referring to the early lines writers use before they get to their point, but should be deleted.

Trolls: Nasty commenters on the Internet who trash your piece or try to cause trouble.

Vertical: The section of a publication with a specific theme, like "weddings" or "real estate."

Webzine: A publication that is only on the Internet and doesn't print hard copies. Also called "e-zine" or "online magazine."

Writing Coach: Someone hired to help you with your work and writing blocks who usually doesn't line edit.

Acknowledgments

Thanks to my amazing agent Ryan Harbage, and WD colleagues Cris Freese, Amy Jones, Zac Petit (for suggesting this book), Kara Uhl (for finding me), Phil Sexton, Melissa Hill, Baihley Gentry, Taylor Sferra, Jessica Zafarris, Samantha Sanders, and Tyler Moss.

Great editors who've said yes: Peter Catapano, Daniel Jones, Mark Rotella, Honor Jones, Julie Just, Eli Reyes, James Taranto, Wayne Hoffman, Natalie Shutler, Whitney Dangereld, Eric Copage, Roberta Zeff, Joanna Douglas, Erin Keane, Paul Smalera, Josh Greenman, Lauren Kern, Megan Greenwell, Adam Langer, KJ Dell'Antonia, Lincoln Anderson, Leigh Newman, Faye Penn, Ali Drucker, David Wallis, Chloe Schama, Matt Oshinsky, Esther Haynes, Rob Spillman, Emma Komlos–Hrobsky, Sherry Amatenstein, Yona Zeldis McDonough, Peter Bloch, Elise Sole, Dave Daley, Ann Treistman, Amanda Chan, Nanette Varian, Jenny Rogers, Kara Bolonik, David Brinn, Lynn Andriani, Louisa Ermelino, Loren Kleinman, Danielle Perez, Wendy Wolf, Jill Rothenberg, Katie Gilligan, Naomi Rosenblatt, Jaime Lubin & Ronit Pinto.

Teaching colleagues I've driven crazy: Deborah Landau, Phillip Lopate, Robert Polito, Nick Allanach, Justin Sherwood, Laura Cronk, Lori Turner, Luis Jaramillo, Nicole Drayton, Ben Fama, John Reed, Joseph Salvatore, Jackson Taylor, David Greenstein, Katherine Goldstein, Michael Zam, Jessica Siegel, Mary Quigley, Clarence Coo, John McShane, Jerome Murphy, Ian Frazier, Bob Blaisdell, Alice Phillips, Elizabeth Maxwell.

Brilliant workshoppers sick of millions of my pages: Frank Flaherty, Nicole Bokat, Kate Walter, Alice Feiring, Richard Prior, Lisa Lewis, Anthony Powell, Haig Chahinian, Judy Batalion, Jeff Vasishta, Amy Wolfe, Tyler Kelley, Amy Klein, David Sobel, Roberta Bernstein, Brenda Copeland, Sara-Kate Astrove, Kimberlee Auerbach, Merideth Finn, Sybil Sage, Suzanne Roth, Jerry Portwood, Candy Schulman, Sharon Mesmer, Doreen Oliver, Hilary Davidson, Harold James, Michael Narkunski, Stephen Paul Miller, Rafiq Kathwari, Abby Sher, Wendy Shanker, Guy Niccoluci, Jim Jennewin, Molly Jong-Fast, Kristen Kemp, Royal Young, Sarah Herrington, and Aspen Matis (thanks for the title!)

Former students who went out of their way for me: Renee Watson, Jakki Kerubo, Enma Elias, Lexie Bean, Hugo Saurny, Katy Hershenberg, Anne McDermott, Helen Chernikoff, Elisabeth Turner, Stephanie Sui, Jessica Milliken, Michael Charboneau, Shoaib Harris, Danielle Gelfand, Ryan Stewart, Jenny Aurthur, Keysha Whitaker, Randle Browning, Chloe Kent, Nick Lioudis, Julie Charnet, Pamela Jacobs, Emily Reub, Lia Monroy, Margo Hammond, Connie Kirk, Court Stroud, Jessica Henriquez, Penina Roth, Estelle Erasmus, and Brenda Janowitz.

Generous gurus: Danny Brownstein, Patty Gross, Fred Woolverton, Bob Cook, Vatsal Thakkar, Carlos Saavedra, Karl Zakalik, Olaf Kroneman, Doug Moss, Saul Pressner, Sheldon Cherry, Susan Drossman, Leeber Cohen, Judi Vitale, Stan Mieses, Eyal Solomon, Karen Salmansohn, Bruce Tracy, Besty Maury, Tom Reiss, Larry Bergreen, Kenan Trebincevic, Grace Schulman, Gerry Jonas, Galen Williams, and the great Harvey Shapiro.

Book event angels: Fred and Nancy Bass, Kaylen Higgins, Peter Enzinna, Gary Kordan, Stacey Greenwald, Alison Singh Gee, Amy Alkon, Tom Zoellner, Mark Axelrod, Gina Ryder, Kathryn Glasgow, Gary Rubin, Jane Wald, Jen Kaluzny, Tracie Fienman, Yael Yisraeli, Michele Filgate, Janine Ditullio, Rachel Fershleiser, Molly Rose Quinn, Donna Rauch, Desiree Nelson, Corrina Gramma, and Bob Contant and Marilyn Berkman from the sorely missed St. Mark's Bookshop.

Michigan friends forever Susan Goldsmith, Karen Sosnick, Lisa Applebaum, Laura Berman, Brian O'Connor, Robin Singer, Andrea Becker, Nancy Newman, Suzanne Altman, Julie Ingber, Karen Buscemi, Arlene and Alli Cohen, EJ Levy, Howard Lyons, Ellen Piligian, Hillary Polon, Cindy Frenkel, Lynne Cohen, Jill Margolick, Lolly Averbuck, Sally Horvitz, the Grants, Solways, Perchikovskys, James and Kathleen Chambers, and Judy Burdick-who are really sick of coming to my book events!

Special thanks to Jack Shapiro, who made my Manhattan life possible, my seven beautiful nieces and nephews and extended family: the Kahns, Zippers, Fasts, Brownsteins, Landsmans, Brinns, Michael Greenblatt, Sivan Ilan, webmaster EB who saves me and my work daily & the incredible CR who has "done wonders with me."

About the Author

Susan Shapiro is a *New York Times* best-selling author/co-author of twelve books her family hates, including *Unhooked, The Bosnia List, Lighting Up,* and *Only As Good as Your Word.* She's written for *The New York Times, New York* magazine, *The Wall Street Journal, Newsweek, Salon, Los Angeles Times, The Washington Post, The Atlantic, Esquire, Elle,* Oprah.com, *Marie Claire,* and others. Since 1993, she's been an award-winning writing professor at The New School and NYU and recently at Columbia University, where she teaches her wildly popular "Instant Gratification Takes Too Long" classes and seminars that help people get published and launch book projects. She lives with her husband, a scriptwriter/NYU Tisch professor, in Greenwich Village. You can follow her on Twitter @susanshapironet or Instagram at @profsue123.

Index

WD WRITER'S DIGEST

WRITER'S DIGEST
ONLINEworkshops
WritersOnlineWorkshops.*com*

Our workshops combine the best of world-class writing instruction with the convenience and immediacy of the web to create a state-of-the-art learning environment. You get all of the benefits of a traditional workshop setting—peer review, instructor feedback, a community of writers, and productive writing practice—without any of the hassle.

WRITE, WORK, AND THRIVE ON YOUR OWN TERMS
The Essential Guide to Freelance Writing

BY ZACHARY PETIT

Zachary Petit, former managing editor of *Writer's Digest* magazine and seasoned freelancer, shares the innumerable lessons he's learned from his time "in the trenches," from breaking in and querying to interviewing, maintaining relationships with editors and publishers, and more. Whether a veteran of the publishing business or a novice, you'll find his tips, advice, and exercises valuable in helping build your career.

Available from WritersDigestShop.com and your favorite book retailers.

To get started, join our mailing list: **WritersDigest.com**

FOLLOW US ON:

 Find more great tips, networking, and advice by following **@writersdigest**

 And become a fan of our Facebook page: **facebook.com/writersdigest**